COLONEL OF THE BLACK REGIMENT

The Life of Thomas Wentworth Higginson

BY HOWARD N. MEYER

Let Us Have Peace: The Life of Ulysses S. Grant

Colonel of the Black Regiment: The Life of Thomas Wentworth Higginson

Editor of *Army Life in a Black Regiment* by Colonel Thomas Wentworth Higginson

Thomas Wentworth Higginson, 1857.

COURTESY MRS. WILLIAM HALLOWELL AND MRS. W. J. WOODIN

Howard N. Meyer

COLONEL OF THE BLACK REGIMENT

THE LIFE OF *Thomas Wentworth Higginson*

Illustrated with photographs and engravings

W·W·NORTON & COMPANY·INC·
New York

JB
Higginson

TO MY FINE SONS,

Andrew, Franklin, Jonathan.

First Edition
Library of Congress Catalog Card No. 67-15445

Published simultaneously in Canada by
George J. McLeod Limited, Toronto
Printed in the United States of America
1 2 3 4 5 6 7 8 9 0

CONTENTS

LIST OF ILLUSTRATIONS

FOREWORD

AFTER LOOKING AT the varied photographs taken over a span of seventy years, my editor, William McMorris, said he felt like asking, "Will the real Thomas Wentworth Higginson stand up?" Minister, author, physical fitness enthusiast, agitator, naturalist, lecturer, soldier, dandy, there was a single thread that ran through his life. The real Higginson always stood up for freedom and for the truth without which man cannot be free. He did not flinch when he could fight the good fight, nor did he ever apologize for peaceful or violent (when necessary) opposition to those who acted in the name of the United States while debasing the ideals of the Declaration of Independence. In his time this meant opposing the Mexican War, violating the Fugitive Slave Law, attacking the Boston Courthouse, smuggling guns to Kansas, financing John Brown's raid on Harpers Ferry, abetting Miss Anthony's attempt to force her way into a polling booth, and speaking out repeatedly against repression of the Philippine Insurrection—the second unjust American war during his lifetime.

He saw that it was not enough to help the oppressed win their freedom. Describing what justice required for women, to whose emancipation he contributed, he stated a simple truth that applies to the heirs of the black regiments whose hard-won freedom was stolen in all but name:

We men have been standing for years with our hands crushing down the shoulders of woman, so that she should not attain her true altitude; it is not so easy, after we have cramped, dwarfed and crippled her, to get rid of our responsibility by standing back and saying: "There, we will let you go; stand up for yourself." If it is true, as these women say, that we have wronged them for centuries, we have got to do more than mere negative duty. By as much as we have helped to wrong them, we have got to help right them.

Colonel Higginson, rebel with many causes, needs no further introduction. I hope I have done him justice.

ACKNOWLEDGMENTS

I HONOR THE MEMORY of Van Wyck Brooks, whose evocative profile of the Colonel in the pages of *New England: Indian Summer* aroused my interest. His exciting summary of highlights of *Army Life in a Black Regiment* inspired my search for that neglected masterpiece. The first copy I located came from the New York State Library at Albany, and for this and many later courtesies I am grateful to the interloan service of the Rockville Centre Public Library and the Nassau County Library system.

The Colonel's numerous out-of-print books, scattered writings, and his second wife's faithful compilation of extracts from his letters and journals, many of which appeared in her own biography of her husband, were my principal sources. I appreciate the gracious courtesy of Mrs. William Hallowell and Mrs. W. J. Woodin, in consenting to the use of some of the photographs in their grandmother's book. For assistance in securing my collection of the Colonel's books and others, I must thank the many dealers in old books, including George Milkey of Greenfield, the Jewetts of Rowley, Pangloss of Cambridge—all in Massachusetts—Isaac Mendoza of New York, and others too numerous to mention. Such dealers deserve greater recognition as custodians of an important part of the neglected American heritage and greater consideration when "progress" commands demolition of the structures housing them.

The tiny handful of contemporary scholars whose imagination was captured by the Colonel made its contribution. They were preceded in their labors by the late Howard Hintz, of Brooklyn College, whose massive unpublished dissertation is a gold mine. The doctoral works of Sister Thomas Catherine Brennan, O.P., of Barry College, and Dean Edgar L. McCormick, of Kent State College, were useful and stimulating. I examined Tilden Edelstein's published essay and benefited from a perusal of William H. Kendrick's study of the Colonel's reading.

My greatest boon has been the generosity of Anna Mary Wells, who literally poured most of her notes onto my desk. It would have been enough that she mined the ore for her lively *Dear Preceptor*. I have unblushingly drawn from its eloquent answer to errors in previous treatments of the relationship between Higginson and Emily Dickinson.

Foremost among others who have helped is Princeton's James McPherson, who gave me many useful leads to scattered post-Reconstruction writings of Higginson's that supplemented the assistance of his *The Struggle for Equality*. Boyd B. Stutler gave help from his unique John Brown collection. Lloyd Robson of the Newport Historical Society furnished material on that period, especially the school desegregation fight. Mary V. Darcy, then of the Massachusetts Civil War Centennial Commission, was helpful, as were historian Louis Ruchames and novelist Truman Nelson, both abolitionist scholars, and George Middleton, Charles Feinberg, and William Armstrong. Upton Sinclair confirmed the old Colonel's role as cofounder of the student Socialist group that became the League for Industrial Democracy. Dorothy Sterling, who has told so well the story of Robert Smalls in her *Captain of the Planter*, gave me a valuable tip, which I was able to run down with the help of Dr. John Morsell and Henry Lee Moon of the N.A.A.C.P. I cherish the memory of my meeting with Ben Huebsch, who showed me his brief 1908 to 1910 correspondence with the old Colonel.

My family rates honorable mention. My son Andrew obtained

extracts that I needed from old Boston newspapers and my wife Sylvette made imaginative suggestions and tedious corrections. Franklin typed, and he or Jonathan asked a question that haunts me: "Dad, what did you do with your spare time before you started writing?"

HOWARD N. MEYER

PROLOGUE

LANDFALL

THE TALL OFFICER in blue paced the deck, stopping often at the starboard rail. There he hoped for a first glimpse of the coastal islands that should now be appearing on the western horizon. He could not conceal his impatience. No traveler had ever approached a mysterious land with more eager anticipation.

It was soon to be his thirty-ninth birthday. That was old for an army captain, especially for a captain of volunteers in time of war. But he strode with the spring and grace of a college athlete. His eyes had the dreamy look of a young scholar.

His life had been devoted to the arts of peace: lecturing, tutoring, writing, even preaching for some years. "War," he had written not long before, is "brutal and disgusting." Now he was on a government steamer bound for a forward combat station. It was November 23, 1862, and the S.S. *Arago* was on the last leg of a voyage from New York to the Sea Islands of South Carolina. The next months in this tiny, obscure region might hold the key to the future of his country.

He thought, as he gazed sternward at the long line of shining phosphorescence in the night waters, of the first time he had ever seen a Negro. Thirty-five years ago as a boy of four on a summer steamer sailing to Nahant, an island resort off his native Massachusetts, he had been startled when he saw a black waiter come along the deck and enter the dining cabin. He had been so frightened by the strange and unexpected sight of a human being with dark skin that he had refused to go in for dinner. The pangs of hunger on the beach that afternoon fixed the memory of the occasion into his consciousness. They gave a point to the retelling of the story since the lesson was that he had suffered more from turning his back on the stranger than had the latter.

Now he was being carried by steamer to Beaufort, South Carolina's popular island resort of prewar slavery days. If all went well, he was to become colonel in command of a regiment of Negroes, the first ex-slaves to be permitted to fight for their freedom. The Civil War had begun eighteen months before and it was not going at all well for the nation.

"As I approach the mysterious land," he had written his wife only the night before, "I am more and more impressed with my good fortune in having this novel and uncertain career open before me . . . the first man who organizes and commands a successful black regiment will perform the most important service in the history of the war."

He could not catch a glimpse of land that night. Early the next morning he rushed out of the cabin as soon as he sensed that the engines had slowed. Stars were still overhead and the gulls were wheeling and shrieking when he came on deck, but there was much to be seen in the hazy light of dawn. Two points of land, a magnificent harbor between them, dozens of transports and steamers at anchor. The shore was flat, mainly sandbanks and beaches backed up by long green masses of foliage. Entering the harbor, the *Arago* steamed up the Beaufort River after the tide became favorable. The river banks were soft and graceful on either side.

There were glimpses of vegetation, shrubs and trees that he did not recognize despite all the botany he had studied and his hobby as a naturalist. They chugged past an old plantation on which there stood a great, decaying house and a long avenue of magnolia trees as well as a tiny church in the midst of the woods. Behind it stood a neat encampment of white tents.

"There," said one of the ship's officers, "is your future regiment."

To Thomas Wentworth Higginson it almost seemed that his whole life had been designed to prepare him for his new experience.

I

OF SALEM AND THE SEA

THE INFORMER STOLE slyly into the Bishop's study. "Francis Higginson is a Nonconformist," he whispered.

"He shall be silenced," said the Bishop.

The English Court of High Commission was scheduled to meet next in the spring of 1629. The Reverend Francis Higginson did not wait to see how the trial would turn out, after friends told him he had been denounced as a Dissenter. The lightest penalty for one who insisted in being guided by his own conscience was life imprisonment. He sailed from England as a refugee and landed at Salem, Massachusetts, two months later as an immigrant.

His son John Higginson became a Puritan minister at Salem and served his flock for fifty years. He did not fear nonconformity or its consequences. He refused to join the witch-hunters in 1692, and because of this his daughter was jailed as a suspected witch. He was too old and beloved by his people to be made a victim himself. Since it was an essential rule of the instigators of the witchcraft persecution "to punish all who were suspected of disapproving of the proceedings," Reverend John was made to suffer by her imprisonment.

John Higginson did not fear, a few years later, to go to the assistance of his friend Judge Samuel Sewell of Boston. The Judge made enemies who were even more powerful than the witch-hunters when he wrote a pioneer antislavery appeal that he called

The Selling of Joseph. He denounced the idea that any race had the right to buy or sell any other, declaring, "God hath made of one blood all nations of men." As the contents of his pamphlet became known he was met on all hands by "Frowns and Hard Words," he wrote John Higginson, who nevertheless supported the Judge and enlisted others in his defense.

John Higginson's descendants turned to the sea for their careers. They were among the townsfolk who, as sailors and shipmasters, made the name of Salem synonymous with America in distant ports. When the colonies were prevented by British occupation or seapower from using many major harbors during the Revolution, Salem became a center for ships fitted out to make hit-and-run attacks on British commerce in reprisal. Called privateers, these ships were too large and costly to be used in coastwise trade after independence was won. They were sent over the oceans to compete with the French and English.

Great merchant fortunes were made and lost on the adventurous voyages of the privateers. China trade was opened by one daring shipmaster from Salem. Another Salem shipmaster was the first to show the stars and stripes at Manila. Still another brought the first cargo of wild pepper from the shores of Sumatra. The ports of the South Pacific came to be as familiar to Yankee sailors as the coast between Cape Ann and Cape Cod.

By 1823, when Thomas Wentworth Higginson was born, all this had become part of the past. An embargo that had preceded the War of 1812 and the war itself had thrown Salem into a period of decline and decay. Weeds grew near the unpainted wharves, and the swarms of blue-jacketed sailors with varnished hats were no longer to be seen. Their former captains dozed in the sun beside the customhouse and told stories of their adventures to any who would listen.

Stephen Higginson, Thomas Wentworth Higginson's father, had been a generous and public-spirited man while his Salem-based shipping trade had thrived. After his ships had been captured or sunk, he had little left. Loyal friends stood by him and secured for him a post as business manager of Harvard University. Cambridge, the village where the university was located, had a seaport from which merchant vessels sailed during the 1820's, when Thomas Higginson was a boy. It could not match the attractions of Salem, however, nor could it furnish stories as fascinating as those his father's cousin Cap'n Cleveland of Salem could tell.

That serene old man, with his apple-shaped head and indelibly sunburned complexion, would charm the children for hours as he rambled on. The whole globe had been his home; no sea or cape was so distant or remote as to have been overlooked in his wandering. His favorite story was about America's first "sit-in" in 1798—a bold gesture of his friend Captain Nathan Silsbee. Captured by a French privateer for the suspected offense of carrying British goods, Silsbee's ship was taken to the French consul at Malaga in Spain. This official had the responsiblity of conducting "prize trials," to determine whether vessel and cargo should be forfeited for carrying goods of an enemy of France. The consul languidly told Silsbee that his case would not come on for months and that meanwhile he and his ship would be detained.

Silsbee would not accept this highhanded treatment. He announced that he would not leave the consular office except by force until his case was settled. He remained in his chair without food or rest for twenty-four hours. At the end of that period the Frenchman silently gave him discharge papers.

When asked afterwards, "Why did you discharge the Yankee so quickly?" he replied, "I found that I must either dismiss him or bury him and I preferred the former."

There was a sea tale in his mother's family history that was more romantic than any story of Stephen's fleet. In 1777, Captain Thomas Storrow of George III's army was on his way from Jamaica, in the West Indies, to England in a British merchantman. The ship was seized by a Massachusetts privateer and brought in triumph to Portsmouth, New Hampshire. There the Captain was taken off and held as a prisoner of war. While on parole, he was allowed to go about the seaport city , where he met and fell in love with Anne Appleton, a beautiful young colonial maiden. Her family was related to the Wentworths, who had been colonial governors and great landowners of New Hampshire. When the Captain was set free in an exchange of prisoners, Anne sailed for England with him over the outraged protests of her family. There they were married despite equally vigorous objections of his kin. The independent young couple was obliged to wander from place to place and country to country for the rest of their short lives.

After Anne and the Captain died one of their children, Louisa Storrow, who was still a young girl, found a home with Stephen Higginson. There she helped care for his children. When Stephen's wife died, he asked Louisa to marry him. She shared his prosperity in the early years of their marriage, then, with cheerful good nature, shared his adversity. After leaving Boston's active social life for a farm, where they remained until Stephen moved to Harvard, she wrote in her diary:

> *I always awake, calm and serene. My children occupy my mind and my heart and fill it with affection and gratitude. Books are my recreation, and, next to my children, my greatest source of pleasure. This exemption from visitors is delightful to me; it gives me time to think and to read, and I only hope that I shall improve all my advantages.*

II

CAMBRIDGE, INDOORS AND OUT

TOMMY HIGGINSON thought it quite an advantage that Mr. Wells' school was a whole mile away from home. Since he returned to his mother's kitchen for lunch each day, this gave him a chance to walk four miles before he even began his round of after-school activities.

He started school at the age of nine. At the beginning he would often trail behind his older brother and the latter's classmate, Jemmie Lowell. The younger schoolboy loved to eavesdrop on their conversations, taken up, as they often were, with discussions of the books they had been reading. At other times he traveled alone. He would make up stories to pass the time as he walked, many of them about romantic heroes from books his mother had been reading aloud each night. In their adventures and achievements, these imaginary heroes made up for the lack of excitement in a peaceful, country college town like Cambridge.

He did not always need a story to distract him, for it was great fun watching robins or bluebirds or insects of all kinds that could be found on walls or fences or clumps of foliage. Nature study and daydreaming would sometimes give place to a solitary, mile-long game of "football," kicking a stone or horse chestnut from the garden gate of his father's house on Professor's Row to the door of the school that was situated on the lane known as Tory Row.

A boy's imagination could find plenty of material in the stories about the houses on Tory Row. The street had been nicknamed after the colonists who had opposed the Revolution against the British crown. Stubbornly opposed to change, they distrusted freedom. Many of these conservatives were members of families of great wealth who were more or less connected with each other. Their magnificent houses and gardens were products of the profit of slaveholding: many owned one or more plantations in the West Indies. When the Revolution began, the Tory families preferred or were obliged to depart with the British. Their row of fine homes found new owners and occupants, but the stories of the original Tory owners were still being retold fifty years later. When the imposing Vassall house, for example, was abandoned it became General Washington's headquarters during the siege of Boston.

Cambridge had a long and honored history even before George Washington took his first command of the patriot's army under the elm tree that still stood when Tommy was a boy. Tommy and his friends did not have to learn at school about the importance of their village during the Revolution or of its traditions of more than a century before. The red brick buildings of Harvard College were always there to remind them that Cambridge owed its name and very existence to books and education. Any boy could tell a visitor the story of the first printing press in the Colonies, and how for forty years Boston, itself, had to send to Cambridge to have books printed.

The old village burying ground was a favorite play area for Cambridge boys of the eighteen twenties. Tommy passed it every day on his way to school. He and his schoolmates played among the old flat tombstones, many of which were covered with long Latin inscriptions. The boys might sit among them and help one another translate them, for Latin was a language that boys in old Cambridge began to study when they were very young. The inscriptions told about the lives of the village worthies, ministers, and early presidents of Harvard and of their achievements as writers and teachers.

Other stories were told by these stones or recalled by their presence. Most imposing of all was the Vassall family monument, relic of the slaveowning Tory family. The boys had heard often the story of one proud lady of that family who demanded that two slaves be buried with her to serve her in another world. Henry Wadsworth Longfellow wrote of that monument later:

At her feet and at her head
Lies a slave to attend the dead
But their dust is white as hers.

Stories of the Revolution were told by gravestones that had empty, diamond-shaped cavities where leaden coats of arms had once been embedded. The insignia had been pried out to be melted down for bullets to supply the Continental Army.

There were other places where history impressed itself on the minds of young Cambridge boys. Winter Hill was one. There boys could play soldier on grass-covered mounds that had once marked trenches, and pretend they were repelling British onslaughts. The idea of Liberty was important to an American boy then and was usually linked with defiance of the British King. Most elaborate of all the sets of breastworks and trenches that had been left behind by the Revolution were those surrounding the foot of Mount Benedict in nearby Somerville village.

There was a special kind of history lesson in the ruins of a convent farther up the slope of that hill. As a boy of ten, Tommy stood outside his front door and saw in the distance the flames of the convent when it burned. Irish immigration to the Boston area was beginning to increase. Deluded and evil men incited prejudice against the Catholic community and circulated falsehoods about the convent. One night a mob of Bostonians surrounded the place, ejected its occupants, and plundered and burned the convent. The boy who watched this as he stood beside his mother, holding her hand, wrote afterwards, ". . . all that I had read of persecutions did not implant so lasting a love of liberty as that one spectacle."

The road that stretched to the west of the Higginson home ran in the direction of Lexington and Concord, a constant reminder of the fight, fifty years before, for political liberty. While wagons rumbled east, carrying farm products to supply Boston markets, other wagons rolled west along Concord pike. These were making a one-way trip to the western lands: Ohio was the destination in the early years, and later they headed toward one after another of the new territories that were opening up.

To the east of the house there were green pastures dotted with groups of elm and chestnut trees. To the south on a clear day, one could see the placid Charles River, twinkling with sails as it flowed through salt marshes to the sea.

Charlie Parsons was Tommy's next door neighbor and his closest friend in his boyhood days. Charlie lived with his uncle, Reverend Abiel Holmes, whose son Oliver Wendell had won fame at twenty with a poem called "Old Ironsides." That poem had saved a ship that had become a historic symbol from being scrapped. The Holmes house had so much acreage that it was practically a farm with cultivated fields and outbuildings sheltering horses and cattle.

On rainy days, the boys played in the garret of the Holmes house or sometimes in the library. There, one cold winter's day, as the window pane was covered with frost, the kindly old parson had scratched an outline of bristling bushes with stars above, and inscribed the motto, in Latin, *Per aspera ad astra* (through hardships one can achieve the stars).

It was natural in a village that produced writers and literary families for each household to be well stocked with books. Even after Stephen Higginson had been forced to sell many of the books in his own library when hard times came, there remained nearly a thousand to line the walls of the home. As he grew up, Tommy collected, in out-of-the-way closets, the classics discarded by his older brothers as they progressed through college. He was always something of a hoarder, and books were his special delight.

Before he had learned to read—and for a time afterwards—his

Stephen and Louisa Storrow Higginson, his parents.

COURTESY MRS. WILLIAM HALLOWELL AND MRS. W. J. WOODIN

His birthplace, Kirkland Street, Cambridge.

COURTESY MRS. WILLIAM HALLOWELL AND MRS. W. J. WOODIN

mother read aloud to the family every evening before bedtime. She covered, in this way, every one of Sir Walter Scott's Waverly novels and many others. Later in life he paid tribute to the value of those evenings, saying that to have lain on a hearthrug and heard one's mother read aloud was a liberal education in itself.

Reading was not confined to the classics. His mother never knew about some of the under-the-desk literature that Tommy read avidly and helped circulate at school. There was a whole flock of little volumes, with contents even more exciting than their titles—*The Devil on Two Sticks, The Three Spaniards,* and so on—that would have brought raised eyebrows from the family.

Music as well as literature was always present in the household. One sister was an excellent pianist, one of the first in the Boston area to play Beethoven's music. Of the Harvard boys who came to visit the house, among the most welcome were three who played flute trios to her accompaniment. One, John Dwight, was to become Boston's leading music critic for many years. Another had a genuine silver flute of which Dwight said, "It has a silver sound." Other visitors included older girls who sang in the living room. They sang one ballad after another, sentimental or dramatic, all pleasing. When Tommy was sent to bed at eight, he never failed to keep his bedroom door ajar so that he might go to sleep with the sound of music.

Outdoor life was no less important to him than the world of books and music. In proper season there were swimming and skating, football, and a kind of baseball. Competitive sports never appealed to him as much as exercise alone. It was swimming that gave Tommy the greatest sense of achievement. There was one proud moment when he swam from one part of the Charles River bank to another through a stream that was well over his head.

Walking was also a favorite activity, quite apart from the daily four miles to and from school. The destinations, as well as the exercise, itself, were attractive. One of the most exciting was Boston's Long Wharf, which projected one-third of a mile into the water so that it could accommodate the many sailing vessels used in coastal and foreign commerce. Sailors still wore earrings; all swore mighty oaths. The ships' masts clustered thickly like a forest whose leaves had been blown off by a gale; the pungent and varied smells of the cargoes of the India trade tantalized and tempted the boys.

The most important part of Tommy's life out of doors was his communion with nature. Whether with butterfly net in summer or nutting-sack in autumn, there was no greater joy for him than the life of a naturalist. He could not and would not be a hunter, as some of the boys his age already were. After one episode of guilty complicity in the shooting down of a bird by bow-and-arrow, he could never again bear the thought of killing an animal or a bird for mere sport. Leaves, barks, insects, and even fish, however, were his constant quarry. It was always a delight to find a field flower he had not seen before or to spy a strange new bird among the herons and ducks while he crouched in the marshes near Fresh Pond.

While home and neighbors were plentifully supplied with

books and field and stream provided a generous education, there was still school to attend. At Mr. Wells' Latin School Cambridge boys prepared for Harvard. There they found discipline of a kind that involved a frequent swish, and then the snap of a rod on back or hand. Between the blows of the birch, Latin and Greek were offered. Tommy took such joy in the classical languages that his performance exempted him from much of the caning. His interest in learning was not confined to the classics; he never approached a new study without eager anticipation. Forty years later he was to remark that he did not see how anyone could find boredom in life while there remained a new language or science to learn.

Tommy Higginson's father died when he was ten years old. He had never been very close to his father and admitted later that he did not feel the loss very much. His mother had always been much closer to him and she and his aunt Nancy, a maiden aunt who was always a part of his household, made up their minds that the boy was to go on and complete his education. He was too good a student to be allowed to go to waste.

III

HARVARD

IT WAS A BLISSFUL moment for young Thomas Wentworth Higginson when he stood, one autumn morning in 1837, on the steps of Harvard's University Hall. The day he had awaited so long had finally arrived. He had just been admitted "without conditions." Not yet fourteen, he was the youngest in his class.

He had always been aware of the presence of Harvard, its faculty, and its students. The college was not yet very large; though almost two hundred years old, it still graduated only about fifty men a year. It was large enough to dominate the tiny village. Almost everyone who lived there knew everyone else. The boys made a special hobby of the college. At the age of ten a Cambridge lad could recite each class roster alphabetically, and prided himself on being able to recognize every undergraduate by sight. They felt like spectators outside a remarkably large glass beehive where it was possible, all day, to watch the busy people inside. They studied their traits, their games, their habits, and the fortunate ones who were slated to enter the hive looked forward to the great day.

For Wentworth (he was no longer "Tommy") the entrance examination was more grueling than difficult. To rise at four thirty in order to present himself at six A.M. for the examination, and then to be detained in various recitation rooms until seven

P.M. was an ordeal. The tests themselves, more oral than written, limited to Latin, Greek, and mathematics, were not difficult for him. Examinations resumed the next day at six and continued until two in the afternoon. After that the boys loafed around the yard (Harvard, uniquely, calls it that and not a campus) until they were called in, one by one, to hear their fate. Only half-a-dozen or so were admitted without being placed on probation, and young Higginson, as star Latin and Greek scholar of Mr. Wells' school, was one of the select few.

The boy who was called into Harvard's corporation room to hear the announcement of his success from the president of the university, himself, in the presence of the rest of the faculty was hardly ready for college. Less than fourteen years old, he was uncomfortably tall for his age and awkward, shy, and reserved. He kept a diary at college and, after one of the first evening parties he attended, he recorded a familiar sentiment: "Played backgammon. Danced. Had a miserable time."

While his social life was to improve as the college years passed, his youth and shyness kept him from having more than a few close friends among the undergraduates. His only real intimate for the first years was a classmate, Frank Parker, with whom he was to compete for the honor of achieving first in the class. Wentworth ended second. It may have been that he spread himself too thin. He was handicapped not only by his youth and immaturity, but by the number and variety of his interests.

The college was trying the experiment, new and daring for those days, of allowing students to take some electives. Calculus was one of the courses that could be chosen. Wentworth picked it and found Professor Peirce, who was still developing the subject, to be inspiring and delightful. He entered with eagerness into the construction of equations and the pursuit of their solutions. He came very close, in fact, to devoting his life to the subject, and probably would have if a tutorship had been offered to him.

Some years after graduation, when it seemed that Higginson might have to spend some time in prison for having tried to help free a fugitive slave, he met the Professor in a Boston street and told Peirce that he planned to use part of the expected prison term to review math.

"In that case," said Professor Peirce, his eyes lighting up with genuine pleasure, "I sincerely hope that you may go there." The Professor was doubly pleased at the thought. Like so many of the wealthy and educated of Massachusetts during this period, he hated antislavery men. At the same time Peirce still hoped to make a professional mathematician of Higginson.

Second to mathematics in its appeal was the English course given by Professor Edward T. Channing. An exacting critic and an inspiring teacher, this professor has the distinction of having instructed more of America's great writers than any other university faculty member. Thoreau, Emerson, Lowell, and Holmes are a few at the top rank of the many who studied with him. For Wentworth it was always a mark of achievement, in a subject that attracted him more and more, to have passages from his essays read aloud with approval by Professor Channing.

The study of French, in the newly formed Modern Language Department, was made especially attractive by the teaching methods of Professor Henry Wadsworth Longfellow. The poet-teacher would sit with his students around a long table and create a rare communication with them and an even rarer love for the teacher. It was a great thrill for Wentworth when he saw, on the seminar table, the proof sheets of a new book of poetry that were being corrected and about to go back to the printer.

The subject that took more of his time and attention than any other was not a part of the official curriculum, and no credit was given for attendance. The college librarian gave a series of lectures that were called Philosophy of Natural History. The subject covered what we would now call botany, biology, and especially entomology, the study of insect life. To young Higginson this field of learning, that was just beginning to develop, was not merely fascinating for its own sake. It also offered the opportunity for many field trips and exploring expeditions to identify plants and insects in their natural surroundings. It gave him a great sense of achievement to discover a new and as yet unclassified specimen.

His activities included studies and hikes with Dr. Harris, the librarian whom the college could not afford to give a professorship. Wentworth was also a member of a student club, the Harvard Natural History Society, and he later became an officer of the group.

The Natural History course and Society did not completely satisfy his lean, six-foot body, which craved activity as much as his mind did. His entrance into college provided an opportunity to increase the number and the length of the walks he took. Day and night he would set out, sometimes with a friend, sometimes alone. When Wentworth was still a freshman, he and his classmate Charles Parker would walk ten miles on a casual Saturday stroll. On one occasion in 1837 they reached Medford and saw railway cars in motion for the first time in their lives. "Astonishing sight!!! Wonderful vision!!!" Wentworth recorded in his diary.

Walking was not the sole physical activity. There were group sports like football and cricket, the latter played with large bats and heavy balls. There was ice-skating on Fresh Pond in winter and swimming in warmer seasons. Leapfrog, hockey, ninepins, and a whole catalog of other activities were rounded out by chopping wood for his home when he lived off-campus as a freshman.

The football they played was not a spectator sport. It was more of an audience participation game. Half a century later, recalling the contests of his youth in which the whole freshman class of fifty would line up against the sophomores, he wrote:

> *To those who loved, as I did, the old time football,—the very thud of the ball, the scent of bruised grass, the mighty rush of a hundred men, the swift and cool defense,—there is something insufficient in the presence of a whole university sitting and shivering in the chill wind around an arena where a few picked gladiators push and wrestle.*

There were contests of the intellect and speech, too, in the debates at the Harvard Union. One of the earliest that Wentworth attended, in September of his freshman year, was on the proposition, "Would it be expedient to abolish slavery in the District of Columbia?" He recorded in his diary, without showing any particular interest in the outcome, that the proposition went down 7 to 1. Another debate that drew no reaction from him at the time was on the subject, "Ought women to be allowed to speak in public?"

With all this physical and mental activity and an increasing social program, books remained his greatest passion. It gave zest to some of his walks when the object might be a bookshop. There was John Bartlett's in Cambridge where the owner was compiling his own book of familiar quotations. There were those in Boston, a few miles away, where there was always something new to see in old books. Wentworth would catch hold of himself with a start, sometimes, and realize that he had spent half a day standing and reading in one of these bookstores. It was no wonder that in his senior year he recorded in his diary, "The Prex sent for me. . . . He found I'd cut 17 prayers. . . . I must look out."

IV

A LOOK AROUND

WENTWORTH'S FAMILY wanted him to become a lawyer. As a boy he had accepted the idea without giving it much thought. When he left college money was short in the family, and it seemed a good idea to interrupt his schooling and go to work and earn enough to pay for the post-graduate education needed for a profession. Supporting himself would provide a chance to look at the world outside before making his final commitment to a lifetime career. He wasn't much more than a boy when he graduated, not yet eighteen.

Shortly before commencement, he was engaged as an assistant instructor at a small boys' boarding school in a region south of Boston called Jamaica Plain. Although not much older than some of the youths who were to be his charges, Wentworth was well qualified to be a teacher. On leaving college he had a reading knowledge of six languages; sufficient achievement in higher mathematics to qualify him as a tutor for Harvard lower classmen; and a continuing passion for both books and physical activity. He described himself as having a "voracious desire for all knowledge and all action."

Though he was only a beginner, he had little trouble teaching the boys and less in making friends with them. In the 1840's, however, making friends with pupils or being on informal terms with them was sternly disapproved. The proprietor of this particular school,

Stephen Weld, was not ready for new methods. He barely tolerated the long rambling walks that the young teacher took with the boys in search of flowers and fresh air, sometimes in the pouring rain. Going out with one of the older boys to call on a pair of young ladies living nearby brought frowns. There was disapproval again when a note came from the director of a nearby girls' boarding school, complaining that one of the damsels had been disciplined after having been caught climbing out her window to take an early morning horseback ride with Higginson.

One day Mr. Weld walked in to find a circle of boys at one end of the dormitory, gathered around as if to see an exhibition. He walked over to the group and saw young Higginson and one of the older boys in the center, standing up facing each other, fists clenched, arms extended, and stripped to the waist. They were squaring off for some sparring.

"What's this! What's this!" demanded Weld.

"Just teaching them self-defense, sir," replied Wentworth. "There's nothing like it for indoor exercise, not to mention the protection it gives when they walk through Boston streets on a dark night."

"Come to my office young man," was the curt end of the conversation, as Weld turned on his heel and walked away.

A few weeks later the young enthusiast recorded in his diary, "February 28, 1842. School for the last time. Bid the boys goodbye quite satisfactorily—they are really sorry to lose me, and I felt so, too. . . ."

The involuntary departure from his position (the first of several during his life) proved to be a gain for young Wentworth. His regret at parting from his friends was temporary. He had not really liked boarding-school life. "I shall be perfectly sick of it before the year is out," he had confided to his diary in September. He was about to enter a period that would shape much of his life.

He soon found a new place as a private tutor. Such positions were common because of the low quality of private as well as public schools. He would take charge of three boys in the Boston suburb of Brookline. They were sons of a wealthy cousin, Stephen H. Perkins.

Shortly after he began teaching the Perkins boys, his widowed mother, his aunt Nancy, and two sisters, who made up the Cambridge household, sold their home to move to Brattleboro, Vermont, where they were to run a modest health resort.

Wentworth transferred his belongings, mostly books, to the Perkins house. It was from there that he was to take his first real look at life in the United States. He had been too young at Harvard and too isolated at Jamaica Plain to be able to understand very much about the world around him.

Seeking to learn about the world, especially what might be wrong with life in America was on the mind of the young people he came to know and mix with in the spring and summer of 1842. For one thing, the United States was just beginning to recover from its second major business depression. Young people had encountered women and children begging on the streets of Boston and had been shocked at the sight. They heard of families with children living in rat-infested rooms behind a stable or in a basement. They contributed to societies for the relief of the poor, but they did not stop at that. They wanted to understand more about the nature of a society that produced such evils, to find out what could be changed in their country to eliminate poverty.

Their interest and their inquiry was not limited to the problem of poverty. There was a whole sisterhood of reforms, as Higginson called it later, that attracted support in the New England he began to discover during his stay with the Perkins family. Rural folk and townspeople, educated and uneducated, were beginning to rebel against the injustice, inequality, and suffering they saw around them. They tried to pry down to the roots of it and they spoke out against what they thought were its causes. They did not mind being called "radical," since, as the good Latin scholars among them knew, the word meant only getting to the root of things.

The beginning of this reforming impulse probably came with

the antiwar sentiments that were America's response to news of the awful toll of the Napoleonic wars. It spread under the influence of new ideas in religion and philosophy. These were summed up by one group, who came to be called the Transcendentalists, as "love of individual freedom and hope of social progress." The desire for change was strengthened as the developing factory system and the growth of railroads created squalid slum conditions, and the life and death of communities came to be dependent on the self-interest of small groups of wealthy men.

One of the first of the leaders who inspired the reformers was the Boston Unitarian, Dr. William Ellery Channing. His fame and popularity were so great that when Charles Dickens visited the United States, he expressed as his greatest wish the desire to hear Dr. Channing preach. In his sermons Channing constantly maintained that the "ideal life was service to others," and many of his listeners enthusiastically accepted the idea. They were stimulated into questioning every social custom and economic institution of the day by sermons such as one saying, "I cannot endure to see one man establishing his arbitrary will over another by fraud or force or wealth or rank or superstitious claims."

Another leader in the growing movement of radical reform was Ralph Waldo Emerson, justly called by one biographer the wisest American. "Morality is the object of government," he told his listeners. When he said that, they knew he meant morality was not the object of the government they had inherited. "There is an infinite worthiness in man," he insisted, giving them hope that they could change the world so that morality would be the object of government. "What is man born for," he asked, "but to be a Reformer, a remaker of what man has made; a renouncer of lies; a restorer of truth and good?" Above all, said Emerson, it was wrong to be bound by the thinking of those who had preceded us. We must not look at God and nature through any eyes but our own; we must have "an original relation with the universe."

Influenced by Emerson and Channing, but the creator of his own ideas, was another inspiring leader of the generation of Wentworth's youth, the minister Theodore Parker. He spoke for many of the youthful reformers in rejecting both of the established political parties of the period, the Whigs and the Democrats. To him one was the symbol of money already acquired, and the other stood for the "Desire to get Money." Again and again he denounced the "itch to get rich," the single most dangerous threat, as he felt, to the democracy and people's government for which his grandfather had fought on Lexington common in 1775.

Under the influence of such men radical reformers multiplied and reached out for new ideas to examine, new evils to oppose, new changes to advocate. "What a fertility of projects for the salvation of the world!" Emerson remarked, when he stopped to survey the scene in 1844:

> *One apostle thought all men should go to farming, and another that no man should buy or sell, that the use of money was the cardinal evil; another that the mischief was in our diet, that we eat and drink damnation. . . . With these appeared the adepts of homeopathy, of hydropathy, of mesmerism, of phrenology. . . . With this din of opinion and debate there was a keener scrutiny of institutions and domestic life than any we had known; there was sincere protesting against existing evils, and there were changes of employment dictated by conscience.*

It was to this ferment of programs for changing the world that Wentworth was now exposed. The rebellious ideas that filled the air were not altogether new to him. He had attended some of Ralph Waldo Emerson's lectures even before he entered college. The great Dr. Channing was a relative by marriage. However, during his stay at the Perkins household, Wentworth was to associate more intimately with the young people who were part of the many reform movements.

Mr. Perkins, himself, the rich cousin who was his employer, was not at all like the predominantly conservative Boston merchants and bankers of his day. He gave active encouragement to an inquiring young mind. He was in a state of "social revolt" himself, he declared. He hated his business and put all his energy and interest into an art collection he was slowly assembling. "Think for yourself," he told Wentworth, "and don't be afraid of any new idea, so long as you examine it all round."

V

A CONTINUING EDUCATION

WENTWORTH DID NOT become a reformer or a radical critic of society overnight. When he went to the Perkins house to live he was more interested in the state of his clothes than the condition of the world. With his first month's earnings he bought an outfit centered on a flashy vest and showed himself wherever he could to display it. On one outing, after reaching Boston, he decided to go on to Cambridge so that he could be seen by his acquaintances there. Halfway to his destination, his new shoes began to pinch so much that he took them off and walked barefoot the rest of the way, new vest, new pants, and all.

Life as a tutor was not unpleasant. Four hours a day was all he had to spend in actual teaching. He was young enough to take part in and enjoy the boys' outdoor games, and his comradeship with them was not discouraged. They in turn were glad to join him on his nature walks and forest rambles. Sometimes he would have classes in the woods. Students and tutor would sit among the trees or in the branches, interrupting their work now and then to watch a weasel winding his way over a rock or to stalk a squirrel or chipmunk through branches and shrubs.

He did not lack activity to occupy his free time. There were always new books to read, and the more he read, the more he realized how much there was left to read. There were meetings of reformers in Boston where he would hear eloquent pleas for remedies for social injustice.

Evenings also provided concerts at which the bold and daring music of a composer named Beethoven was being introduced to the American public. Many afternoons and evenings were spent at a little bookstore in Boston that specialized in French and German books that introduced new thinkers and new ideas. One learned much from exchanging views with the patrons who frequented it. Proprietor of the bookstore and one of the best conversationalists was Miss Elizabeth Peabody, sister-in-law of Nathaniel Hawthorne and Horace Mann.

There was a lively social life at the Perkins house, enough to keep a young man busy even if he had no other interests. In the summer, especially, there was a constant round of visiting and entertaining among the suburban-type homes of the more prosperous Bostonians. Lawn parties and outdoor games helped fill out the program of activities.

Two of the visitors were unusually captivating: Barbara and Mary Channing, daughters of a physician who had married an aunt of Wentworth. They were nieces of the great liberal church leader. Both were attractive and serious, and Mary's conversation came to be especially interesting.

Soon after their first visit, Barbara announced a novelty: she had invited some friends who were members of the Community. All summer there had been talk of this Community, also known as Brook Farm. It was supposed to be quite radical and daring. The founder and guiding spirit was George Ripley, who had been inspired by their uncle, Reverend Channing. Ripley set out to prove that human life could be made happier, more productive, and more culturally rewarding if the effects of competition for profit were removed.

The Community was a small-scale cooperative association, the members of which had bought land and buildings, out of their pooled funds, in the nearby town of West Roxbury. Each member was pledged to do manual labor and could at the same time continue his own education or help to educate others. A school, at which some of the members taught, was a part of the Brook Farm Community. Children from outside were eligible, and many attended because of the high caliber of the teachers. The revenue helped to support the radical experiment.

Young Higginson was to have only a passing acquaintance with Brook Farm. He was impressed by Barbara's guests on the sunny Sunday summer afternoon when they first visited. They proved to be serious and well-bred young men, wearing gaily colored shirts and tasseled berets. They were looked upon with disapproval by Mr. Perkins, who conceded, however, their right to make fools of themselves.

Later Wentworth and Barbara visited the Farm itself and saw its members at work and at play. He felt a stirring of sympathy when they talked of how they would prove that labor could be dignified and free, and that exploitation, the preying of one human being on another, was not a necessary part of life. He was not frightened when some of them described what they were doing as Socialism. Years later Nathaniel Hawthorne, who had been a member of Brook Farm and had lost his savings when it failed, poked fun at it in one of his novels but conceded generously, "We had struck upon what ought to be a truth. Posterity may dig it up and profit by it." Higginson agreed.

Mary Channing began to take more of his time and attention than her sister Barbara during the Brookline months. She had a lively and irrepressible, if sometimes sharp, sense of humor, and they had great fun teasing each other. Although Mary was three years older—Wentworth was then only nineteen—she made a fine companion and good friend for the lonely boy whose family was now so many miles away. In his free evenings and week ends they would travel to Boston together. There they would listen to the sermons of Mary's favorite minister, James Freeman Clarke, whose leading themes were social justice, peace, and dignity and freedom for the common man, black or white. Sometimes they would attend a concert or an Emerson lecture and spend hours together afterwards, walking and talking about books or ideas for social reform.

Books and more books. There never seemed to be enough of them. His reading ranged far and wide in the world's literature: the great Greek and Roman classics; the polished British essayists; and most important of all, the new European writers of the day, children of the French Revolution and exponents of the ideas of freedom and brotherhood. Wentworth did not limit himself to social questions or politics in his reading. He had a hunger for information and a thirst for ideas that were never satisfied. The lonely and quiet hours with his books took most of his free time. They seemed more important than the many attractions and distractions that surrounded him.

He often dreamed of following the examples of the writers he admired. The idea that appealed to him above all others was that it was a man's duty to use his talents to help lead the world to a better way of life. He came to despise the belief that accumulation of wealth was the foremost object of life. He made up his mind that come what might poverty would never hold any terrors for him as long as he could keep body and soul together and throw his energy into the things he wanted to do.

It was not easy for him to decide upon a career. At one point, it seemed enough to dream of having "books and nature" and no more. Even at nineteen he could see after a while that that was impractical. Then it occurred to him to go off and rent a plot of ground in the midst of the woods where he could grow peach trees. His plan was to raise just enough to make it possible to have freedom for study and thought in a lonely confrontation with nature. Two years later, a few miles away, a Massachusetts man named Henry Thoreau was to do something very similar.

The prospect of isolation from people was too unpleasant and caused Wentworth to drop the idea. Even if it had not been for his increasing affection for Mary Channing, he liked society too much to cut himself off from it. He was not interested in the company of the Boston aristocrats and the merchants that he often saw and met at Brookline. It was the society of plain people of all sorts and varieties and conditions of life that he liked.

"I cannot live alone, I long to come out and obtain a working place among men." He confided his troubled thoughts to a dairy:

> *I crave action, unbounded action. I love men passionately. I feel intensely their sufferings and shortcomings and yearn to make all men brothers. There is no man too small to be useful, so he be true and bold.*

Such reflections would have pleased his relative, the celebrated Doctor Channing, who had written during his last year in reflecting about the number, variety, and seeming extremism of the New England Reformers, "Nothing terrifies me in their wildest movements. What has for years terrified me and discouraged me is apathy."

One outlet Wentworth began to explore during these months was writing. Writing poetry particularly pleased and appealed to him as a way of expressing himself on the brotherhood of man and at the same time winning the approval and respect of his fellow men. He began to write verses and was very excited when some of them were published in the little magazines to which they were sent. His words looked better in print. It thrilled him even more when a distant relative would ask, "Did you write that beautiful thing?" However, his poetry wasn't really good, and although one noted editor admitted, in rejecting some, that it showed "truth and earnestness," Wentworth, himself, recognized after a couple of years that his mark would have to be made in a different way.

While experimenting with poetry, Wentworth continued to wonder what he would do to make a living. Neither a poet nor any other artist, with rare exceptions, could sustain himself in America by his art alone. It did become clear to him before very long that what he did *not* want to do was to become a lawyer.

He had let his family choose for him before he entered college, when he did not have the slightest idea what it meant to practice law. He looked through some law books one day during this Brookline period, when he was supposed to be saving money to put himself through law school. At first he was interested. They were books, and that was to their credit, but as he reflected on their contents, he could see no more to them than a system of rules for the protection of the property of those who already had more property than they needed. There was nothing he could find about the rights of those who needed protection: the poor, the Irish, whom he saw so badly treated, or the sailors, whose lot, he had learned from his cousin, Richard Dana, was so hard. There was no tool in Blackstone or any other law book for combating the evils of the society he saw around him. The idea of giving up his freedom of thought and action to become the servant of persons of property and help them hold on to their property and make it grow repelled him. The law, he told a friend, was but a "fossilized system of injustice."

The organized system of rules for the protection of property interests that the courts seemed set up to administer was not for him. He would not surrender his life to what Blackstone represented. Not once during the rest of his life did he regret this decision. He was free to be a nonconformist like his ancestor Reverend Francis Higginson, who had fled from England two centuries before as a radical political refugee.

VI

STUDENT FOR FREEDOM

ONE FINE AUGUST afternoon in 1843 Mrs. John Farrar, an old family friend, saw an odd sight on the road from Brookline to Cambridge. A tiny wagon was lumbering through the mud, laden with clothes, a desk, a cot, and miscellaneous baggage. The driver, spattered and dirty, whom she hardly recognized at first, was Wentworth Higginson. He was returning to Cambridge to enroll as a resident graduate student. He did not know what he wanted to study at Harvard. "Indeed," he said, "I came here to find out."

Of one thing he was certain. He wrote to his mother after having given notice to Mr. Perkins, "Regard it as from this day settled! That I need not study a profession. NO LAW! Hurrah!" Then, as if he anticipated what she might be thinking when she read the letter in far-off Brattleboro, he added, "By the various old gentlemen who ask me every time they see me what my profession is to be, I do not expect my plans to be understood or approved."

Wentworth did have a vague notion that he might prepare for a professorship in mathematics or literature. He was in no great hurry to commit himself to a course of study. He had, however, just before his return to Cambridge, committed himself to Mary Channing. She was twenty-two and he was nineteen, and she was sufficiently older and wiser to understand his need to find himself. She was patient and agreed to the long engagement that seemed inevitable.

It was possible then to register as a graduate student without being assigned to any particular faculty or course of study. As a free-lance scholar, Wentworth began to browse about in the enormous wealth of the world of knowledge. At about this time he became increasingly aware that one of his outside interests took precedence over all the others. His state and his country were beginning to divide and his friends to take sides in the growing controversy over slavery. As heated words were exchanged in print and at meetings, as the issue seemed to become more urgent, Thomas Wentworth Higginson soon found his place.

Neither the slavery controversy nor his own interest in it began in 1843. The debate was at least as old as Judge Sewell's pamphlet of 1700, which Wentworth's ancestor John Higginson had helped distribute. Wentworth's personal consciousness of a great wrong had begun when he heard the story of his mother's visit, before his birth, to the family of a southern Harvard student with whom the Higginsons had become friendly. While being driven from the plantation to a nearby home by a well-dressed, handsome Negro coachman who seemed better off than many teamsters in Massachusetts, Mrs. Higginson had turned and remarked that his life seemed very happy though he was a slave. At this the driver gave her a long, lingering, sorrowful look and said simply, "Ah missis! Free breath is good."

Slavery might be mild in some places and harsh in others, but it was the institution itself and what it did to people that so grievously injured the United States. Wentworth came very soon to see this, while the conflict sharpened between those who opposed slavery, on the one hand, and those who favored or were indifferent to it, on the other. It was not only, or even primarily, the system of forced labor and the violation of human dignity that made slavery obnoxious. The Irish around Boston and the poorer classes in the North had no choice but to work at low wages and in miserable circumstances. Their conditions of life in the factory towns and along the railroads were abominable. Slavery superimposed on involuntary servitude the spread of a poisonous sentiment of racial prejudice: a belief that bondage was the natural and proper condition of the Negro. From this developed the idea that flourished as widely in the North as in the South, that the white race was superior, the Negro inferior and unfit to associate socially with the white.

To recognize that slavery and the ideas of racial prejudice it fostered were evil and endangered free America was one thing. To do something about it was quite another. It was an institution that was entirely legal in the states where it was practiced, and to those among whom Wentworth grew up it seemed a normal part of their country's social order and economic organization. Nevertheless, voices of protest had long been heard. During the first part of our history, they were even louder in the South than in the North. Then, as slavery began to become especially profitable, after the invention of the cotton gin, these voices were heard less often.

As if to compensate, a new source of protest opened up in the northern states. In 1827, four years after Wentworth was born, the free Negroes of the North, who in their scattered and segregated communities never forgot their brothers in the South, began a fighting newspaper called *Freedom's Journal.* Two years later a southern-born black Bostonian named David Walker wrote and published a pamphlet, *Appeal to the Colored Citizens of the World,* calling on his people to fight for freedom. Shortly after this William Lloyd Garrison founded a newspaper named *The Liberator.* This newspaper was to continue, until the end of the Civil War, to demand the abolition of slavery and to combat prejudice on grounds of color.

As means of communication improved, as railroads and canals were built, we came more and more to be a single nation instead of a loose group of separate states. Business and trade flourished, and an important part of the expanding economy was the marketing of raw cotton and its export, and the domestic manufacture and sale of cotton products. More and more people in the northern states began to have a direct financial interest in the continuance of slavery in the southern states. Bankers and merchants, millowners and exporters, and the many who worked for them and

THE LIBERATOR.

OL. I.] WILLIAM LLOYD GARRISON AND ISAAC KNAPP, PUBLISHERS. [NO. 22.

OSTON, MASSACHUSETTS.] OUR COUNTRY IS THE WORLD—OUR COUNTRYMEN ARE MANKIND. [SATURDAY, MAY 28, 1831.

Masthead of Garrison's Liberator.

depended on the cotton trade united to defend slavery and to spread the belief in racial difference that was used to justify it.

What gradually happened to America was strange and shocking. Fifty years before, in a world ruled by monarchies and aristocracies, the idea of liberty had been an American idea and the love of liberty an American passion. After our own Revolution was won, we were quick to hear the call of the oppressed—when it came from foreign lands. If a people were victimized by another, whether because of recent conquest or ancient wrong, we would lend spiritual and material help, as long as it was outside our borders. But from Maine to Minnesota and down the Mississippi, most Americans tolerated oppressors at home. Color prejudice had become so widespread that most white Americans were literally deaf and blind to mistreatment of one-sixth of their people. In northern states, persons with enough African ancestry to darken their skin were not treated as free citizens. They were excluded from schools, jobs, and professions and subjected to indignities in places of amusement, inns, and transportation facilities.

Prejudice and profit were the two chief barriers in the way of those who sought to abolish slavery. The combination of profit and prejudice produced a third obstacle: repression of dissent. As a boy Wentworth Higginson had stood before his Cambridge home, clutching his mother's hand and watching the flames of the

Ursuline convent in the distance. That had been an early and eloquent lesson concerning the danger of mass prejudice to liberty, that a lawless mob could be as great a threat to freedom as a dictatorial government.

Within a year after the attack on the convent another Boston mob taught another such lesson. This time a meeting of the Boston Female Antislavery Society was broken up and the mob almost lynched William Lloyd Garrison. His newspaper, *The Liberator,* had a tiny circulation. It was read and supported financially by more Negroes than whites. Nevertheless it had a tremendous influence in helping mold public opinion in support of the antislavery cause. The response to that early success in combating bigotry was the mob attack, a mob described as composed of gentlemen of property and standing, in an effort to still Garrison's voice.

Wentworth's conversion from mere sympathetic observer of the abolition movement to an active member was completed during his first year of graduate study at Cambridge. Among the many and varied groups working for social change in New England in the early 1840's, the abolitionists had seemed the most worthy and the most persecuted. He instinctively felt that there must be something fine and admirable in the little band of devoted men and women who feared neither the violence of mobs nor the loss of friends, jobs, or economic opportunities.

Once, while he was still trying to decide whether to pass from the ranks of the sympathizers to those of the active members of the abolitionist cause, he described to a guest in his uncle's Brookline home his admiration for William Lloyd Garrison. His listener was an old gentleman of fine and delicate bearing who always presented himself with the sweetest courtesy and who was said to cultivate the finest roses to be found near Boston. He listened attentively, continuing, during Wentworth's enthusiastic praise, quietly to sip his glass of wine. "It may be as you say," he responded gently when the young man finished, "I never saw him, but I always supposed him to be a fellow who ought to be hung."

The hostility of such men—who still, in 1843, spoke for most of Boston—may have been due to a financial stake in slavery or color prejudice or fear of insurrection, or a combination of all three. Their opposition did not deter Wentworth in his search for the right road. His interest grew each time he attended a meeting or convention in Boston. There he saw mixed audiences mingling without any self-consciousness. He saw and heard eloquent Negro speakers, some of them ex-slaves, as well as Garrison's white allies, agitators who had given up family life or middle-class careers to enlist in the cause and dedicate themselves to its service. Many in the audience were low-paid white factory workers, who united with even more poorly paid free Negroes to help meet the expenses of the movement.

What completed Wentworth's conversion to the abolitionist cause of fighting slavery in the South and prejudice in the North was his study of two books. Each had been written by a woman, a factor not without a related meaning. In the white-ruled nation the female sex was itself an oppressed group. Women could not vote, were not permitted to own property, were excluded from many professions and occupations and restricted in others.

Lydia Maria Child, author of the work that most impressed him, was one of the first American women to attain success as a writer. A few years after first hearing Garrison she risked and lost her hard-won popularity by publishing a work called *An Appeal in Favor of That Class of Americans Called Africans.* This was a careful study of slavery and its evils and an attack on discrimination in the North as well. "Our prejudice against colored people," wrote Mrs. Child, "is even more inveterate than it is at the South."

The other book that helped determine Wentworth in his course was written by Harriet Martineau, a very successful English writer who had toured the United States as a celebrity and who was visiting Boston at the time of the mob attack on Garrison. This had helped inspire her to write a short study of the abolitionist movement called *The Martyr Age in America.* This book described the nobility and courage of the antislavery agitators as

Frederick Douglass Statue in Rochester, New York.

COURTESY OF ASSOCIATION FOR THE STUDY OF NEGRO LIFE AND HISTORY

having a remarkable character, one that "has perhaps never been witnessed" in the world before.

The title of Mrs. Child's book was obviously inspired by the *Appeal,* the pioneer work by the free Negro, David Walker. Her *Appeal* was a calm, strong, systematic, careful study of the history of slavery, its influence on politics, and of the feelings of the community against the Negroes who were its own victims. Miss Martineau described the effect of its publication on Mrs. Child's reputation. She was "a lady of whom society was exceedingly proud before she published her *Appeal*, and to whom society has been extremely contemptuous ever since." Wentworth studied the *Appeal* early in 1843, and it left him with no doubt whatsoever as to his course; when he then read Miss Martineau's little book on the abolitionists, he resolved to join them. He regretted only that, as it seemed to him, the most important, heroic, and self-sacrificing part of their work had already been done, and there was so little left for him to do.

This was not quite true, as he was to learn during the next twenty years.

VII

INTO THE MINISTRY

"DEAR MARY," began the letter, "I have been worrying a great deal lately as to what is to be done for this preposterous world." It was not difficult to get from Cambridge to Boston or even Brookline to see Mary at least once a week, but those few hours together did not give him half a chance to do all the talking he wanted to do. There was so much to say, always, and Mary was a wonderful listener. He felt as though he were speaking to her now, as he sat up late in his lonely room, rambling on about the future.

"The great reason why the apostles of truth don't make any more impression is this—" he went on, continuing with the subject that he now thought about most often, "the moment any person among us begins to broach any 'new views' and intimate that all things aren't exactly right, the conservatives lose no time holding up their fingers and branding him as an unsafe person—fanatic, visionary, insane and all the rest of it—this has been the case with all reforms great and small and moreover there is often some ground for it because it is the enthusiastic (i.e. half cracked) people who begin all reforms. Mrs. Child you know has long been proscribed as an entirely unsafe person and as for Mr. Emerson and Mr. Alcott, it doesn't do for a sober person even to *think* of them."

The one thing he was certain about, as his first year of random graduate study drew to a close, was that he was going to continue to insist on speaking out in favor of new ideas if he thought they were any good. The more he thought about this, the more he realized he would have to find a life's work that would make it possible for him to do so without fear of what people might think. Companionship with Mary helped him find the answer. For some time she had belonged to a congregation whose minister, James Freeman Clarke, preached the Unitarian creed, "He loves God most who loves man best." It did not take too many Sundays of listening to Clarke before Wentworth saw a future for himself.

It was true that Theodore Parker, his own favorite, and Clarke were an exceptional pair. Most ministers, even in New England, refrained from facing the great issue of the day. Some gave aid and comfort to those who insisted that slavery must, for the sake of the country's peace and harmony, be left undisturbed. Only a few years before, while Clarke was still a young preacher in far-off Kentucky and Parker in a suburb, it had not been possible to find a church in Boston where a memorial service could be read for Karl Follen, who had died in a tragic steamboat fire. Dr. Follen had been a professor in Germany, driven from there because of his stand for political freedom. He found intolerance here after he joined the abolitionists and lost his post at Harvard in consequence. The vast majority of Boston ministers shrank from Clarke and Parker and refused them the common courtesy of exchanging pulpits.

On the Sundays when Mary took Wentworth to Clarke's Church of the Disciples, the student found himself more and more inclined to the idea of the liberal ministry. He knew he had the answer to his problem of choosing a career when he heard Reverend Clarke's lecture to his congregation, relating the experience of his seven years in a slave state. The Reverend said:

> *Abolitionists have stated the evils of slavery very strongly, but they never have been overstated. It is a condition of perpetual warfare. Not only are untold cruelties inflicted on*

the slaves almost as a matter of necessity; but among the whites deeds of violence, duels, street-shootings, death by lynch-law, mob violence in all its forms are common. The young men grow up in the midst of license and self-indulgence of all kinds.

He went on to tell of the exceptions, the honorable and upright men and women who felt responsibility for the care and comfort and spiritual well-being of their slaves. "But the system itself is so evil," he concluded, "that it made their best efforts almost useless."

As Wentworth listened with rapt attention, he realized that he had the answer to his own problem. A person could accomplish something for his fellow man, could really lead a manly life in the pulpit. All that was necessary was to win the honor and love and respect of the congregation, as Clarke obviously had. Then it would be possible to defy the few who attempted to control the minister's conscience because they dominated the source of his income. Could he win such love and admiration from enough parishioners in a community? Wentworth decided it was worth the effort to find out. He enrolled at the Harvard Divinity School.

The months went slowly, the work was hard, and funds were short. He economized by cooking in his room, boiling water over his study lamp. He would go on bread and milk all week, without a square meal until Sunday, when he and Mary could have dinner with one or another prosperous friend.

Although Wentworth spent much time with the heavy and sometimes dreary theological treatises required in Divinity School, he never ceased to study and discuss the perpetual flow of radical ideas that reformers proposed for the improvement of society. One day he wrote to Mary on a new subject:

I do go for the rights of women as far as an equal education and an equal share in government goes. . . . I think it a monstrous absurdity to talk of a democratic government and universal suffrage and yet exclude one-half the inhabitants without any ground of incapacity to plead.

On another occasion, there was thrust in his hand at a public meeting a little booklet advancing the idea (quite novel in those days) that workingmen would never get fair wages or decent treatment unless they united together to deal as a group with the mill and factory owners. The thought electrified him. "I have read the articles on the organization of labor," he wrote Mary, "and if I were a rich man would have 30,000 printed and distributed."

Neither his schoolwork nor his interest in Boston agitators and reformers could diminish Wentworth's love for physical exercise and activities that would bring him close to nature. If he could not interest his fellow religious students, he would find younger undergraduates with whom he could play football or baseball. In summer, he went as often as he could to swim in the Charles River. If there was no time during daylight hours, he would slip out alone at night and return to his room at two A.M. to write to Mary how he had found it "beautiful to lie back on the water and gaze at the midnight sky." In winter there was Fresh Pond to skate upon, where he had spent many hours in his boyhood. At odd times, there were nature walks, with or without botany students, to the many haunts where there were still new lichens or mosses to study or insects to discover and impale and bring back triumphantly to the natural history collection he had helped start as an undergraduate.

Toward the end of his first year of Divinity School a growing mood of doubt and self-questioning overwhelmed him. Was it right for him to imprison himself within the narrow, sheltered confines of a minister's life? His hopes for a career of devotion to humanity in liberal religion were overcome by fear of the limitations imposed on a minister. "Preaching alone I should love," he reflected, "but I feel inwardly that something more will be sought of me.—An aesthetic life—how beautiful—but the life of a Reformer, a People's Guide 'battling for the right'—glorious, but, Oh how hard!" After much inward debate, he withdrew from the Divinity School when he had completed his first year.

During the next year he read and studied widely in philosophy, poetry, and European literature. He continued with his own tentative efforts at writing poetry and review essays for the nonconformist radical and religious magazines. He enjoyed the companionship of the men of letters and learning to be found in the Cambridge community. One direction in which he continued unchecked during his twenty-second year was the agitation of dissenting views on public questions, especially those questions having to do with slavery.

In the autumn of 1845, men of conscience in America awoke to find their country on the road to a war of aggression against Mexico. Theodore Parker thundered from his pulpit, "War is treason to the people, to mankind, to God." He and others like him believed that the threatened war with Mexico was to be a war of naked conquest for the benefit of slavery, a totally discreditable and dishonorable war. All agreed that it was the duty of a patriot to denounce and to oppose a war in which their nation was in the wrong.

Wentworth concurred with all his heart and plunged into the antiwar fight. He composed antiwar poems, one of which was published in Garrison's *The Liberator*. He collected hundreds of signatures to petitions, going from door to door in the poorer quarters of town to explain patiently and quietly at each house why one who truly loved his country must resist government efforts to plunge into an unjust war.

The war went on in spite of the signatures and poems and protests and such acts of conscience as the refusal of Henry Thoreau, a few miles away, to pay his two-dollar poll tax. Wentworth shuddered at the decision of President Polk to order troops to cross into Mexican territory, forcing the unwilling Mexican government to fight back. He saw the power of an unholy alliance between the southern planters—who allowed no freedom of speech or press on issues having to do with slavery—and northern merchants and mill operators. With the North divided and the South united, slaveowners would always dominate Washington, he feared, and the Constitution, written with built-in provisions to protect slavery, could never be changed.

The antislavery movement was becoming divided in the 1840's. The political abolitionists believed they could depend on democratic means alone and the Disunion Abolitionists held that the Constitution could never be amended to protect genuine liberty as long as the slave-states remained in the Union. "To Disunion I now subscribe," wrote Wentworth, "in the full expectation that a time is coming which may expose to obloquy and danger even the most insignificant of the adherents to such a cause."

His participation in the abolitionist movement as an active advocate was an education in itself. There was at first, as he wrote to his mother in Brattleboro, "the excitement of the great Abolition convention." Then there was the pleasure of the discovery that he had gotten "the run of slavery argumentation now and can talk Abolitionism pretty well." The thrill of warning his family was next, "Do not be afraid of seeing my name signed to pieces in papers."

His idealism and his sense of commitment increased at the meetings at which white and Negro shared the platform, and Negro and white sat side-by-side in the audience. His mother saw this as she read his weekly letter:

> *The most interesting and moving speech of all I have heard this week was by an old colored woman, Mrs. Thompson of Bangor. This old lady rose among the crowd and began to speak—all stood up to gaze on her, but she fixed her eyes on the chairman and burst out into a most ardent, eloquent and beautiful tribute of gratitude from herself and her race to Garrison; her voice was clear and her language fluent and easy; when she sat down there was a spontaneous burst of applause. It was a truly beautiful and noble scene, one which opened to one's view the prospect of a future*

when American Brotherhood shall be a reality of daily life and honor and respect be given where they are truly due.

As his year's leave of absence drew to a close, he began once more to realize the need to have a platform for the message he wanted to convey. His application for readmission was granted, and he plunged into his final year of Divinity School. He was soon to report to his mother:

Am busy on two dissertations—one on the erroneous views of the Scriptures—the other on the early history of the Trinity—both of which give an opportunity for original and "unsound" views. . . . Nothing keeps a man so fresh as abolitionism and kindred propensities, I observe.

VIII

ON TO NEWBURYPORT

ELDER HOLLAND was a respectable Christian minister from Buffalo. He was considered a liberal, as ministers went, and made no secret of the fact that he read the essays of Ralph Waldo Emerson (then considered a radical intellectual) as fast as they were published. During a convention that brought him to Cambridge in December, 1846, he attended a Friday evening Divinity School debate and heard a fiery young student argue against setting up the scriptures as "absolute master of reason and conscience."

When Wentworth had finished, Elder Holland pursed his lips and turned to a nearby member of the faculty. "Does that young man ever expect to find a pulpit to preach in?"

He was expressing a concern that Wentworth shared, though the young agitator did not worry as much about his future as did his more conservative older brothers and sisters. They had been having many uneasy moments as to what the baby of the family might do next. The Mexican War was disturbing even conservative Bostonians, and so they had a certain sympathy with his antislavery opinions, if not with his methods of expressing them. They shook their heads anxiously, however, over his ideas on the rights of women. Even his mother, who was always more sympathetic and understanding, wrote in bewilderment to her son, "You don't want women to vote, do you, or be lawyers, or go to Congress?"

Senior at Divinity School, 1846.

COURTESY MRS. WILLIAM HALLOWELL AND MRS. W. J. WOODIN

The time came for members of the senior class to scout around for congregations that would accept them after graduation. Wentworth responded to an invitation from a New Hampshire church to come one week end for a couple of trial sermons. Their minister was scheduled to leave that June for another town. The student-preacher received high praise from the minister's wife, a fellow radical. "A real Parker sermon," she declared. The rest of the congregation was more cautious, and Wentworth did not hear from them again. "I can't make up my mind," he wrote his mother, "whether my radicalisms will be the ruin of me or not."

Later on in the spring he was asked to preach as a candidate at Newburyport, a Massachusetts seaport village near the New Hampshire border. His mother was visiting Boston that week, staying with his older sisters, and Wentworth went to call before catching the stagecoach. He wore, with great pride, a very dashing tweed overcoat with matching cap, quite the thing for the man-about-town but not the usual Sunday garb of a would-be minister.

"You aren't going to wear anything so unclerical, are you?" asked his sister, "It will ruin your prospects."

"Let him wear it by all means," answered his mother for him. "If they cannot stand that clothing, they can never stand its wearer."

His mother's opinion prevailed, and so it was an unusually fashionable-looking young radical who sailed in to Newburyport for the first of his guest sermons. It was possible that the raiment obscured the radicalism. Those noting his appearance, he was later told, felt that at worst it meant that there might be "some pleasant admixture of heresy" about him. Even more protective were the weather conditions in a wet March in Newburyport. Only the hardiest (and probably not the well-to-do conservatives) waded to the church to hear the new candidate under the conditions he described to his mother:

> *My second visit to Newburyport was singularly analogous to the first. Then the state of matters overhead made going to church impossible—this time ditto ditto underfoot. Sunday the sun rose triumphant, however, but what was my horror on finding a state of slosh compared to which the direst experiences of Boston, Cambridge, or Brattleboro are peace and pavement! A few undaunted females were seen picking their way hen-like along, while anxious men were seen in all directions jumping across puddles and plumping into the middle of deeper ones. Of course the audience was not much greater than the Sunday before, and great were the lamentations, of course, of the saddened parish committee.*

Clothes, weather, or limited audience, whatever it was, the parish committee overlooked the young candidate's outspoken views. The Newburyport invitation seemed to be definite, and Mary and Wentworth made plans to marry and set up housekeeping.

Time seemed to drag between Wentworth's return from Newburyport in March and his graduation in July. He was now twenty-three years old and had been a student for what had been a long, long, time. Most of his classmates at college were out making their way in the world, and he had hardly started. Before him, at last, there was the prospect of being able to put his energy and his talent to the use of mankind. The vision of the Transcendalist, that man was perfectible and that the human condition could be improved by ceaseless striving, seemed very real to him, and its realization within reach. He needed only to preach and lead, and the people of Newburyport, he thought, would learn and follow.

When, in July, graduation day arrived, the twelve new young ministers were each to deliver a sermon to mark the event. They spoke in alphabetical order. Wentworth was seventh to rise and if, perchance, some of the audience were by then nodding drowsily, he woke them up. A little stir began with the announcement of his title, "The Clergy and Reform," for reform in 1847 meant radical social change. Wentworth spared no feelings, used no soft words. He worked up to his climax:

> *There are social evils against which we know that Christ, if alive, would have protested with the whole strength of his soul—evils which require the Christ-like spirit of love and moral indignation to put them down; and yet those who fall to the office of minister of Christ—(I speak not of particular denominations)—have not only left them untouched and even unmentioned, but have actually lent their influence by threatening, by slander, and even by satire, against those who would touch them.*

It was not until later on that the young agitator was to learn that some of his shafts, too well directed, had struck home, that his sermon was a "rock of offense" to many of his listeners. All he heard on graduation day was praise. Even Mary, usually a very restrained commentator and often a severe critic, was pleased and excited. Others agreed that the young radical had stood head and shoulders above his classmates. Theodore Parker shook his hand. Parker told his young admirer that he had made the trip especially to hear him and that he was not disappointed by what he had heard. Edward Everett Hale, too, had some kind words. He was glad, he said, to hear that there was someone who was going to electrify the world.

A Divinity School graduate who has found his first pulpit has a great advantage over the graduates of most other professional schools. He does not have to descend from the giddy heights of the senior class to the bottom of his profession. He begins at once to have the responsibilities and the status of a full-fledged practitioner. Especially pleased with this aspect of his choice of life's work, Wentworth began his new ministry with self-confidence and courage.

His installation was presided over by two other liberal unitarian ministers, his cousin W.H. Channing and his model, James Freeman Clarke. The latter's exhortations to the beginner to devote himself to reforming the evils of mankind and combating slavery were hardly necessary. Two weeks later Mary Channing and Thomas Wentworth Higginson were married, and they settled down to their new life.

In 1847 Newburyport was already quite an old town. The original parish in nearby Newbury had first been settled in 1635. The seaside section, where construction of small vessels and coastal trade had become important, had broken away in the early years of the seventeenth century. When Wentworth arrived, he was most impressed with High Street, the town's main thoroughfare, lined with the handsome dwellings of sea captains and foreign traders. The Unitarian church he was to preside over had an old-fashioned dignity, with its tall white spire, but it did not please him as a building. The pulpit particularly bothered him. It was raised so high over the congregation that he could not have the feeling of talking *with* them. The high elevation gave him always the feeling of preaching *at* them.

In his first weeks at his post, the parishioners showed a certain regard for him by a full and attentive presence at church. Personally and socially they were standoffish. New Englanders in smaller villages, then as now, tended to regard as strangers newcomers who came from as far as ten miles away. The newcomers might live in a place for many years and yet never be accepted as fellow townsmen. But Wentworth felt they were listening to him, and that was what was most important. One rich member of the congregation greeted him laconically when they met and then unexpectedly remarked. "That was a right good whipping you gave them Sunday afternoon on freedom of speech."

"I have not yet found one," he wrote his brother, "who approves the war or disapproves free speech on the minister's part and I begin to feel somewhat confident that they will stand the trials I have ready for them." The Reverend T.W. Higginson was too optimistic. He had not yet seen that week's Newburyport *Herald,* the town's conservative paper. The editor had listened to a sermon or two and found much to be concerned about in the "radical and imaginative notions" of the young preacher. You can no more change a world whose destiny has been determined by God, he warned, than a farmer can control the weather. Having sounded his warning, the editor was not heard from again for some time.

A new minister, even though a young stranger, will usually find that there is a special social standing that goes with his position, and he will associate with the most "respectable" elements of a community. Wentworth found himself, because of his interests and convictions, mixed up as well with "all that was most radical."

Wentworth had become an abolitionist at Cambridge without having committed himself to any definite opinions on any of the other new ideas that percolated around the community. In Newburyport he found there was an expectation that a bold thinker on one subject would recognize an affinity between his belief and the beliefs of others who were trying to change the world for the better. One who concentrated on pacifism was expected to be sympathetic to the temperance movement, which was considered then to be a necessity for improving the condition of the poorer classes, and these overlapped with antislavery, vegetarianism, and so on. Wentworth's cousin W.H. Channing had warned him against vegetarianism as sapping a man's strength, and so he never went that far.

There was a special area for the concern of reformers that was new to Newburyport, and it did not take long for his friends in the antislavery movement to draw him into it: the condition of factory workers, who worked at miserably low wages for unbelievably long hours—fourteen hours a day, many of them, six days a week.

It was not at all unexpected for a minister to interest himself in the conditions of the poor. The usual thing, however, was for the man of the church to make sure the pressures of poverty did not too seriously impair the morals of the underprivileged, and to help make available such charity as might be solicited for the especially needy cases that developed. This was not at all the limit of Reverend Higginson's concern. What were the causes of this poverty that he saw around him, he wanted to know, and how could the poor be helped to change their condition? He wrote to his aunt Nancy, in Brattleboro, "This charity is *unnatural,* I think. It seems so much easier to prevent, than to cure poverty. It isn't because I sympathize too little that I find charity painful, but because I sympathize too much."

Reverend Higginson went on to take an active interest in the working people of the factory district and to concern himself about their conditions and long hours of labor. For the rest of his life he was to ponder about the root cause of such conditions and how they could be eliminated. He saw that the problem was complex. One could not, as with the slaves, simply say at one stroke, "You are free," and thus end the matter. He realized that the social structure of the America of small independent farmers and craftsmen in which he was born had been changing before his eyes. Ralph Waldo Emerson, leader of Transcendentalist thought, had put the case in a nutshell:

The nobles shall not any longer, as feudal lords, have power of life and death over the churls, but now, in another shape, as capitalists, shall in all love and peace eat these up as before.

On the practical and immediate side, the young minister saw two ways in which he could help. Some of the workers began to agitate for the passage of a Ten Hour Day Bill by the Massachusetts State Legislature. Higginson supported this vigorously. He also established an evening school for the adult education of the working people, many of whom had little or no schooling, even the native born. It was Higginson's belief that with education and a better understanding of the nature of the world in which they lived these people would find ways to help themselves. One of the bright young girls he enlisted to work as a teacher in the workers' evening school wrote of the youthful minister, "Mr. Higginson was like a great archangel to us all then, and there were so many of us! Coming into the humdrum life of the town, he was like someone from another star."

IX

OUT OF THE PULPIT

THE NEW MINISTER preached hard and worked hard in behalf of the causes that commanded his loyalty. His experiments at poetry and prose were forgotten for the time being. Writing sermons used up his productive energy. In his early years in Newburyport his literary interests were indulged by his contacts with many of the noted American writers of the day. Some of these meetings occurred during Wentworth's excursions away from Newburyport; others when these writers visited his town. In the New England of 1848, a literary figure was likely to lead another life as well: either as a lecturer for hire or as a reformer-agitator.

One whose home was not far off—near enough for a pleasant hike, sail, or row—was John Greenleaf Whittier. Rural poet and reformer, Quaker and abolitionist, he was a people's bard unmatched by any in our history for his activities as a friend of mankind. Whittier's first poem in honor of the abolitionist leader William Lloyd Garrison was written when Wentworth was eight years old. For decades every new verse he wrote was recited at workingmen's meetings, rural picnics, and church socials. When he did not deal with antislavery subjects or antiwar crusading, his poetry concerned itself with the life or work of the shoemaker, shipbuilder, fisherman, or farmer, or the activities of the "barefoot boy." Wentworth, who did not make friends easily as yet, found relaxation and inspiration in frequent visits to this veteran of the freedom movement of the thirties and forties.

Sometimes an engagement that took Wentworth farther away provided a welcome change of scenery and audience. Traveling was still primitive in the United States in 1848, and even a visit to Concord, nearby in Massachusetts and hardly an hour's drive today, could result in a variety of adventures. "I had a queer time going to Concord," he wrote to his mother, "part in stage and part in sleigh and was upset once in each, together with a slight concussion on the railroad, coming back."

Whatever the hazards, Wentworth's journey from Newburyport to Concord was well worth while. Concord had been the headquarters of the Transcendentalist group, the intellectuals who had faith that society might be improved because man, being divine, must be perfectible. They had published a magazine of short life and small circulation, *The Dial,* to which Wentworth had unsuccessfully offered his early verse. In its pages he had first met a Concord writer, Henry David Thoreau, who was to become much more widely recognized. Later, in Newburyport, he had read Thoreau's first book, *A Week on the Concord and Merrimack Rivers,* and was one of the few readers who thoroughly enjoyed its unusual combination of love of nature, wide-ranging appreciation of the world's great books, and thoroughly radical criticism of society and its institutions. Here, thought Wentworth, was a soul in tune with his own on every point, nature, books, and reform. True, the man's style was different, Thoreau wrote with an unaccustomed sharp, dry wit. When he first went to call on the Concordian Wentworth wondered how he would be received.

Wentworth was pleased and flattered at the reception given him by the thin little suntanned man whom he found making pencils in the family workshop. "I've heard Mr. Emerson speak of you," said Thoreau in a voice that was much more warm and friendly than Wentworth had expected. The conversation moved along nicely. The little pencil-maker's clipped, nasal tone of voice was much like Ralph Waldo Emerson's, his Concord neighbor, but "his thoughts are quite his own," decided Wentworth. He was especially proud to report to his mother about the visit to the Thor-

Garrison's birthplace in Newburyport (house on right). Unitarian Church in background.

eau house, "I saw his mother, a gaunt and elderly Abolitionist, who had read my Thanksgiving sermon with comfort, and told me anecdotes of Henry's ways, which are more domestic and filial than one would suppose."

There was stimulation, pleasure, and intellectual profit in the company of writers and others who visited Newburyport as lecturers. With no radio, television, movies, and very little theater, Americans were widely interested in what we might now call adult education. People were conscious of their limited knowledge of the world about them and its science and culture. The thirst for learning of those who had not been fortunate enough to attend one of the few colleges was satisfied somewhat by a seasonal lecture series of programs that were called Lyceums. Mary and Wentworth, starved for the educated Cambridge and Boston set with whom they'd grown up, made sure to find out who was scheduled to visit Newburyport and to invite many to be their house guests for the necessary overnight stay.

Such varied personalities as Louis Agassiz, first important American natural scientist, Charles Sumner, soon to become Massachusetts' senator and his nation's most magnificant human rights statesman, and Lucy Stone, tirelessly agitating for the emancipation of women, all came their way.

The frequency of lodgers was accounted for by the wretched quality of the inns for tourists. "Mr. Emerson comes on Friday," Wentworth proudly wrote his mother one day, "and will stay here—as will also probably the minor star Dr. Oliver Wendell Holmes, the week after. 'Tis a nice way of seeing great people, for they can't well be otherwise than complaisant when you rescue them from a dirty tavern and give them hominy for breakfast."

Another sort of visitor, not part of the Lyceum lecture circuit, was the traveling agitator for the abolitionist movement. This tiny handful of men, Negro and white, persisted in their effort to convince all Americans of the evils of slavery and discrimination. "The worst trait of the American race seems to me this infernal colorphobia," Wentworth wrote once. Another time, as if to show he practiced what he preached, he described the night's lodging at the Higginsons' that was provided for a Negro who stopped in Newburyport during a trip to raise money for a Michigan school for fugitive slaves.

> *He spent the night here and was very good company, told plenty of stories about slaves and slave-catchers. He was a man of superior intelligence, information, and humor. I entirely forgot he was black.*

Storm clouds were gathering for the young minister, however, and there was one visitor he invited who helped to bring to a head the rising tide of feeling against him among an influential minority of his flock.

Wentworth knew, when his ministry began, that among the important financial supporters of his parish were a number of retired sea captains and shipowners who had engaged in coastal trade south to such points as Charleston and New Orleans. These men had not scrupled to participate in the illegal slave traffic and thought nothing of putting back to a southern port during their voyages if, perchance, some runaway slaves were discovered in the ships' holds. Most of the group refrained, at first, from openly objecting to the new minister's plain-spoken denunciation of the institution that had been the source of their wealth. They had a certain admiration for straightforward speech and tolerated the brash young man. The tolerance had its limits. When the minister accepted a "draft" to run for Congress on a third-party, Free-Soil ticket, the grumbling grew.

Soon after his candidacy was announced an incident occurred that produced additional resentment. Wentworth was not content to have his parishioners tolerate his talk because they liked him as a man. He wanted to shake them up and change their opinions. His idol among clergymen, Theodore Parker, was a logical choice for one to administer the medicine, a stronger dose in an unfamiliar package that would attract attention. Because of his insistence on radicalism in religion Parker had been forced to resign from the Boston Ministers' Association; and at a time when exchange of visits among clergymen was a common practice, no minister in the Boston area would invite Parker to his pulpit.

Wentworth looked forward to the opportunity to invite Parker to Newburyport in exchange for a visit of his own to Roxbury. Not wishing to risk being turned down, he failed to notify the lay leaders of the Newburyport congregation in advance. One Sunday morning, those present in the First Religious Society church were startled to see, striding up the aisle, a prematurely bald-headed stranger, a head shorter than their minister. By the time he reached the pulpit, those who recognized Theodore Parker began to spread the word, and an excited buzz filled the church. The episode passed without immediate reaction, but it increased the number of those who had determined that Higginson must go.

As if to make sure no one doubted where he stood, Wentworth spoke out sharply at the time of the election of Zachary Taylor as president of the United States in 1848. Taylor, a hero of the war against Mexico that Wentworth had opposed as a student, was a southerner and the owner of three hundred slaves. This irked the abolitionists, who had thought it quite bad enough to have the country run by proslavery men from the free states, "northern men with southern principles," as they called them. In a sermon based on the Biblical text "Man Shall Not Live By Bread Alone," Wentworth reproached his congregation for their greed and love of material things and for their sympathetic tolerance of slavery and for having helped to elect a slaveowner as president. The anti-Higginsonians grew in determination and numbers.

Oblivious to the gossip and intrigue against him, Wentworth went about his duties. Typical of his insistent interest in the underprivileged of the community was the Christmas party about which he wrote his mother that year:

> *For two or three dollars I had bought toys enough at a wholesale store in Boston to supply all the children that good King Herod slew. . . . As you must know, all statistics fail in the presence of Irish children. The children were invited at Three; that the majority came soon after One it is needless to say. The piano was populous with little blue and gray legs and radiant with red and yellow speckled hands with no perceptible fingers.*

His love for the children was genuine and not merely a pose for the sake of the work he had to do. Years later one recalled that the minister was connected with many of the most joyous experiences of her childhood. "He was a genuine playmate to us," she wrote, "Many were the bright winter afternoons when we went coasting together on the long hills back of the town, when we had no doubt he enjoyed himself as much as we did."

None of this deterred the group of rich supporters of the church who took advantage of the independence and autonomy of Unitarian congregations to unite to oust him. By the summer of 1849 they felt confident there were enough of them—even though they were in a minority—to threaten the financial survival of the congregation if they should withdraw their support at once and together. They had no objection to his conduct of the services. His religious views were sound and his sermons always interesting. His tactless persistence in trying to put ideas of Christian brotherhood into practice could not be tolerated. One kindly old gentleman, a member of the proslavery clique (whose heart, as Wentworth wrote, was "divided between General Taylor and me"), was finally sent as emissary. It was a case of resign or have the financial support of the church removed, and Wentworth resigned.

His departure was mourned most bitterly among the ladies of the congregation, who had come to love their handsome young firebrand. Some of them went home in tears the Sunday he announced his resignation. "We didn't expect *this,*" they cried. "Somebody ought to have told us."

Wentworth took the news better than his loyal followers, the majority of whom had been outvoted by the minority of wealth. "An empty pulpit," he defiantly proclaimed, "has often preached louder than a living minister." To one old friend he wrote words of consolation, addressing him as "Dear but Agitated Brother," and pointing out, "I *had* resolved to release myself from the whole thing next year, for various reasons. I could carry off half the society and many urge it—but I will not. . . . I intend to give lectures here by and by or something of that sort. We are to board for the present at Mrs. Curson's, Artichoke Mills, 3 miles from town and the loveliest place on earth. . . .

"Not a dozen are really opposed to me, but they have all the *wealth.* Oh Christian Church!"

X

FREE LANCE

THE SPECTER OF unemployment and possible unemployability would have terrified an ordinary young minister who was less than three years out of Divinity School. The word blacklist had not come into vogue, but the idea of starving into submission one who voiced discontent with society's injustices was as old as injustice itself. Wentworth thought it futile to hope he would receive a call to another church; however, since he was not an ordinary young minister, this did not frighten him at all.

There was a bit of money that Mary had from her family, and other ways of rounding out their income presented themselves to him. He felt confident that he could support himself by the combined use of his talents as a speaker and a writer. A sympathetic local newspaper editor offered to take a weekly column. Other friends expressed immediate interest in his giving private classes in literature and history, to be paid for by subscription. Taking his cue from the informal arrangements he had observed at some branches of the Lyceum lecture circuit, he also hired a hall from time to time, and announced lectures. Selling tickets was easy, and each time he felt he had something to say he was able to take in a tidy profit. His popularity was not merely unimpaired by the forced resignation, it was enhanced. One lady who had wept in the sanctuary of the First Religious Society's imposing edifice gave voice to her feelings after she had begun to attend these lectures at the cruder hall, "We sat on the steps of the platform from which he spoke, and worshipped him instead of God."

Loving children as he did, Wentworth had been restless and unhappy when Mary failed to become a mother early in their marriage. Their childlessness at least made possible a style of living that was as economical as their circumstances required. Freed from the necessity of living in the village, near the church, they were able to share the beautiful lodgings of a relative. The house was part of an already ancient country grist mill at a charming spot on the river three miles out of town. Here Higginson had the pleasure of living near nature and the opportunity to enjoy the variety of buds and blossoms, breezes and dancing waves that provide the unique charm of a seaside New England rural retreat. The place, Curzon's Mill, was close enough to Newburyport to enable him to walk back and forth for a class or lecture or to stroll to a stagecoach station when he had an out-of-town engagement.

There were visits to Boston for business and pleasure, and there were trips to the many moderate-sized New England towns that formed the heart of the national Lyceum lecture circuit. On one such visit he called at the home of Ralph Waldo Emerson at Concord. Emerson was not at home when the unemployed minister called, but Wentworth walked into the study, nevertheless, and later confessed a moral lapse, "I borrowed an especially tempting first edition of Tennyson, promising myself to return it in a week. Alas, that the conscience should be so hardened by time, but I have kept it six weeks, and do not feel so guilty as when I first pocketed it."

During the same year, Wentworth shared a special pleasure with many of his generation. In the memoirs that have come down to us and the records of the American stage, there is agreement on the tremendous charm and talent of Fanny Kemble. She was a British actress who conquered audiences here with ease. Wentworth saw her in Shakespeare's *Midsummer Night's Dream* and was overwhelmed. "I had never even seen her before," he wrote his mother, "and the tones of that unequalled voice and the myriad expressions of that unequalled face were all new to me." It was not just her great beauty that captivated Miss Kemble's fans. Wentworth confessed that he could not find words to describe "the immense animal spirits, the utter transformation of voice, face, and gesture, with which this extraordinary woman threw herself into the comedy."

As the midcentury mark was passed, it became evident that there was much more serious business calling for his constant attention. The cause of human freedom was moving to the center of the national stage. He would soon see how foolish was the boyish regret he had expressed, on entering the abolitionist ranks, that all the important battles had been won without him and before his time. Events of 1850 were to push the frontier of slavery into Boston itself, and in such a way that many of the propertied and prejudiced sympathized with that minority of radicals they had reviled, rejected, and even mobbed at the beginning.

During Wentworth's boyhood the struggle for freedom of speech for abolitionists had gained allies as well as sympathizers. Those who had come only to defend the basic Americanism of a citizen's right to speak out stayed to be convinced by the talk they heard. Wentworth himself helped gain new converts to the antislavery cause when, as a graduate student, he circulated petitions opposing the Mexican War. Cambridge citizens who had never supported abolitionism itself gladly joined in voicing their opposition to the acts of aggression along the Rio Grande that had been promoted and led by slave interests.

Now Wentworth was to take a direct part in a new phase of the battle. Again the less radical, who would avoid attacking slavery itself, would be glad to help combat one of its consequences. The issue was joined after the conflict between the free and slave states over control of the conquered Mexican territory was settled by passage of a series of laws that were to be known as the Compromise of 1850. Politicians with no feeling for human rights dominated Congress, and one item in the compromise was a new severe and stringent federal Fugitive Slave Law.

Communities of free Negroes had long existed in northern and western cities, although they were relatively small, compared to those of the present day. Some were descendants of men who had won their own freedom in helping to gain their nation's liberty during the Revolution of 1776. By midcentury, Negroes in increasing numbers had migrated to these communities from the slave states. Some were the free Negroes of the South who had been permitted to work on the side to save money to buy their own freedom or who had been bequeathed their emancipation when their masters died. Other arrivals in the North had given effect to their resistance to enslavement by running away. To become a successful fugitive from slavery involved great ingenuity, courage, resourcefulness, and persistence. Even when the would-be runaway had the help of the free Negroes along his route or of white men and women of conscience and courage, notably among the Quakers, the dangers and difficulties were enormous.

These fugitives struck a double blow against slavery. Their departure in itself undermined the stability of a property system based on their ownership. Each arrival in free territory was living proof of the falsity of proslavery propaganda that proclaimed the slaves to be content and well treated. More significant, they provided a reservoir of freedom writers and speakers whose ability as agitators struck at the society from which they had escaped. They provided living and highly persuasive proof, as they had to young Wentworth Higginson at the first abolitionist meetings he attended, of their dignity and manhood, their right to be free and equal.

This was especially objectionable to politicians placed in Congress by the slaveholders. The increased activity of free and escaped Negroes and freedom-loving whites who helped southern property to escape was dangerous. The slaveholders thought to stop it by the same type of repressive measure with which they had ended free speech in their territory. Increased patrols, rewards, and penalties all failed. A national law of 1793, providing that state officials should cooperate in the return of fugitive slaves had become a dead letter over the years. It was no longer enforced because so many resisted sending back to bondage men and women who had endured such dangers to win their freedom. Talk of secession, or of violence, began to be more frequent. Representatives in Congress of northern commercial interests thought national unity at the expense of the freedom of the fugitive was worth the price.

When Wentworth read in September, 1850, of the provisions of the new federal law for efficient and speedy recovery of fugitive slaves, he denounced it as "most cruel and unrighteous." The claimant to a fugitive slave could have a man arrested and practically kidnapped back to slave territory without the slightest semblance of due process of law. All the owner had to do was swear to a statement identifying a supposed fugitive. A special federal commissioner would pass on the claim without any opportunity for the man accused to testify. The commissioner received a fee of ten dollars if he upheld the claim, only five dollars if he rejected it. Heavy fines and penalties were levied on those who helped a fugitive to escape and on those who, when called upon by a federal marshal to help return a fugitive, refused their aid.

Widespread opposition to the law was voiced at once. It provoked public meetings by those who had not in the past been heard to speak on the issue of slavery. Community leaders who had been tolerant of the idea of appeasing the southern slaveowners, recoiled in horror when they realized that the letter and the spirit of the law were retroactive, that is, intended to reach back and affect men and women who had long settled in the North, who had become respected and admired citizens in their community, and who had been safe against apprehension until then. Wentworth wrote to a classmate, Charles Devens, who had become a United States Marshal at Boston and would be obliged to help enforce the new law, ". . . there is something in the thought of assisting to return to slavery a man guilty of no crime but a colored skin, at which every thought of my nature rebels in horror." These were the feelings of many of his neighbors and friends. Unwilling to interfere with slavery at the South, they abhorred the idea of surrendering to slavery on free soil. They were appalled by the methods of enforcement embodied in the new law.

Daniel Webster was the leading northern politician who had been instrumental in the passage of the Fugitive Slave Law of 1850. He had begun his political career as a lawyer admired for his eloquence and established himself over the years as the outstanding spokesman and statesman of New England. He ended his career with his reputation stained by his role in the forging of the Compromise. Wentworth's friend and neighbor John Greenleaf Whittier voiced the sentiments of men of conscience in New England when he learned of Webster's betrayal, ". . . from those great eyes/the soul is fled;/When faith is lost, when honor dies,/The man is dead!"

XI

SHADRACH, SIMS, AND ON TO WORCESTER

THERE WERE AMERICANS who had concluded that talk and persuasion alone would never destroy slavery. Hope that it could be ended by peaceful agitation grew dimmer as the slave states eliminated abolition societies that had flourished first in the South, where slavery could be seen firsthand. The Constitutional provisions that the slaveholders had demanded in 1789 as the price of national unity precluded national action to end slavery peacefully.

The first to recognize that nonviolent change was not to be hoped for were the Negro leaders themselves. Henry Highland Garnet, a Presbyterian pastor, told his fellow Americans of African descent that "there was not much hope of redemption without shedding of blood." In 1849, a New York Negro newspaper editor, citing the Louisiana legislature's resolution, which had expressed warm sympathy with Hungarian revolutionists, urged: "Slaves of the South! Strike for your freedom *now*, at the suggestion of your enslavers." Later on, as leader of a body of soldiers who had themselves been slaves, Thomas Wentworth Higginson was to learn at firsthand why they had not kept the slave states in a "perpetual flame of insurrection."

White abolitionists, too, now realized that the rights of property based on racial injustice would not be given up peacefully. Some did not hesitate to admit this openly. Dr. Samuel Gridley Howe, whose aid and comradeship Wentworth was to appreciate, said in 1843 that "some movement of actual force would have to be made against slavery." Dr. Howe was qualified to judge. An early American freedom fighter on the world stage, he had enlisted in the Greek war of independence in the 1820's and had later been imprisoned by the Germans for his efforts for Polish freedom. Most of the abolitionists, however, were pacifists as well and espoused a doctrine called nonresistance to evil, similar to the nonviolent doctrines of today. A few went so far as to refrain from any political action. To vote or participate in politics, they held, was to support and be a part of a sinful political system.

Dr. Howe, as a man of action, led other antislavery Bostonians of varied points of view into joining an organization that was ready for action in the fugitive slave period. The group was called the Vigilance Committee, and its purpose was to protect fugitive slaves from pursuit and recapture by informers who had been stimulated into action by the new law. Early in its career the Vigilance Committee learned that William and Ellen Craft, a married couple who had escaped some years before were in danger. Their pursuers arrived with a warrant almost as soon as Daniel Webster's law was passed. The Crafts were hidden, and members of the committee formed squads to pursue and expose the slave-catchers in the very streets of Boston. After five days of being hooted at wherever they went the would-be kidnappers departed.

The first man seized in Massachusetts under the new law was Frederick Jenkins, who had come to be known as Shadrach. At the time he was taken, he was employed in a Boston coffee house. In later years, Wentworth used to enjoy telling the story of Shadrach's rescue, a pleasure marred only by the fact that he did not participate personally. The aftermath of the Shadrach affair was to affect his own later career.

His cousin Richard H. Dana, Jr., legal defender of fugitive slaves and mistreated seamen was summoned at once. Distrusting the federal commissioner who was empowered to pass on the claim of Shadrach's alleged owner, Dana sought to persuade a state court judge to issue the ancient writ of Habeas Corpus as a tool for winning the victim's freedom. While Dana was bogged down in these legal methods, Lewis Hayden, leader of Boston's Negro community and himself a one-time fugitive, used more direct action. He walked with a group of sympathizers into the courthouse where Shadrach was being held, and during a recess in the hearing they signaled the prisoner, swarmed around him, and hustled him out to a carriage that drove away before the federal officials realized what had happened. The Negroes in the carriage drove Shadrach to Concord, where there was a change of vehicle, and the regular route of the Underground Railroad carried him to safety in free Canada.

As Higginson remarked later, if it had been a minor pickpocket who had been swept off so by accomplices, it "would hardly have furnished a press item, yet it was treated in Washington as if it had shaken the nation." Daniel Webster, resentful at the blow to his own prestige in his own state, called it a case of treason. Prosecution of the men accused of complicity in the rescue was begun. Attorney Dana won freedom for accused members of the Vigilance Committee when the jury were unable to reach a verdict, even though the prosecution's case was strong. Years later, a single dissenting, hold-out juror, a blacksmith from Concord explained his vote to Dana: he had personally driven the carriage that took Shadrach from Concord to Sudbury, second leg on the escape route. He argued that he had given the prosecutor a fair hearing but that not enough evidence had been offered to convince him that one man could own another. In this he perhaps echoed the sentiment of a New Hampshire judge who had insisted, some years before, in releasing a fugitive slave, that nothing less than a bill of sale from God Almighty could convince him of the justice of a slaveholder's claim.

After reading about the Shadrach case and hearing the details, Wentworth joined the Boston Vigilance Committee. He had previously done his part by quietly aiding fugitives to slip on through Newburyport to points north. Now that the problem was no longer transportation, but rescue from northern slave-catchers, he wanted to be in the thick of the fight. He did not have long to wait. One April day in 1851 a messenger came to his house in Newburyport and said simply, "Another fugitive slave is arrested in Boston, and they wish you to come."

Wentworth traveled to Boston that same day with the messenger, and they proceeded directly to the office of Garrison's *Liberator,* where a meeting of the Vigilance Committee was in session. Thomas Sims, a young man of seventeen, pleasant, good looking, and well liked, had been seized and taken at night to be held at the courthouse in a room in the upper story. The so-called hearing before the fugitive-slave commissioner was to begin the next day.

Not long after his arrival, Higginson began to realize that the members of the committee, however admirable their antislavery dedication, were not temperamentally fitted for the kind of action that was needed. He predicted correctly that the authorities would take greater precautions with Sims than they had with Shadrach. The discussion at the meeting was rambling and indecisive: half the members were dedicated to the principle of nonresistance; many of the others to political action, primarily through the antislavery Liberty Party, which, for them, excluded a clash with the law. Only a handful seemed mentally and spiritually ready for the direct action required to bring about the result which all agreed they wanted.

Higginson outlined and argued in favor of a plan of attack, and when some of those present murmured that their principles would not permit them to engage in acts of violence or combat the forces of the government, he declared defiantly, "The Negroes of Boston have done it before, and they doubtless will do it again." Lewis Hayden, the free Negro leader who was present, answered, "Of course they will." Soon afterwards he drew Wentworth aside and whispered, "I said that for bluff, you know. We do not wish any one to know how really weak we are. There are hardly any colored men left in Boston; the Shadrach prosecutions have scattered them all."

Higginson and the more militant members of the committee were disappointed. Yet they could understand how the threat of kidnapping under the Fugitive Slave Law could have dispersed the bravest. The next morning they went out early to survey the scene. As they feared nothing seemed possible at the courthouse. More than a hundred armed police maintained constant guard around the building, which was also protected by heavy chains looped in front of the doors. Even the judges had to stoop and squirm under the chains to enter, a fact that Wentworth said was precisely just and symbolic. In the courtroom they observed a squad of burly deputies surrounding the young man; these deputies had orders to permit no one but the attorney retained by the Vigilance Committee to come near the captive.

Fantastic and desperate schemes crossed Higginson's mind. One was to snatch from the courtroom table and destroy the Georgia court warrant that agents of Sims' owner needed to clinch their case. He was dissuaded from this as he was from the idea of plotting to board and raid, pirate style, the brig *Acorn* in which the kidnapped man was expected to be carried off. He attempted unsuccessfully to persuade his classmate Charlie Devens, the United States Marshal, to resign abruptly so that the guards and deputies would be dispersed and the coast clear for rescue.

That night there was a crowded protest meeting at which Horace Mann, one of the more timid abolitionists, was the chairman. After several hours of eloquent, but ineffective oratory, Higginson gained the platform. His speech, carefully planned by a man who had learned how to sway audiences from a pulpit, held the audience spellbound. One observer declared there was a fire in the eye that "made him tremble." Wendell Phillips, most renowned abolitionist orator of all, agreed with Dr. Howe that when Wentworth concluded the audience could have been led to revolution. But the next speaker, a conservative antislavery attorney who would not be a party to violation of law, arose and "threw cold water on all action."

The one definite plan the minority of freedom-plotters agreed upon was frustrated at the last minute. They conceived the scheme of having Sims jump through his window at a pre-arranged hour, when they would have a stack of mattresses in place on the sidewalk below. The prisoner was to be told of the plan during a visit by a Negro clergyman. All was ready for the attempt, when early in the evening, Higginson and a fellow-conspirator observed two men at work installing bars across the window of the detention room. Either they had been betrayed by an informer or an extraordinary coincidence ruined their only chance.

In the predawn hours of a quiet Saturday three hundred armed constables surrounded the courthouse exit. Sims was taken out and surrounded; the detachment marched to the dockside and placed him on a southbound ship. There were spectators along the route to express their contempt and cry "Shame!" but Wentworth was not among them. He had returned to Newburyport, depressed and chagrined, unable to bear the sight of the final defeat. He did not immediately realize that in this defeat lay one of the seeds of ultimate victory. Less than two weeks later, partly as a reaction to the Sims kidnapping, Massachusetts elected Charles Sumner to represent it in the United States Senate. Sumner was to be the golden voice of freedom in Washington for the next quarter of a century.

Higginson unhappily recognized the reasons for the defeat of a committee that had been formed to prevent such tragedies. He remarked on "the great want of preparation, on our part, for this revolutionary work. Brought up as we all have been, it takes the whole experience of one such case to educate the mind to the attitude of revolution. It is so strange to find one's self outside of established institutions; to be obliged to lower one's voice and conceal one's purposes; to see law and order, police and military, on the wrong side, and find good citizenship a sin and bad citizenship a duty, that it takes time to prepare one to act coolly and wisely and courageously, in such an emergency."

His participation in the work of the Vigilance Committee as well as his many expeditions as a Lyceum lecturer were making his name and personality more widely known. It was always a pleasure for him to meet a new audience and communicate with its members. He recorded on one trip the mutual pleasure of contact between audience and speaker in an age unblessed by electronic communication. His destination was Milford, Massachusetts, halfway from Boston to Worcester, in December, 1851:

> *I observed an excitement among railroad officials about the lecture—conductor asked passengers if they were going, and brakemen asked each other if they were. As I moralized on the good effects of lyceums among the people, the conductor came along; I asked some questions which revealed me as the lecturer; then the mystery came out. "Sir," said he, "do you know that the President of the Lyceum is absent, and the Vice-President, who will introduce you, is the engineer of this very train!" The engineer turned out quite a character, and our acquaintance ended in my riding down with him on the locomotive the next morning; as novel and exciting a steed as a man can well bestride, I assure you.*

Worcester, Massachusetts' second city, was then the center of antislavery feeling in the state. Boston itself lagged behind in the developing moral crisis, its conscience somewhat paralyzed by the influence of wealthy bankers and merchants tied to the southern economy. Worcester, as trading center for many of the small farmers of the state and location of new factories, whose workers took turns reading abolitionist tracts aloud during working hours, was not so handicapped. Moreover, it was a key junction on the fugitive slave route from the South, which provided a continuing educational experience for the community. It was the town in which, in 1848, the Free Soil Party had been founded. This was a third party movement initiated by men who found it intolerable to participate in the two existing parties, which seemed to vie with each other in trying to please the slaveholding groups who dominated southern and a good deal of northern political life. It was at Worcester that the first National Women's Rights Convention met, a new emancipation crusade of which Wentworth was a charter member.

Leaders of progressive and radical thought in the politically pioneering town knew and were envious of Theodore Parker's militant, independent Free Church of Boston. Worcester radicals were scattered among several denominations, but they would have liked to quit them and unite in a real People's Church, like Parker's, if they could only get the right preacher. At an organization meeting one inspired member spoke up, "Why not Thomas Wentworth Higginson of Newburyport?"

The proposal was carried unanimously. Much to his own surprise and pleasure, Higginson was to return to the pulpit. He and his new congregation were meant for each other.

XII

WORCESTER AND WOMEN'S RIGHTS

BEFORE LEAVING NEWBURYPORT, the childless Higginsons had acquired a young boarder. She was Margaret Fuller Channing, six years old in 1850, and she was so welcome when she first came that they looked forward to the longer and longer visits that followed during the years to come.

The girl, whom they nicknamed Greta or Gretchen, was the daughter of Mary's brother, Ellery Channing. He had rambled on Cape Cod with Henry Thoreau, written some mediocre poetry and was an unstable husband and father. Greta's mother was a sister of Maragaret Fuller, for whom the child was named. It was the sudden death of this aunt that occasioned the little one's first long visit to the Higginson household.

Margaret Fuller had died tragically when the ship on which she was returning to America, after four eventful years abroad, struck a reef and sank off Fire Island. Long before her namesake niece stayed with Mary and Wentworth in the aftermath of her death, Margaret Fuller's path had crossed Wentworth's and her influence helped to shape his life. Born in Cambridge thirteen years before him, she had been the friend of his older sisters, and he had been the playmate of her younger brothers.

Most of Margaret Fuller's forty years had been marked by resistance and rebellion against the condition of women in the nine-

Margaret Fuller.

An artist's interpretation of her last moments: Shipwreck off Fire Island.

teenth century. When she was a young girl she learned that by law and tradition American women were kept in a kind of bondage that was not too much better than slavery itself. Their lives were subordinated to the interests of brother, husband, or son. Regarded as fit for nothing but domestic occupations, they were prevented from attempting to qualify for anything better by being forbidden higher education.

Higginson was as inspired by women like Margaret Fuller as he was by the Negroes he saw spearheading the movement for their own emancipation. In her struggle to gain for herself and her sisters the right to live in freedom she overcame the handicaps of bad health, troubles at home, poverty, and ineligibility for college. She had gained, by 1840, sufficient respect and recognition from Emerson and the Transcendentalists to be appointed to edit their magazine, *The Dial*. This magazine had inspired some of Wentworth's own early and unsuccessful literary efforts.

Shortly after leaving *The Dial*, Margaret set herself to writing a book that was to become an inspiration to the women who transformed the wish for equality into an organized movement. This was *Woman in the Nineteenth Century*, a work that argued the justice and the historical necessity of equal rights. After pioneering in 1845-46 as America's first woman literary critic, she took on a unique position as roving reporter for Horace Greeley's New York *Tribune*. In this role she went to Europe on assignment.

After travels and interviews in England and France, she arrived in Italy. There she became involved, first as journalist and then as participant, in the unsuccessful Italian revolution of 1848. During the struggle she met and married a radical young Italian nobleman who had fought on the side of the people. She was returning with him and their baby in 1850 when they met a tragic death together off the south shore of Long Island.

When he wrote her biography many years later, Wentworth declared that Margaret Fuller "through her writings" had, on him, "a more immediate intellectual influence than anyone except Emerson, and possibly Parker." Her restless fight for freedom set up for him the ideal of a "career of mingled thought and action." With her namesake, Margaret Fuller Channing in his own household, he carried on at Worcester an important part of the fight for which the child's aunt had prepared the leaders of American women.

The test of a book, he said of her *Woman in the Nineteenth Century,* is not whether it has been a best seller, but is "in the number of passages that have really taken root in younger minds." Surveying those who had the courage to initiate the long hard struggle for equality and the extent to which they had been inspired by Margaret, he could say her book had met the test. "Margaret Fuller ranks high, and if I should judge strictly by my own personal experience, very high indeed."

While still in Newburyport Higginson had been one of the signers of the call to the historic Seneca Falls convention that marked the transition from talk to action in the revolution Margaret Fuller had helped to inspire. The young minister had tried to put theories of the new movement into practice. He gave a course in English poetry for young women who might not otherwise get beyond the rudiments of reading. He offered prizes to bring out the talent he saw in many Newburyport girls. Several of his early protégés became writers, including Harriet Prescott Spofford, who was afterwards well known and successful. After his transfer to Worcester his efforts for the cause moved to a broader stage.

His very first impression of Worcester, after he arrived with Mary and Margaret Fuller Channing, made him feel he had made a wise choice. The people he saw made up for the coastal landscape he missed. "People look busier and happier here . . . there is much more air of country, too, the main street is filled all day with country wagons, and you buy your firewood from the carts. . . . Everything prospers in the Free Church and I like it very much. The people are a very wide-awake set; and we have a neighboring parishioner in Bloomer dress who sends us squash pies and alarms Mrs. H. continually." The Bloomer costume he mentioned was itself an expression of social protest. The simplified, then unfeminine garment introduced by a rebel named Amelia Bloomer became a sort of uniform for those American women who were especially militant about fighting for their rights.

Reverend Higginson, as his new congregation of radicals might have expected, persisted in his activity in behalf of the women's rights revolution. He was not deterred by the treatment that influential newspapers like the New York *Herald* had given to the October 1850 Worcester convention. In the style of that day the paper's headline read: AWFUL COMBINATION OF SOCIALISM, ABOLITIONISM, AND INFIDELITY. As far as Higginson was concerned, there was partial truth in the accusation and he was proud of it. An abolitionist element participated in the struggle for the rights of women, and there had been an important female fighting force from the first in the abolitionist crusade. Brook Farm socialists were in both movements.

Many of the women working in the abolitionist branch of the sisterhood of reforms were aroused to an awareness of the injustice of their own position. Higginson's mentor, Lydia Maria Child, had been a charter member of Garrison's movement for "immediate and unconditional emancipation." Their offers to help, credited by one agitator to the fact that "their moral instincts made them quicker to discern the right than most men," were accepted in subordinate matters behind the scenes. This was changed with the arrival from the South, in 1836, of two sisters who had known slavery at firsthand.

Sarah and Angelina Grimké were unusually qualified to testify on slavery as a special atrocity against both the Negro and white women of the slave states. It was an atrocity against the former because Negroes were defenseless in the face of the passions of the owners and overseers, and against the latter because of the degradation and infidelity of their menfolk. Abolitionist leaders wanted the Grimké sisters to speak from their platforms and the girls had the courage to do so. Outside of the movement and to some extent within it there were rigid bars against participation by women in such unfemale matters as public meetings. By 1840 the result was a split in the American Antislavery Association itself.

Shortly afterwards, while Wentworth was still a Harvard student, the issue erupted again at a World's Antislavery Convention in London. Women were barred as delegates and some Americans present withdrew in protest. Among them was the Negro abolitionist, Charles L. Remond, who insisted, ". . . the emancipation of the American slave from the sepulchre of American slavery is not of more importance than the rejection of females from the platform of any anti-slavery society or conference."

Higginson was pleased and impressed when, at the 1848 Seneca Falls founding convention, a deadlock over whether to go so far as to demand the right to vote for women was broken by the response to a stirring speech by an unusual delegate from Rochester. This was Frederick Douglass, a slave in Maryland only ten years before, who had become the most eloquent speaker after Wendell Phillips, and the most effective writer in the abolitionist movement with, perhaps, the exception of Garrison himself.

Early in 1853, shortly after the Higginsons arrived in Worcester, the women's movement had grown and its leaders wanted a newspaper to carry its message. Wentworth was a charter member of the editorial staff, and for the next sixty years his talents as a writer were at the disposal of the cause. In the fifties, however, he was primarily an agitator at first, and one maneuver that he masterminded drew the country's attention to his name as well as the cause.

This arose from his interest in still another reform campaign, the temperance movement, motivated by the debasing effect of strong drink on workingmen. In May, 1853, he was invited to New York to help make arrangements for what was called a "World's Temperance Convention." He was accompanied on the trip by Abby Kelley Foster an abolitionist-feminist from Worcester, and Lucy Stone, whom he had first met as an antislavery lecturer when she visited Newburyport, and who had now transferred the center of her interest to feminist work. He had described Lucy to his mother as "a little meek-looking Quakerish body, with the sweetest modest manners, and yet as unshrinking and self-possessed as a loaded cannon."

When the trio arrived at the meeting place, they found feminist leader Susan B. Anthony present with other woman delegates. It became evident that some agitation was necessary that was more important than the temperance work itself. Miss Anthony was nominated by one of her group for the business committee. This horrified many of the male delegates who dominated the meeting. They sought to dispose of the question by ruling the motion out of order on the ground that the committee in question was full. Higginson, who had already been named a member, promptly withdrew and chose Lucy Stone to take his place. There followed an uproar, which subsided while the question was referred to the credentials committee. When that committee ruled that ladies had not been invited, Higginson rose and protested that the ruling was "disgraceful."

From his seat in the audience he turned and faced the rest of those present, shouting to make himself heard while the chairman angrily hammered with his gavel. "All persons who wish to call a *whole* world's temperance convention," he said, "are invited to meet with us this afternoon at Dr. Trull's." The split in the meeting created a sensation. The New York press, which might otherwise have ignored the Temperance Convention, found that there was irresistible news value in the prospective competition between the "half-world's" and "whole world's" temperance conventions. And Thomas Wentworth Higginson became a national celebrity.

When the two competing September conventions met, one New York paper expressed its horror at the participation of women on a basis of equality at the meeting Wentworth had initiated. "We saw, in broad daylight, in a public hall in the City of New York, women publicly propounding the doctrine that they should be allowed to stay out of their appropriate sphere and mingle in the busy walks of every day life, to the neglect of those duties which both human and divine law have assigned to them. . . . Is the world to be depopulated? Are there to be no more children?"

Another daily journal, more sympathetic, thought it *not* unfitting to find "William Lloyd Garrison, Wendell Phillips and Thomas Wentworth Higginson eloquently pleading for the black man's freedom on the antislavery platform, and for the equality of their mothers, wives and daughters on the woman's rights platform, and for both the woman and the black man on the temperance platform."

Meanwhile, in Worcester Wentworth had been selected by the national leaders of the feminist movement to write and present their position at a Massachusetts State Constitutional Convention, which convened to consider rewriting the state's entire basic law. It was to be seventy years before the fight would be won, and the successful and complacent men, lawyers, and politicians who had assembled in Worcester were startled. There came before them the young, tall, and handsome preacher who dared to stand up and tell them that they were violating the original Bill of Rights of the state, which had conferred on "All the inhabitants of this Commonwealth . . . an equal right to elect officers."

Women were a majority in Massachusetts, he argued, and unless the Convention granted his demands, they would "disenfranchise the majority." He succeeded in creating quite a stir, but no action resulted.

XIII

BURNS AND BUTMAN

NEVER, WHILE HE WAS in Worcester, did Wentworth relax his efforts in behalf of the antislavery cause. Pulpit, pen, and platform were all employed in winning converts. What made him an especially effective abolitionist was not merely his eloquence or his style. It was a sense of commitment that had come with the abolition, within himself, of whatever traces of prejudice he had acquired in the course of his growth and education.

His extensive reading as well as his personal experiences in the movement had helped him to understand the nature of the problem. More northerners than would admit to it had the stubborn, almost unconscious, feeling that Negroes were not members of the same human family. To Higginson this was nonsense. If God was our father, the Negro was our brother. It was unjust and barbaric to keep him from riding a streetcar in Philadelphia or to keep his child from attending the same school in Boston. Once one recognized the Negro's common humanity, he must admit that no one had the right to own another man in Virginia or Alabama.

What Wentworth saw clearly, most men hardly saw at all. They could hardly be blamed, he felt, when most of the press was under the influence of the bankers and merchants who profited from the cotton trade. The struggle against slavery, he told his listeners at a meeting, "must be fought first by battling with the money powers of the city and the conservative power of the state." They dominated both of the major political parties as well as the press, and he saw the two-party system as a barrier to social progress. "What difference is it to the anti-slavery movement," he asked, "whether the Whig or Democratic parties take this or that position?"

He lived as he would have others live. Even such things as the first Free Church Christmas party: one hundred fifty children invited and twenty of them Negroes. There was also more dangerous work: he and the Free Church were an important factor in strengthening Worcester's link in the Underground Railroad. Not far outside town lived Abby Kelley Foster and her husband Stephen. She had been a fiery little Irish Quaker abolitionist speaker and participated in the feminest coup that took over the Whole World's Temperance Convention. Her husband was an agitator of unusual durability. His specialty had been interrupting New England Church services to inquire what they had been doing about the sin of slavery, and he had been physically ejected from more churches than most men knew existed.

Wentworth would occasionally receive a fugitive at his Worcester home and then drive out to the Fosters' at midnight to make ready for the predawn departure for the north on the next leg of the journey. He also owned stock in a yacht, the *Flirt,* which operated in Boston Harbor in aid of the cause. A typical effort would be to board a ship known, from Underground correspondence, to have left a southern port with stowaways aboard and to remove them to facilitate escape in case the Captain should be tempted to turn the fugitive over to the zealous, slaveowner-serving federal authorities.

Life in Worcester was interrupted in May of 1854 by serious news from Boston. Anthony Burns, born in Virginia, had been living in Boston and was employed in the store of a clothing dealer. One evening, as he was leaving work to stroll home, Burns was accosted by a man he had seen lurking about the store earlier in the day. The man accused Burns of a jewelry theft. He said he was Asa O. Butman, a Boston policeman and a deputy United

States marshal. As Burns, thrown off guard by the unexpected accusation, walked with Butman, six men rushed out from an alleyway, picked him up bodily, and rushed him to a Boston courthouse, where he learned from the visit of one who claimed to be his owner that he was held as a fugitive slave. Butman had lied to him to prevent him from giving the alarm that might have resulted in instant rescue. Burns was imprisoned in the very room with barred windows from which Thomas Sims had been taken back to slavery after having been seized on the streets of Boston three years before.

A messenger arrived at Worcester the next day with a personal letter from Wendell Phillips to Wentworth Higginson. "Another kidnaping case; you'll *come* of course." Another note, from an active abolitionist clergyman, Reverend Samuel J. May, Louisa May Alcott's uncle, said it was important that Worcester be well represented at a protest meeting to be held the next night.

There was no train to Boston until early the next morning. Higginson made good use of the time by sending word to reliable friends in Worcester. One whom he particularly wanted to come was Martin Stowell, who recently told him the story of his personal participation in the forcible rescue of a man in Syracuse, New York. Thoughts of independent action had begun to enter his mind, as he remembered Sims' fate. Public opinion had turned more strongly against the Fugitive Slave Law, but the President and all federal officials were persistent in their efforts to enforce it. The greatest fault of men interested in human rights was their inability to take united action.

When Wentworth arrived in Boston and walked into the session of the Vigilance Committee he found his fears were justified. The spirit of the meeting was not essentially different from those that had been so disappointing in the past. There was neither plan nor prospect of unified action. The temper of the group was reflected in the one concrete proposal that received enthusiastic support. This was that the members proceed to the hotel of the claimant and his Virginia henchmen and point "the finger of scorn" at them.

When the meeting adjourned without taking action and the members began to file out, some thirty remained in excited discussion. Someone moved that Higginson be chairman of those who stayed, and the discussion of possibilities for action was renewed. The group heard spirited advice from Dr. Howe, but were as incapable of agreeing on a plan or a leader as they were united in agreeing on the need for action and effective leadership. An executive committee of seven men was finally chosen, including Wentworth and his expected associate from Worcester, Martin Stowell.

When the executive committee reconvened in the afternoon and still could not agree on a course of action, Wentworth made up his mind to act in any case. "Better a failure," he said, "than to acquiesce tamely as before and see Massachusetts henceforward made a hunting-ground for fugitive slaves." Stowell arrived that evening and Higginson met him at the station. After listening intently to a review of the situation in Boston, the new arrival gave a quick and convincing appraisal.

"We must rescue him from the Court House itself," Stowell said, "afterwards, it will be no use even to try. It will be too late. What's more, we cannot do it quietly or peacefully or in cold blood. There will be too many officers there, protected by walls and bars. But you have a public meeting tonight, and if you can get them to swarm around the place, the momentum and the excitement will give us our chance."

"That won't do," said Higginson. "An attack at the end of the meeting would be hopeless. The Marshal will be expecting us then and he will be sure to be reinforced."

"Why not attack during the meeting, then, while it is at its very height?" asked Stowell. "Let all be in readiness; let a picked body of men be distributed near the Court House and Square; then let some loud-voiced speaker stand up in the gallery at Faneuil Hall and announce that Negroes are attacking the Court House and need our help."

This seemed the ideal plot to Wentworth. They could have one of the platform speakers prepared for the interruption, preferably

Phillips, arrange for him to break up the meeting and signal the audience to head pell-mell for the courthouse long before its scheduled closing time and before reinforcements could get to the Square. Even before getting agreement to the plan he took the first step by going to a hardware store, where he bought a dozen axes. He figured that the job that had to be done would require the breaking down of doors, and when asked by the dealer what name should be placed on the receipt, revealed his inexperience as a conspirator by saying "Higgins." Next he went with Stowell to look for the committee, which was scheduled to meet once more in the lobby of Faneuil Hall before the meeting began.

The rush of Bostonians and visitors from out of town who had been summoned by their friends on the Vigilance Committee was so great that the lobby filled much earlier than they anticipated. The expected committee meeting could not take place. Higginson and Stowell caught first one member, then another, to attempt to explain their plot and to take an informal poll. They could not reach Wendell Phillips. They did think Howe and Parker had given their consent to the plan, but it turned out later that in the rush and confusion these two important leaders had hardly understood it. One of the committee members, Kemp, an energetic, antislavery Irishman, understood it very well, approved it, and could barely wait for the moment he could put his fists into play against the type of underworld character he knew had been deputized by the United States Marshal and United States Attorney. It was agreed that Stowell, Kemp, and Higginson would each select five followers, and that Lewis Hayden, leader of the Negro community, would join them with ten picked men to lead the attack.

Faneuil Hall, a meeting place on many historic occasions in Boston's past, was filled with the largest gathering Wentworth had ever seen there. Seats had been brought onto the platform and galleries; the aisles and outer staircases were filled. This success was to contribute to the failure of what Wentworth was to insist for the remainder of his life was one of the "best plots ever."

He left the meeting place with his squad, and they separated on the way to the courthouse, so that they would not attract attention. Wentworth planted himself on one side of the building, near an open door and waited. After the alloted time, the passing moments seemed endless. The crowd from Faneuil Hall that should have been surging into the square never came. Instead, a few idlers from the outer edges of the meeting came strolling over, a few at a trot, some with hands in their pockets, none of them looking very menacing. It was obvious that something had gone wrong, that the man they had planted in the gallery had called out, but that the leaders on the platform had not successfully signaled or unleashed the audience. Enough people did enter the square to worry the courthouse guards, and the door nearest to where Wentworth was lurking slammed shut.

He mingled with the small crowd that had formed to see what could be done with them and ran into Stowell, who had been unable to find the axes. "Some of our men are bringing up a beam to the west door," he whispered, "come on." They ran around together, and Reverend Thomas Wentworth Higginson, descendant of Puritans and merchants, took the lead position in swinging the massive beam against the courthouse door. Opposite him, as his partner, stood a sturdy Negro, one of Hayden's men. It was not many minutes before the door gave way and swung crazily to one side. There was room for only one to enter at a time. As Wentworth instinctively glanced across at his parner to see which should be the first to enter the other sprang in without hesitation. Wentworth followed, and they found themselves faced by at least half a dozen policemen, who began hammering away at them with their clubs. Wentworth had often heard of clubbing by free-swinging police, but never knew how it felt to be on the receiving end. Although he received a cut on the chin so deep it scarred him for life, the excitement of the moment seemed for the time being to insulate him from pain.

More important was an occurrence of which he was not aware at the time. A shot had been fired after he and his Negro partner had

Night attack on the courthouse. Illustration by an artist who was an eyewitness, from Anthony Burns, A History *by Charles Emery Stevens, Boston 1856.*

entered the doorway, and one of the marshal's deputies had fallen dead. At the same time, a squad of police, swinging their clubs, swept the steps behind them, pushing off Stowell and most of the men who had swung the beam. The crowd held back, and the marshal's posse inside withdrew with the body of the man who had fallen. Wentworth and his Negro comrade, found themselves alone, and Wentworth stepped outside to the head of the steps and called out to the crowd, "You cowards, will you desert us now?" Only one young man, a lawyer he had known in college, joined him and was all for going in again, but Wentworth stopped him, pointing out that they had to have more people. In the few moments of silence that followed, Bronson Alcott, aging Transcendental philosopher, father of Louisa May, ascended the steps and called out, "Why are we not within?" There was still no response from the crowd. By now, the approach of expected reinforcements of troops could be heard and Higginson and the attackers withdrew.

Butman and the slaveowners he served had won this crucial

engagement. Boston, particularly in the vicinity of the courthouse, remained an armed camp for a few days, while legal maneuvers were exhausted. By the time Burns was brought into the courtroom to hear pronounced in the name of the United States the words that would send him back to slavery, there were elements of twenty-two companies of troops in Boston to insure execution of the verdict. At the center of a square of armed deputies he was marched down to the Boston docks to be forced aboard a ship for Virginia.

The procession passed through streets lined with a thousand soldiers, each supplied with eleven rounds of live ammunition. Store fronts had been draped in black by their owners, and suspended over the corner of Court and Washington Streets was a large coffin labeled Liberty. Thousands stood in silence behind the line of American troops serving slavery.

"There was lots of folks," Anthony Burns is reported to have said, "to see a colored man walk through the streets."

Marshal's posse with Burns moving down State Street. Illustration by an artist who was an eyewitness, from Anthony Burns, A History *by Charles Emery Stevens, Boston 1856.*

Meanwhile Wentworth, somewhat battered and bandaged, had been returned, over his protest, to Worcester. That city was full of excitement and indignation, and frustration as well. Men considered tolerant of slavery in the past, the moderates, were now talking of arming five hundred men to go to Boston. The Sunday after Burns was marched to the docks, Wentworth preached a sermon, "Massachusetts in Mourning," in which he declared that "each reverberating throb" on the courthouse door "was a blow upon the door of every slave prison of this guilty republic."

This was hardly a way of keeping secret his participation in the attack on the building, which was after all a violation of law. He had no fear. He was confident that he would be arrested and quite as confident that he would be released. Mary expressed the limit of her own concern very testily by asking whether his letters to her from prison would be read by the jailer.

Greta interjected, "Not if he writes them in his usual handwriting."

His confidence that no jury would convict him was increased when his conservative friend, James Russell Lowell, patted him approvingly and said, "This is a traitor's head." The charges against Wentworth and his fellow conspirators were dismissed without a trial.

A few months later, Asa O. Butman, the man who had arrested Anthony Burns, was presumptuous enough to visit Worcester on similar business. He was searching for information on fugitives reported to be in the vicinity. He registered at a hotel on a Saturday and by Sunday his identity and presence had become known. An angry crowd began to gather. Butman fled from the hotel to the City Marshal's office, where he spent Sunday night. By Monday morning there was a crowd around City Hall so large and unruly that it did not seem that local police could disperse them by force. George F. Hoar, later a United States senator, then the City Marshal's attorney, looked around and concluded that unless the crowd could be pacified, "something was likely to happen which we all should have regretted."

With Higginson by his side the attorney went out to address the crowd. Hoar was well known and respected as a Free Soiler, pioneer in the party that led to the disintegration of the Whigs. He reminded the crowd that his father, Squire Samuel Hoar, had almost been lynched in Charleston, South Carolina, when he went there ten years before as official Massachusetts commissioner to defend the rights of free Negro seamen on Massachusetts clippers in Charleston Harbor. "Do not give the mobs of South Carolina the right to excuse their own conduct by citing an example from Massachusetts," he pleaded. The crowd quieted down, somewhat, although there were angry shouts.

"Will he promise to leave Worcester and never come back?"

Butman heard this from inside and called out, "I'll promise. Tell them I'll promise," but Hoar wanted to control the crowd without yielding any conditions.

There was a train expected soon for Boston, and to take advantage of the quieter mood of the crowd, they started for the station. Hoar took one of Butman's arms, Higginson, the other. A few policemen preceded and a few followed them as they departed from the back door of City Hall. The crowd of at least two thousand quickly caught up with them. Most of them wanted to continue to badger the cringing Butman, some to inflict at least some injury. Stones were thrown and Wentworth received a few minor blows. Soon some of the abolitionists of the Free Church gathered around to guard the convoy, recognizing the need for consistency in their advocacy of nonviolence. One kept calling out, "Don't hurt him, mean as he is. Don't hurt him, mean though he be!"

Wentworth was more successful in his attempt to rescue Butman than he had been in behalf of Burns. He wrote a friend, describing it all:

> *I was not seriously damaged in the Butman trouble. . . . It* was *a time of peril, however, though it ended in nothing worse than frightening a bully into a coward. I wish the poor creature's face could have been daguerrotyped as he*

crouched into the bottom of the carriage when the stones came crashing in. I never saw such an image of abject fear. Our City Marshal had to drive him the whole way to Boston, too frightened to get into the cars; when they changed horses half way, he hid himself in the woods and could hardly be found again; he would not enter Boston till after dark. They have arrested a few persons for riot, chiefly those who were most instrumental in saving him! so that not much will come of it.

XIV

WORCESTER DAYS AND NIGHTS

WENTWORTH WAS A SUCCESS as a minister, and his sermons fulfilled his Worcester parishioners' expectations. The effect of his performance in the pulpit, the president of the Free Church wrote to Wentworth's mother, was that ". . . common sermons appear weak and stale, and our people will not go to hear them." He added that her son had a quality that "called out the masses."

Wentworth was proud of his church and of what he had achieved. "Would you like to look in at the Free Church?" he wrote Harriet Prescott, the young lady he had drawn into writing at Newburyport. "The people are bright and earnest, rather than cultivated." To his mother he confessed, "my transplantation to this new soil has enriched and strengthened me immeasurably, and given me many steps toward maturity."

His love for children, frustrated in his own home, was released in the Sunday School he conducted. There were no compulsory recitations of memorized verses from the Bible, as in most schools of that period, with tiny prizes and large punishments as motivation. Instead, Wentworth gathered the children round him and told stories illustrative of the moral principles he sought to instill. Truth, Generosity, Love, and Loyalty were his favorites. His Sunday School was not confined to indoors. He would take groups of

Higginson's Worcester home as it looked in 1938.

COURTESY AMERICAN ANTIQUARIAN SOCIETY, WORCESTER, MASSACHUSETTS

children to play games on the village green. His effect on the boys and girls was disclosed in the report of one little girl that she and her sister had "played Mr. Higginson the previous afternoon." For a childless young minister who had once recorded in his diary that it made him "uncomfortable to be for five minutes in the room with a strange child, without winning it to love me," this was a precious achievement.

The radicalism of his politics at first prevented his exchanging pulpits with other Worcester ministers, with one exception. That was Edward Everett Hale, later to win fame as author of the story *The Man Without a Country*. Hale did not shrink from giving support to some of the causes Higginson joined. He was able in time to bring Higginson into amicable relations with the other ministers in town. The battle for human rights came to seem less radical during the fifties and one day Wentworth was invited to serve on the public school board, an invitation he was delighted to accept.

Soon after he joined the school committee, he took the lead in bringing about an increase in teachers' salaries. He took advantage of his new position to launch a movement for a free public library for the city. These innovations were more acceptable than a campaign Wentworth began after receiving the complaint of a Roman Catholic parent who believed his religious freedom had been violated. It was part of Catholic religious instruction that the Douay translation of the Bible be read, rather than the Protestant King James version. The irate parent protested that Catholic pupils should be permitted to read the version authorized by their faith. Higginson plunged into the fight for freedom of religion that he saw endangered by the compulsory use of the King James Bible.

This was a battle, like the Burns case, in which Wentworth was to lose the first round badly. The hostility of some Americans to Roman Catholic immigrants, which Wentworth had seen flare up in the burning of the Ursuline convent, had reached alarming proportions. A Native American Party, also called the Know-Nothings, had gained such strength that he lost his argument in behalf of the rights of the Catholic family and was summarily removed from his position on the school board.

"What matter, if the Governor removes you from office?" he wrote soon afterwards, "he cannot remove you from the lake." The love for boating that had begun on the Charles River and continued on the Merrimack, between Newburyport and Whittier's farmstead, continued on the waters of Lake Quinsigamond, near Worcester. He had his own slender wherry in which he would go out to row, to glide, and to dream. For him this was not merely an opportunity to exercise and relax, but also a time to renew the study of nature he had so ardently pursued at college. Afloat and ashore he did a great deal of field observation, and not only for his own pleasure and instruction. He organized, with Hale, a local Natural History Society, one branch of which, the botanical club, still bore his name years afterwards.

It had not occurred to many residents of Worcester before Wentworth arrived that boating on the lake was a pastime with rewarding results. Higginson organized a boating club for young men from the city and, what was practically unheard of in those days, one for young women and girls as well. He devoted many patient hours to coaching the female contingent. Having taught them how to use their neglected muscles, he instructed them in the use of their senses for the full enjoyment of nature. One night he brought to the lake a bevy of maidens and their boats which they launched to camp all night on a tiny island. The night was cool and a fire of twigs was kindled, around which the boating-club members circled in communion with stars and sky.

Precisely at half past three, while it was still dark, a song sparrow gave the signal for a symphony that seemed to make the whole shore and lake alive with song. The campers bathed and breakfasted and then headed for their predetermined objective. They were seeking to spy out and surprise a water-lily pond at sunrise. As they glided through the placid water the veils of mist were gradually lifting around them and stray sunbeams lent a magnificence they had never seen before to the tops of chestnut trees along the shore. They were too late to see the entire drama of the lilies unfolding. Part of the pleasure they had sought was theirs, however, as they could sense the air around them grow more and more fragrant and see a scattered few of the buds expanding visibly before their eyes.

At other times Higginson would walk for miles as he had in Cambridge. Sometimes he was alone, sometimes accompanied by his friend and neighbor, H.G.O. Blake, who was not only an accomplished naturalist in his own right, but also a friend and regular correspondent of Henry Thoreau. On rare occasions when Thoreau visited Worcester, he and Wentworth would go out together. There were occasional delightful mornings when Harry Blake would call in a few chosen friends and read aloud extracts from Thoreau's latest letter. The series of letters from Henry Thoreau to H. G. O. Blake were to form a large part of the text of *Walden.*

Lecturing occupied many of Wentworth's days and nights. His lectures on subjects of general interest, literature, history, nature, often required a great deal of research and study. Others, on abolition and women's rights dealt with subjects more familiar and, yet always were prepared with thought and care. The flourishing mid-century Lyceum activity carried him to many points in the middle Atlantic states and the Midwest and, on occasion, to Canada. There were even two occasions when he took the steamer to Brooklyn. "My lecture stirred them up a good deal in Brooklyn," he reported once, "and brought special appeals and insults to Sam [Reverend Samuel Longfellow, an old friend] from his flock."

During this period he was keenly aware of his own growth and self-fulfillment. "I am almost terrified," he wrote in his diary, "when I consider the sudden expansion and inspiration of my whole nature since I came to Worcester. Every thought, word, look, and action seems to belong not to me, but to some new being which I am. . . ."

Later in the decade he was particularly impressed by a visitor to Worcester who helped prove his radical theories. He wrote to his mother in great detail:

> *We have had the greatest heroine of the age here, Harriet Tubman, a black woman, and a fugitive slave, who has been back* eight times *secretly and brought out in all sixty slaves with her, including all her own family, besides aiding many more in other ways to escape. Her tales of adventure are beyond anything in fiction and her ingenuity and gen-*

eralship are extraordinary. I have known her for some time and mentioned her in speeches once or twice—the slaves call her Moses. She has had a reward of twelve thousand dollars offered for her in Maryland and will probably be burned alive whenever she is caught, which she probably will be, first or last, as she is going again. She has been in the habit of working in hotels all summer and laying up money for this crusade in the winter. She is jet black and cannot read or write, only talk, *besides acting.*

Harriet Tubman continued to succeed in avoiding capture and she and the minister were to meet in four years, at a time when both were aiding the government, something that neither would have predicted in 1859.

On another occasion Wentworth received a visit from a college classmate, Henry F. Durant, who had become a successful attorney. Because of his own choice to reject that profession, Wentworth wanted to compare notes with the visitor on their respective careers.

"Have no regrets, Higginson," said Durant, "I am now working only to make enough to permit me to retire from the practice."

"I'm surprised to hear you say so," replied Wentworth. "You've gone so far, I should think you would want to go on to the top of your profession, and have the joy of achievement, like Rufus Choate."

"Nonsense, don't believe it for a minute. I've heard him say a thousand times that he has no enthusiasm for it, that he cares for nothing but literature. There isn't enough in the whole science of law to occupy a mind like his for a month. It's all petty maneuvering, like hare hunting in England, splendid horses and men, dogs with pedigrees of centuries, and when all is done, it is only a rabbit. We all know that in nine cases out of ten it is not of the slightest real consequence which way the verdict goes, and yet here are thousands of the finest minds in the nation absorbing themselves in such trifles and led on by mere avarice or habit or love of victory."

The one serious impediment to his happiness was his concern for Mary, who had begun to have severe and prolonged attacks of rheumatic or arthritic pains in addition to other, miscellaneous ailments. There was no hope that she could become a mother; she was on the path to becoming a hopeless invalid. Her wit and conversation remained spontaneous and lively, and often furnished him with a thought or a theme. She shared some of his interests and was tolerantly amused by others. Her interest in the antislavery cause was increased when *Uncle Tom's Cabin* was published. She became a more avid propagandist for the book than for her husband's own work.

One happy occasion she shared with him was his participation as both agitator and clergyman at the marriage of Lucy Stone to Henry Blackwell. "I am glad," he wrote to Brattleboro, "the world should see her as a wife and a mother. Still, there was something so powerful and beautiful in that lonely life of hers, nothing in history more so." Before the wedding, he met the ardent feminist and antislavery lecturer in Boston. "I have good reports about the groom," said Wentworth to Lucy. "He is a man of tried worth, a leader in the western anti-slavery movement."

"You will laugh when I tell you what I came to Boston for," Lucy replied. "To buy a wedding dress, *and* to put my little property into the hands of trustees, so that my husband shall not control it. Harry says that I ought to be very thankful that a woman has this much freedom, but that is like telling a fugitive slave to be thankful there is a Canada, when he knows he ought to be free without going there."

On May 1, 1855, Mary and Wentworth went by train to West Brookfield, Massachusetts, to attend the wedding and perform the ceremony. With them, as an invited guest, was one of the more intense antislavery lecturers, Charles Burleigh, who was noted for wearing his hair and beard in the manner of a fierce and uncompromising Christ. They rode in a cart among rocky hills until they reached a high little farmhouse with a landscape of rocks and barns and cattle. Lucy stood beaming in the front door, and after they entered, while Wentworth was uncloaking Mary, Lucy left

Lucy Stone, 1855.

COURTESY MRS. WILLIAM HALLOWELL AND MRS. W. J. WOODIN

for a moment and returned with a fine, hale, sturdy, stout old lady, and said with an air of love and pride, "Mr. and Mrs. Higginson, this is my mother, my *own* mother," and the old lady looked as happy as she did.

Lucy's father chuckled before the ceremony, "Our Lucy thought there wasn't anybody in these parts good enough to marry her, so she had to fetch somebody from Worcester for it, hey." Wentworth was really there for a prearranged propaganda feature of the wedding. Not only was "obey" to be omitted from the marriage ceremony—a pioneering action then—but bride and groom were to read aloud together a "Protest." This Wentworth endorsed after the ceremony and sent to the Worcester and Boston newspapers with his own introductory remarks:

I never perform the marriage ceremony without a renewed sense of the iniquity of our present system of laws, in respect to marriage; a system by which "man and wife are one and that one is the husband." It was with my hearty concurrence, therefore, that the following protest was read and signed, as part of the nuptial ceremony; and I send it to you that others may be induced to do likewise.

> *While we acknowledge our mutual affection by publicly assuming the relationship of husband and wife, yet, in justice to ourselves and a great principle, we deem it a duty to declare that this act on our part implies no sanction of, nor promise of voluntary obedience to, such of the present laws of marriage as refuse to recognize the wife as an independent, rational being. . . .*
>
> *We believe that personal independence and equal human rights can never be forfeited, except for crime; that marriage should be an equal and permanent partnership, and so recognized by law; that until it is so recognized, married partners should provide against the radical injustice of present laws by every means in their power. . . .*

In writing to his mother to describe the scene and setting in full, Wentworth added "that, after this, Lucy, the heroic Lucy, *cried*, like any village bride!"

XV

LITERATURE AND LIFE

BEFORE HE ENTERED Divinity School, Wentworth had hoped to be a poet. The verse he wrote, though creditable, did not win critical approval and he was himself impartial enough to realize his limitations in that medium. The result was only to postpone his self-fulfillment as a writer. Many influences in Wentworth's life combined to take him back to a literary career.

To have started life in a college town, to have "tumbled about in libraries" as playrooms, to have frequent childhood associations with books and their authors, all had a part in making of him a potential author. There was a need to express himself that came with his developing sensitivity to the beauties of the world of nature and the unattractive features of the man-made world. A further impetus came from the encouragement of the Harvard English professor under whom Emerson, Holmes, Thoreau, Lowell, and other great writers of the era had studied. In Wentworth's undergraduate and graduate days, he responded warmly to the call of the Transcendentalists who urged that our native literature stand on its own feet.

The nation that had won its political independence in 1775-1783 remained for many decades in a colonial, or dependent, condition in its arts and letters. Great statesmen and political orators, seamen and frontiersmen, all were in demand in the first half century of the building of the Republic. Writers and playwrights and poets were not. Unquestioning acceptance of British models and standards was to persist for a long time.

"Life in America was hard for all literary people" in those days, Wentworth recalled later, "from the absence of remuneration, the small supply of books . . . and the lingering prevalence of the colonial spirit." Dependence on Great Britain began to diminish in the 1820's when, partly as a result of the discovery of the German romantic idealist writers, the spirit of Transcendentalism began to flourish. Its recognition of the infinite value of the dignity of individual man was in turn to launch the movement for literary independence.

Higginson credited the change primarily to the influence of Ralph Waldo Emerson. Emerson had called on the American Scholar to "enjoy an original relation to the universe," that is, to see the world for himself and not to be bound by its description in books and tradition. He had also insisted that this country must make its original contribution to the literature of the world. "Self-reliance" in literature was as important as it was in life.

As a Harvard undergraduate, Wentworth Higginson had sat in the audience during the 1839 commencement, two years before his own, and had been moved by the valedictory of one of Emerson's disciples. The speaker, Robert Bartlett, first in his class, was to die a few years later; Higginson was to help his words to live. "We are looking abroad and back after a literature. Let us find now, here, the elements, and in our good souls the fire . . . our own age and land shall be classic to ourselves." Shortly afterwards, Emerson and Margaret Fuller were to launch *The Dial* in response to the new demands on literature that such young men as Bartlett voiced. It was never to have a great circulation, but like any radically pioneering literary publication, it attracted good writers and inspired others. One was Higginson, who recorded his debt in words that also described the beginnings of his literary life:

> The Dial *expired after four years of precarious life . . . perhaps those who best recognized its power were not those who created it, and who, as parents, recognized with anxious*

eyes the defects of their child,—but rather those who, like myself, came too late upon the scene to do more than have some boyish copy of verses judiciously rejected from the last numbers, and who yet drew from the earlier volumes a real and permanent impulse.

While writing some of the poetry that was to be rejected, Wentworth's attention was diverted and his life influenced by another book by Lydia Maria Child, whose *Appeal in Favor of that Class of Americans Called Africans* had helped push him into militant abolitionism. Her new book was entitled *Letters from New York,* and was a collection of dispatches she had sent to a Boston newspaper, after having moved to New York to edit an abolitionist newspaper.

Mrs. Child proved to be a good reporter, and her dispatches put together an impressive book. She had an uncanny knack for finding her way directly to the heart of what Wentworth called "the stern tragedy of city life," always most tragic and stern in New York City. She reported with warm human sympathy on the conditions of the poor and outcast, the scandal of prison mismanagement and the corruption of politicians. Wentworth could hardly put the book down; it made good reading and was a further inspiration for the passion he acquired in these early days in Boston to change the world. One night, a day or two later, he was suddenly carried away by the importance of telling others about the book. He sat down and wrote until midnight. His enthusiastic review, his first published prose essay, appeared in the *Present,* a small religious and literary periodical.

During his Divinity School and Newburyport years he did not try again to write a straight essay intended to be published as such. Early in his Worcester ministry, he was to receive a communication that ultimately was to change his life. Francis H. Underwood was looking for contributors to a new project, "a literary and antislavery magazine" that he hoped would unite "the strongest forces of expression in the joined causes of letters and reform." There was, as yet, no serious and at the same time popular literary magazine in the United States, but there were those who felt the need to build upon what *The Dial* had begun. Would the Reverend Mr. Higginson be willing to be listed among the regular contributors? He promptly agreed, although, as he wrote the prospective publisher in an understatement, "I am very much absorbed by necessary writing, speaking and studies, and it is hard to do collateral work." The projected periodical, *The Atlantic Monthly*, did not become a reality for several years. When it did Wentworth was to find that the demands of writing for publication made it so difficult to continue as a minister that he had to make a choice.

There was nothing surprising in the invitation or in Wentworth Higginson's ready adaptability to a career as a serious writer. Though his entry into Divinity School terminated his career as a would-be poet, it was also to mean the beginning of years of self-expression, as both a minister and agitator, which were to mature and season him for his lifelong work as essayist and critic.

One important lesson gained from the ministry and his frequent public-speaking engagements was that it was the discipline of practice that improved his performance. No one taught him to speak in public. He had been shy and awkward, as he reached six feet before he was fourteen. For years it was painful to face an audience except with a prepared text to read from. In Worcester he became aware that he had developed the ability to speak effectively and well without advance preparation, which he had never really possessed before.

The technique of speaking spontaneously, easily, and freely was not easily acquired, even with practice. As he reflected on it in later life and young people came to him for advice on public speaking, he told them the best way to learn public speaking was to join and support a cause. "Engage in something which you feel for the moment to be so unspeakably more important than yourself as wholly to dwarf you, and the rest will come." On another occasion he said, "My teachers were men whom I saw first walking clumsily across the platform, just arrived from the South, as if they still bore a hundred pounds weight of plantation soil on each ankle, and whom I saw develop in the course of years into the dignity of freedom. . . . We learned to speak because their presence made silence impossible."

Practice in composition came from his occupation as a minister. Some of his brethren in the cloth, he knew, used short cuts, sermon guides, digests, proposed texts, volumes of sermons of past worthies that could be excerpted and rearranged. He had too much self-respect and too much sense of obligation to his congregation to do anything but prepare his sermons the hard way. That was a program so exacting that it was years before he could find the time to spare for much else. The result was rewarding. The favorable reception accorded some of his sermons encouraged him to have several reprinted, for sale at five cents each, as little pamphlets; some were reprinted in periodicals.

His style and content were subjected to exacting tests when he entered the Lyceum lecture circuit after he was forced out of the pulpit at Newburyport. He would realize that the laboriously worked-out text of a talk, rich with quotations, perhaps, and the product of many hours of conscientious work in a library, might still stand in need of much improvement. An audience reaction could show up the weak points of a composition that looked good on paper and turned out stiff and boring in parts when delivered as a lecture. Facing an audience was stimulating, too. It might provide the occasion for acquiring a fortunate phrase, inserted in the talk on the spot, or the spontaneous development of a line of argument or illustration that he might have groped for in vain after hours at a desk.

The richness of his experience as a traveler provided an education in itself. He acquired a ready store of anecdotal and illustrative material, some of which he might not use for years, but which remained a part of his inventory. Literature, he once said, "needs for its material only men, nature, and books. . . ." But his emphasis was always on human life itself. He never ceased to feel that the literary man could use "the large vistas of knowledge" that books could give him, but not as a substitute for actual experience.

There was an ample store of experience and book-learning behind Thomas Wentworth Higginson when his career as professional writer began with the new *Atlantic Monthly*. It was an advantage and certainly a convenience to start by invitation, without having to endure the ordeal of repeated rejection that he had tasted with his poetry. He had no difficulty finding subject matter; the reverse was true—"there were so many interesting things to write about."

He joined a distinguished circle of contributors, including Emerson, Thoreau, Hawthorne, Whittier, Holmes, Longfellow, and Lowell. He did not lack ambition or individuality and fancied himself destined, perhaps, to unite all their virtues "and avoid all their faults" in his own work. He had great pleasure in seeing his first contribution printed in the fifth number of the new magazine, and it pleased him even more to have had Oliver Wendell Holmes call it an "admirable paper." There was to be a bit of joshing after Holmes' reference to Higginson as his "young friend." Wentworth was already thirty-three, and at the next meeting of the Worcester Gymnastic Club, of which he was then president, he was hooted at by one of the *really* young members of the Club—one so young that later, when he was killed in the Civil War, he was only twenty, but by then a brevet brigadier-general.

XVI

FITNESS PIONEER

Who, in this community, really takes exercise? . . . to ride sixty miles in one day, to walk thirty, to run five, or to swim one, would cost most men among us a fit of illness and many their lives. Let any man test his physical condition . . . and his enfeebled muscular apparatus will groan with rheumatism for a week.

These were Thomas Wentworth Higginson's words, in "Saints and their Bodies," first of the essays he wrote for the new magazine. His invitation to write for *The Atlantic* marked a turning point in his intellectual life, and he, coincidentally, had decided to try to help make it a turning point in the nation's physical life.

For years he had seen the symptoms of a declining state of physical fitness among American men and women. One contemporary writer had described the young America of the day as "a pale pasty-faced, narrow-chested, spindle-shanked, dwarfed race." His friend Emerson had remarked on what he called the "invalid habits of the country." Wentworth had long sought to overcome those habits, on occasions such as the day he had lost his first teaching job because he gave sparring lessons to his pupils. This kind of radical reform program would face obstacles. It was as true in the 1850's as it was in 1961 that to "change the physical habits of millions of Americans," was, as President John F. Kennedy said when he launched his own physical fitness program, "far more difficult than changing their tastes, their fashions, or even their politics."

Wentworth's Lyceum lecture tours took him to Canada on several occasions. There he was struck by the contrast with the New England and the Middle Atlantic cities he had left behind. It was visible on the faces and the figures of the crowds encountered in the street. The glowing faces of the girls and the straight and manly figures of the youths and men were impressive. They were a keen reminder of his own country's weakness. The reason for the difference was evident in the shop windows, the posters on street corners, the conversation of the groups with which he mingled. Everything he saw indicated that Canadians had out-door habits and athletic constitutions.

The difficulty he faced was, principally, in the prejudices Americans had to overcome. There was moral disapproval of out-door games; and athletic amusements were considered to border on the sinful. The root of the matter was in the stern Puritan tradition that taught, one fellow Bostonian recalled, that it was one's duty to spend Sunday in "sombre idleness." Charles Francis Adams, descendent of two presidents, complained he had suffered all his life from the rigid limitations of a Puritan upbringing. "My father saw no good whatever in athletics; and he had a prejudice against the gymnasium."

As long as the necessities of frontier life had kept them agile and active, the prejudice against activity in the out-of-doors in leisure time did not have serious effects. As the frontier moved beyond the Appalachians, the people of the villages and cities of the East began to suffer the consequences of a mode of life that provided no opportunity for bodily activity. With the exception of immigrants, who brought their native games with them, Young America refrained from play.

All this Higginson knew, as he sat at his Worcester writing-desk, and began to give shape to his first *Atlantic* essays. While there was no organized movement in support of this particular crusade, the need was so obvious, the evidence so strong, that it required only skillful presentation of the case to win. His pen was deft and his knowledge deep. He was able to organize and present his material so as to get to the heart of the matter. He achieved the dream of every crusading agitator, a dream rarely realized, of receiving a response so prompt and overwhelming one felt all that had been lacking was his summons to action.

In the title and initial paragraphs of his opening essay, "Saints and their Bodies," he skillfully exposed the misguided religious element that was in part to blame. The saints, he complained, "by spiritual laws, have usually been sinners against physical laws." Why, he asked, should physical vigor and spiritual sanctity be considered incompatible. The reader might well have asked himself, reflecting on this husky, six foot man of God, boatsman, skater, swimmer, gymnast, hiker, and field naturalist, who but Thomas Wentworth Higginson is better qualified to ask this question?

In his discussion he put to work his classical education and the fruit of his wide-ranging reading. He did not forget the other reforms he espoused not even overlooking the opportunity to take a good poke at militarism. "Everybody admires the physical training of military and naval schools. But these same persons never seem to imagine that the body is worth cultivating for any purpose except to annihilate the bodies of others."

In his evocation of the "wild joys of living," he was able to infuse a poetry into his prose that he had never been able to attain in his verse, "skating, while the orange sky of sunset dies away over the delicate tracery of gray branches, and the throbbing feet pause in their tingling motion, and the frosty air is filled with the shrill sound of distant steel, the resounding of the ice, and the echoes up the hillside—sailing, beating up against a stiff breeze, with the waves thumping under the bow, as if a dozen sea-gods had laid their heads together to resist it."

Above all, he shrewdly appealed to the self-interest of the thrifty Yankees in his audience. "Are not fresh air and cold water to be had cheap? . . . and is not good bread less costly than cake and pies? Is not the gymnasium a more economical institution than a hospital? . . . and is not a pair of skates a good investment if it aids you to elude the grasp of the apothecary?" This admonition to the practical interests of his readers was topped off by a warning and appeal to them as Americans. "Physical health is a necessary condition of all permanent success. To the American people it has a stupendous importance, because it is the only attribute of power in which they are losing ground. Guarantee us against physical degeneracy and we can risk all other perils. . . ."

The effect of the evidence that Higginson and others brought back from abroad was aided by the example of the growing immigrant elements of our population at home. The new arrivals from Germany were outstanding in the pre-Civil War era, as examplars and exponents of physical culture. They came in successive waves, refugees who had failed to achieve political freedom by revolution.

One of the intellectual leaders of an earlier generation of German immigrants had been Karl Follen, who as student and then professor of philosophy resisted the tyrants in his native land. He arrived at Cambridge while Wentworth was still a boy and introduced gymnastics on the campus. This was to prove as premature as Dr. Follen's own conversion to active abolitionism. He was forced out of Harvard and by 1850 his gymnasium was but a vague memory, which Wentworth revived in "Saints and their Bodies."

German immigrants of 1848 and afterwards brought a combination social, political, and athletic club called the *turnverein*. Based on gymnasia and centered on activities for recreation and physical fitness, these radical organizations continued for a period after transplantation here to be centers of activity for freedom and social justice. Their contribution, in the fifties, to inspiring the first physical fitness revolution was matched by their contribution, in the sixties, to their adopted country in its self-defense against the slave state assault.

There was a native character to the most immediate response to Wentworth's crusade against America's physical decline. Ice skating, the virtues of which he had advocated so eloquently, was an activity for which the facilities were readily available. The myriad creeks, ponds, and rivers of the northeastern United States, the long hard winters (and the absence of the polluted contribution of factories that later interfered with natural freezing) offered a broad invitation to practice of the sport on a scale unknown except, perhaps, in Holland. It was an activity, moreover, that women as well as men could enjoy. This equality of participation was an added incentive for women's-rights advocates to take up the sport. One abolitionist lady disclosed the rate of growth in a letter to a friend after she visited Worcester in February, 1859:

> *What do you say to nineteen cars being loaded with twelve hundred men, women, boys, and girls, all bound for the ice, equipped with skates, hand-sleds, and the like? We went about three miles to a beautiful sheet of ice covering "Long Pond." The ladies in their bright dresses of scarlet, crimson, blue, green, and high-colored plaids made the scene a gay and animated one. . . . Mr. Higginson's articles in the* Atlantic, *"Saints and their Bodies," "Physical Training," and his lectures and personal efforts seem to have stimulated everybody, old and young, grave and gay, to participate in this excellent and fascinating exercise. Last winter some rigid-minded people called it "Higginson's Revival." This winter he marvels at the excellent skaters among the ladies, and declares they must have learned last summer.*

Boating and swimming, too, gained popularity in these last years before the Civil War. Each, like skating, marked by individual and noncompetitive participation, met Higginson's standards for an outdoor activity that would help combat mass, wide-spread decline in fitness. Baseball, coming into vogue at the time, he was inclined to question because of its primacy as a spectator rather than participant sport. It was contrary to the American spirit, he said, "both as a consumer of time and as partaking too much of gambling." If only there were more players and fewer watchers he would have welcomed it, approving as he did its "briskness and unceasing activity," as more congenial to our national temperament than "the comparative deliberation of cricket."

In one of the last of his physical fitness essays, published six months after the Civil War had begun, Higginson was a century in advance of his time. One essay does not make a crusade, and the coming of the war changed much in American life, and perhaps effaced completely the memory of his 1861 attack on smoking. "A New Counterblast," he called it. With a combination of humor, history, and gentle irony, he tried to set the stage for a crusade against tobacco. This was a conspicuous failure measured by immediate response but his "Counterblast" makes fascinating reading in an era that has erupted in a wave of intensive action against the evil he sought to oppose in 1861.

"America is especially responsible to the whole world for tobacco, since the two are twin-sisters, born to the globe in a day." Beginning with Western man's introduction to tobacco, he reviewed the history of its use. It was thought at first, he reminded his readers, to be a medicinal panacea, referred to by one early writer as the "most sovereign and precious weed that ever the earth tendered to the use of man," and mentioned in Spenser's *Faerie Queen* as "divine tobacco." Even during the first half of the nineteenth century, "it was familiarly prescribed all over Europe, for asthma, gout, consumption, catarrh, headache." The weed passed through phases of excessive use on the one hand, and persecution, on the other. "Indeed," he recounted, "some of the most royal wills that ever lived in the world have measured themselves against the tobacco plant and been defeated."

Higginson discounted some of the exaggerated and unsubstantial arguments that had been used against smoking in his day. The claim that it predisposes "to more dangerous dissipations," he rejected. On the other hand he demolished some of the stock arguments that were given in favor of the use of tobacco. Was it soothing? Hardly, he answered, could anything have a soothing effect if, when it is not available, the "nervous system is more susceptible," the "hand more tremulous," the "temper more irritable."

Coming closer to the most important point, he referred to a forgotten statement by a neglected president:

> *John Quincy Adams used* [tobacco] *in his early youth, and after thirty years of abstinence said, that, if every one would try abstinence for three months, it would annihilate the practice, and add five years to the average length of human life.*

To confirm Adams' statement, Higginson produced medical proof of the terrible local diseases that followed use of tobacco:

> . . . *as, for instance, cancer of the mouth, which has become, according to the eminent surgeon, Brouisson, the disease most dreaded in the French hospitals. He has performed sixty-eight operations for this, within fourteen years, in the Hospital St. Eloi, and traces it entirely to the use of tobacco. Such facts are chiefly valuable as showing the tendency of the thing. Where the evils of excess are so glaring, the advantages of even moderate use are questionable.*

He reviewed a premature and likewise forgotten controversy in England that followed publication in the medical journal, *Lancet*, of a paper in which one great surgeon declared "I know of no single vice which does so much harm as smoking." The debate in the pages of the English periodical included many telling items of evidence, especially one brought back from an interview with an American Indian chief, "those Indians who smoked gave out soonest in the chase."

Higginson summed up the two incontrovertible arguments against tobacco, the theoretical—that it is admittedly a poison—and the practical—that even its devotees abandon it when, as for boxing or college crew, it is necessary that the body be in top-notch physical condition.

There is not a regatta or a prize-fight in which the betting would not be seriously affected by the discovery that either party used the beguiling weed. The argument is irresistible. . . . If a man goes into training for the mimic contest, why not for the actual one? If he needs steady nerves and a cool head for the play of life . . . why not for its earnest?

Yet with a wry forecast of the future fate of his efforts Higginson closed by quoting a British clergyman whose answer to the weighty arguments pressed on him by those seeking to have him quit is still valid:

He sent a message to Dr. Clarke, in return for a pamphlet against tobacco, that he could not possibly refute his arguments and could not possibly give up smoking.

XVII

TO KANSAS FOR FREEDOM

IT BEGAN TO SEEM, around 1850, that every victory for slavery and its sympathizers was destined to turn into a defeat. When they won the drastic Fugitive Slave Law as part of the Compromise of 1850, it aroused the conscience of many who had been deaf or hostile to the arguments of abolitionists. The cruel deportation of Anthony Burns was a seeming triumph for the property rights of all the slave states. "Another such victory and I am undone," they could have said, when many thousands joined the antislavery ranks as a result. During Burns' ordeal and the military occupation of Boston, while the last ditch legal fight was being carried on after Higginson's failure at the courthouse door, Congress gave slaveowners another such victory in the Kansas-Nebraska Bill.

It had been supposed that by the Missouri Compromise of 1820 there had been gained, in exchange for concessions then made to the white South, the principle that slavery should not be permitted in the unsettled territory west of Missouri. The new bill of 1854 broke that promise and aroused intense and widespread opposition, notably among the many clergymen whose neutralism toward slavery had so often exasperated Wentworth. The conscience of the North, paralyzed by the prejudices of most of its own people, began to stir. The 1850 compromise with slavery had degraded Boston in deporting Burns, and now the news from

Washington was that the pledge of the Compromise of 1820 had been broken. Wentworth preached bitterly to his flock, "If this nation attaches no more importance to its compromises than to its principles, then what have we left to trust to?"

Once more a setback for freedom was to bring the end of slavery closer. So many more of the previously unconcerned saw the growth of slavery menacing their own liberty that there developed a major political realignment. The remnants of the Whig Party, which before 1850 had been one of the two major parties, crumbled away. The free-soil politicians of Whig and Democratic background united with the leaders of the third antislavery party to create a new second party, which they called the Republican Party. It was born pledged to resist further expansion of slavery, but uncommitted on the subject of abolition of slavery.

The new law that organized the Kansas territory and opened it to settlement provided that when it was populated sufficiently to apply for statehood, its voters should decide whether it should be slave or free. This pleased the slave states, since one of them, Missouri, had the longest common border with Kansas and most of them, being nearer, could more easily send new settlers than the abolitionist regions. They did not expect the reaction among the midwestern and northern states that followed repudiation of the Missouri Compromise by Congress. An active, organized movement arose to encourage free settlers. Higginson was involved in the resulting conflict but only after an interlude that found him across the sea as the fight for freedom in Kansas was building toward its 1856 climax.

Wentworth had become increasingly concerned about Mary's chronic bad health and her failure to respond to medical treatment. By 1855 she was thirty-four years old and bedridden for increasingly longer periods of time. It was necessary to forget, for the time being, his efforts to cure the ills of his fellow men and to concentrate on hers. There was little medical knowledge concerning her condition, and they had experimented with a great many kinds of treatment. Finally they decided to try the latest remedy that had been recommended, a long sea voyage and a stay in a different climate. Fayal, an island in the Portuguese Azores, was to be their destination.

His congregation did not begrudge a year's leave of absence to the handsome young minister, even though he had been with them only since 1852. They seemed to realize that in those three years he had done the work of seven. He furnished a substitute, quite as independent and as progressive, and he and Mary started on their voyage.

Neither the passage over the sea nor the change in climate did very much for Mary's health. For Wentworth, whose travels on land as a lecturer never satisfied a persistent restlessness, it furnished something of a compensation for his not yet having been to England or France or Germany, as had so many of his Cambridge contemporaries. It was an opportunity for him as a writer, too, and in one article he wrote he described his feelings, "Every man, when he first crosses the ocean, is a Columbus to himself, no matter how many voyages by other navigators he may have heard described or read recorded."

On the homeward voyage there was a feeling of rising tension as the ship approached Boston Harbor. The story of the contest for Kansas had reached them in letters from home and in occasional newspapers. Mary and Wentworth had known before they sailed of their townsman Eli Thayer's project to finance the settlement of new villages in the midwest territory with emigrants whom the soil of New England could no longer support. The new Kansas town of Lawrence and villages like Topeka and Manhattan had been built by the eastern settlers. Missourians near the Kansas border responded by raids from their privileged sanctuary. Few of them were tempted to settle in the undeveloped land; many felt they could accomplish as much for slavery by fighting there—and voting, too. Legitimate antislavery settlers outnumbered their opponents, but they were outvoted by those who swarmed across the border on election days, brandishing rifle and Bowie knife.

A proslavery territorial government owed its existence to the votes of the invaders. The antislavery settlers denounced the product of a tainted election as a bogus government and set up an administration of their own. The question whether the nation could endure half-slave and half-free was no longer abstract, and the contest forced itself on the minds and hearts of many who had been indifferent or silent until then. Those whose conscience could abide a distant slavery, and who were not moved even when fugitive slaves were seized nearby, became concerned when their own friends and relatives, bona-fide settlers, were forced to live under the shadow of a reign of terror.

Not only Missourians, but groups of men from other slave states harassed the free Kansas settlers. The aggressors believed, as a Charleston, S.C., newspaper had told them, that the safety of slavery in South Carolina depended on its success in Kansas. The free settlers were dismayed and almost demoralized by attacks of the raiders and repressive actions taken in the name of the bogus government. Unused to settling personal and political differences by violent means, they did not fight back at first. The news that reached Fayal was ominous, and Wentworth was anxious lest the new territory be lost to slavery when he and Mary sailed for the United States.

The pilot boat hailed their ship off the coast of Cape Ann, and Wentworth waited at the rail with eager interest. The Boston newspapers that the pilot brought would provide the first information they had had for many days. Wentworth anxiously opened the first newspaper. From Kansas there was word that the free settlers' pride, the town of Lawrence, had been sacked and many buildings burned by marauding Missourians. From Washington there was the terrible news that United States Senator Charles Sumner from Massachusetts, foremost abolitionist spokesman in Congress, had been the victim of a brutal beating. The assault by a cane-wielding congressman from South Carolina had taken place on the very floor of the United States Senate as Sumner sat defenseless with his knees pinned behind his desk.

Sumner's offense had been the delivery of a speech that he called

"The Crime Against Kansas," placing the responsibility for the outrages where it belonged. Two years before, at the time of the passage of the Kansas-Nebraska Bill, Sumner had forecast all that had come to pass when he denounced the new law by saying, ". . . it puts Freedom and Slavery face to face and bids them grapple."

One headline attracted Wentworth's attention. It reported that the Missouri River had been blockaded by the border ruffians to prevent entry by new settlers from the northeast. The emigrants who had called for help were not fighting men, but families who had been encouraged to sell their homes and most of their possessions to head for the new territory. There were two parties stranded, one at Iowa City and one at St. Louis, and the former was running low on food and supplies. To Wentworth the stories meant that there was a need for action and an opportunity for him to act.

The little group that greeted Wentworth and Mary at the Boston dock related the latest news. When they told their minister that a meeting had been scheduled at Worcester for that evening to welcome them home, he responded at once that it should be a Kansas aid meeting. There was more time spent at the meeting in an appeal for volunteers, food, rifles, and blankets than in the usual welcome-home speeches. It had not been the policy of the Emigrant Aid Society to arm settlers, but events at Lawrence and at the border had made them reconsider. There was need for a new organization that would not shrink from meeting violence with violence. Higginson was named secretary of the Worcester Kansas Committee.

At the committee's first meeting it was decided that the new secretary should take an inspection trip before devoting himself to the work of expanding the organization. The parties that had been turned back from the Missouri River by threats of force needed funds and guidance, and it was decided that Higginson was the man best fitted to go. He set forth on a journey across half the continent, pondering whether to break the blockade by force or to outflank it by leading the emigrants on a roundabout overland route that would avoid the proslavery sections of Missouri. It took little inquiry among those whom he met on his way, especially during a stopover in Chicago where there were many sympathizers, to convince him that he must restrain his unpreacherlike desire to face and force the issue at the river's edge. He reported to the committee that only the overland route was available "as yet."

Before he left Worcester, Higginson had made arrangements to act as correspondent for the New York *Tribune*, whose readers were anxious for sympathetic firsthand accounts of the fight against slavery in Kansas. Edited by Horace Greeley, who had been daring enough to employ Margaret Fuller as a critic and then foreign correspondent, the *Tribune* was the first major metropolitan daily newspaper to agitate against slavery.

In one of his first dispatches to the *Tribune*, Wentworth defended the party of migrants he had been sent to rescue from charges of cowardice that had been loosely passed around. They had turned back from the river crossing, he reported, because they were outnumbered by three thousand to forty.

"I had almost hoped to hear," he wrote, "that some of their lives had been sacrificed, for it seems as if nothing but that would arouse the Eastern States to act. This seems a terrible thing to say, but these are terrible times."

He proved by his actions during this first trip to the Kansas wars that he was not indifferent to the loss of human life. He met another New England group that had been organized in Worcester, in response to the call for volunteers made at his welcome-home meeting. The party was led by Martin Stowell, the same man who had been his comrade in the attempt to rescue Anthony Burns from deportation to slavery. Stowell and his lieutenants went to Higginson and begged him to let them try to fight their way through Missouri. One said, the others nodding agreement, that their honor as men of Massachusetts must be redeemed, and that they were ready to die, if need be, to prove that Americans need not flinch in passing through American soil.

"From the bottom of my heart I felt with them," he reported;

"one word from me would have done it, but I did not feel authorized to speak that word."

At St. Louis he chartered a steamboat for the long trip up the Mississippi to Davenport, Iowa. Stowell's group was to follow by the same route. After the river passage across Iowa to Davenport, they would proceed by stage coach down to Iowa City on the Missouri River. From here the party would have to travel by foot to Topeka, Kansas, while Wentworth reluctantly returned to the East.

Although new groups were avoiding trouble, they were no longer unprepared to meet it. Unlike the settlers who had set out previously without the means of protecting their settlements, the latest arrivals were well provided by Higginson's committee with rifles and revolvers.

Meanwhile there was a noticeable change in spirit among the settlers already in the territory, who had not significantly resisted previous aggressions of the border ruffians and acts of the fraudulent legislature. A new leader had come to the fore, a guerrilla chieftain who was determined to fight slavery to the death. He had resolved as a youth that all men were children of God and that he would give his life, if necessary, to free his brothers. He was to win from America's greatest Negro abolitionist leader, Frederick Douglass, the tribute, "His zeal in the cause of my race was far greater than mine. . . . I could live for the slave, but he could die for him." His name was John Brown.

Five of John Brown's grown sons had gone to Kansas as settlers in good faith in 1854 and 1855, but Brown declined at first to join them. When his sons, who had suffered through a difficult year, called upon him a second time, he could not refuse to go. He was a natural leader, a brave and determined man. He was accepted as captain of one of the few guerrilla bands fighting back against the raids of the ruffians during the winter of 1855-56, while Wentworth and Mary were in Fayal.

Brown and a small company of mounted men were on their way to the defense of Lawrence, but reached there too late to help stop the raid and destruction. Brown decided a blow of desperate violence must be struck to arouse the timid free-soil men to sharpen the conflict so that the peaceable settlers would no longer stand by and permit such outrages. Five days after Charles Sumner was struck down and two days after the sack of Lawrence, Brown and a group of followers murdered five proslavery men who had been terrorizing the neighborhood. While the previously timid free-state men repudiated and condemned the deed, suspecting but not knowing who was responsible, they benefited. It confused and terrorized proslavery men and put backbone into the ranks of victimized free settlers. The Kansas conflict was no longer one sided. "I heard no one who did not approve of the act," wrote Wentworth after his journeys to Kansas, "and its beneficial effects were universally asserted, Governor Robinson himself fully indorsing it to me and maintaining like the rest, that it had given an immediate check to the armed aggressions of the Missourians."

Wentworth did not cross the path of John Brown on his first trip to aid the Kansas settlers and probably not during the later trip on which he was actually to enter the beleaguered territory. What each had heard about the other insured that they would meet later on in connection with Brown's "greatest or principal object."

XVIII

A RIDE THROUGH KANSAS

WENTWORTH RETURNED FROM his first Kansas aid trip with determination to redouble his efforts to break down the apathy he felt dominated New England. He had told friends, after seeing the extent of the organization for a free Kansas in Chicago, that New England was disgraced. "The busy give no time and the leisurely no energy and there is no organization," was his complaint.

During the summer of 1856 he and other abolitionists worked hard to remedy this. For most of them it was, except for occasional participation in the work of the Underground Railroad, the first time they could throw themselves into the antislavery struggle in a tangible and effective way without being limited to mere words. Soon after Wentworth's return to Worcester a meeting was held at the City Hall, crowded with listeners eager to hear reports of the events on the troubled Missouri River. He found that he was beginning to lose his reputation as a radical: not because he was less ardent but because public opinion was catching up with him. "I am particularly popular in private just now for what I am doing about Kansas," he wrote his mother, "and it is rather pathetic to have them thank me for doing what they ought to have taken hold of themselves, but have not."

It was not only in Worcester and New England that the Kansas Aid Committees sprang up during that summer of 1856. A National Kansas Aid Committee was formed, dedicated to coordinating activities of the local groups that raised funds, shipped rifles, and recruited men to help the free staters who were fighting to defend themselves. Each state sent a delegate to the National Committee, and the first name from Illinois was that of an obscure ex-congressman, Abraham Lincoln.

Wentworth worked hard that summer in fund-raising and speechmaking. But he had had a taste of action in June and hoped he would have a chance to return to the scene and enter Kansas itself. By the end of August he received the news he was waiting to hear. He was to return, not as unofficial volunteer from Worcester, but as an agent of the National Kansas Aid Committee.

He wrote to his mother that it would not be dangerous—not any more, he assured her, than "setting foot in a ship or in the [railroad] cars, or in running fast downstairs or (if feminine) in meeting a drove of cows." However she may have been comforted by these assurances, the effect must have been lost when he told her that letters to him had to be addressed to "James L. Armstrong," at Topeka. This was a fictitious name, chosen by Mary. To have used his own would endanger the mail addressed to him; the post offices, being federal agencies, were in the hands of the proslavery sympathizers. Every civil servant sent to Kansas from Washington, every secretary, every judge, every Indian agent, every land surveyor sympathized with those who were trying to make Kansas a slave state.

Later Wentworth was to hear how John Brown, early in his guerrilla fighting days, took advantage of the known proslavery bias of government men in Kansas. One May morning, surveying instruments in hand, Brown sauntered boldly into a camp of newly arrived invaders from Georgia. Four of Brown's sons accompanied him as chain carriers and markers, while he preceded them with surveyors' notebook and telescope. Looking the part of government technicians, they were credited with being sympathizers. They listened carefully as they walked though the camp, taking careful notes of the numbers and equipment of the enemy and his plans.

When Wentworth traveled west the end of the railway line was in Iowa City. For those taking the northern route, as he did, the next part of the trip was by coach and by foot. For four days and four nights he rode across Iowa on top of a stage coach, watching the sun rise and set over the treeless, uninhabited prairie, very much like the same scene viewed on the ocean. When he arrived at Nebraska City he felt as if he had crossed the entire continent, for when he had studied geography, Council Bluffs was the farthest western outpost of the United States, and the stage had passed through it before the end of his journey.

He soon learned that even in Iowa and Nebraska, in those troubled times, one was obliged to behave as if living in one of the contemporary European dictatorships like France or Austria. Men were very cautious in revealing their sympathies and waited first to hear what others would say. He was told that one could lose his life in places like Council Bluffs and Sydney, both proslavery, for saying the wrong thing at the wrong time.

Shortly after arriving, it was necessary for him to go from Nebraska City to Tabor on an errand. He had to travel alone over twenty miles of ground that had been taken and retaken by the hostile factions who were giving a preview of the Civil War. He knew, as he rode, that every swell of the rolling prairie offered a possible ambush. Never before had he been so distinctly outside the world of man-made law. Previously the law had always been ready to protect him even when he disobeyed it. Organized society had ceased to exist on the Nebraska-Kansas prairie. His rifle, his revolvers, his ingenuity, and his intelligence were all the protection he had.

In Kansas itself a summer of guerrilla warfare marked by constant raids and reprisals had reached a climax. Nothing in the sense of a military decision was determined by any of the clashes. Although few realized it, however, the invaders from the slave states, had lost. They had failed to drive out more than a few of those who had settled in Kansas as free farmers, and they had not been able to discourage the response across the nation to the call for immigrants. The battle for Kansas was being won by the continued arrival of men who wanted to settle on free soil.

Wentworth busied himself immediately upon his arrival at the border, distributing and buying more supplies. Soon after his arrival in Nebraska City he had bought all the cowhide boots in town and very nearly all the flannel shirts and blankets. The equipping, or rather re-equipping, of the parties of settlers was as vital a part of the battle to win Kansas as the summer-long efforts to arouse them to migrate.

It was a "crowded, dusty, dirty life" he led in the miserable conditions of the frontier. As he performed his routine tasks of rebuilding morale, handling food rations, and distributing clothing and shoes, he ached for action and danger. He wrote the *Tribune*, for the benefit of those whose stinginess in giving to the cause he still hoped to overcome:

> *I can only wonder at the patience and fortitude which the present emigrants have shown. . . . There is plenty of genuine tragedy. . . . Coming from a land where millionaires think themselves generous in giving fifty dollars to Kansas, I converse daily with men who have sacrificed all their property in its service, and are ready at any hour to add their lives.*

One day there was a hubbub in the street. People ran out of doors, some in fear, some in hope. A distant dust cloud resolved itself into thirty rough, tired-looking men riding a motley array of horses and mules. The leader was a thin man of middle age in a gray woolen shirt, and when Wentworth observed his keen eyes, smooth tongue, and courteous manners, he knew who it must be. General Jim Lane, later to become United States Senator James H. Lane of Kansas, then called himself "Major-General commanding the free State Forces of Kansas."

Lane had first attempted to win Kansas for freedom by peaceful political advocacy and action. His eloquence and ability had advanced him in free-state councils, and he had been elected United States senator that spring by the "unrecognized" legislature of the territory. He had taken to the saddle as guerrilla fighter and leader when he saw that in no other way could free government be brought to Kansas. He had foreseen the proslavery blockade of the Missouri River and helped to chart the overland route for free settlers through Iowa and Nebraska that some now called "Lane's Trail," marked with piles of stones that were called "Lane's Chimneys."

Lane and his men remained in Nebraska City two days to rest and re-equip, and they used some of the supplies Higginson provided. While his men were resting, Lane addressed a meeting of the citizens, and Wentworth praised his eloquence in a report to a Boston paper. The two men, minister-turned-agitator and politician-turned-partisan, took to each other and rode together on a tour of inspection of the emigrants that Higginson was about to lead into Kansas. After making some suggestions as to the route, Lane marked the end of the meeting by handing Higginson a bit of crumpled paper. Wentworth looked at it as Lane rode away and learned he had been appointed to Lane's staff, with the rank of brigadier general. He was less impressed with himself the next day when a civilian who had ridden out from Lawrence to help guide the entering group of immigrants managed to exhibit casually a similar bit of paper. They rode on together, feeling now that they might soon run into other brigadier generals.

It was six days' ride and walk across the prairie from Nebraska City to Topeka, Kansas. The responsibility of leading a group of one hundred and sixty men and twenty women and children took the edge off the excitement of actually entering Kansas soil. Twenty-eight wagons lumbered along. They camped out nights, and while they never were attacked, they always had to guard against danger. "Imagine me also patrolling as one of the guard for an hour every night, in high boots amid the dewy grass, rifle in hand and revolver in belt," the churchman wrote home, with obvious pride.

On one of his first mornings in Topeka he arose before daybreak with an uneasy feeling and peered through the window. Outside there was a squad of United States Cavalry, each rider sitting silently on his horse. When he went to investigate he was startled to hear the Captain call out: "Reverend Higginson!" The captain proved to be an acquaintance from Harvard, but he gently and firmly announced that his orders were to investigate the new arrivals, and if they proved to be a group organized to fight for the free-state side, to arrest them. Satisfied of the good faith and peaceful intentions of the immigrants that the Worcester men had brought in, the Captain let them go. Wentworth reflected that if the cavalry had had the wit to discover the rifles and cannon the settlers had brought with them, all might have been arrested.

The governor who had ordered the investigation had just taken office late in August and had instructions from President Franklin Pierce that the internal warfare in Kansas must be brought to an end. There was to be a presidential election, and the great fear of the administration and its supporters was that continued warfare and atrocity stories would so arouse the North that the first national candidate of the new Republican antislavery-extension party might be elected.

The forceful actions of Governor Geary seemed outrageous to the new arrival. He wrote the *Tribune*, "The bravest young men of Lawrence were put under arrest, charged with treason, murder, arson, robbery and what not; while not a proslavery man was seized." Wentworth was to revise his opinion of Governor Geary later on, for while the Governor was not sympathetic to the antislavery cause, he did not believe in violent imposition of minority rule. His repression of the Free State guerrillas was only a prelude to a major effort to restrain the border ruffian groups.

As he traveled among the free-soil settlers Higginson came to know at firsthand the quality of the courage and determination that made it possible for these people to endure. He saw young men he had known in Worcester who had left prosperous homes. Now they were ragged, hungry, almost barefoot, some debating whether to retreat. He had heard Lane praise these young men, declaring that the world had never seen such courage. Lane had told him the story of one Worcester boy who had charged, alone, to within thirty yards of a band of one hundred and fifty raiders to bring down the leader with a single shot and get away. When he met a group, Higginson addressed one. "Will you give up Kansas?" he asked.

"Never," was the reply from bronzed and bearded lips, "we are scattered, starved, hunted, half-naked, but we are not conquered *yet*." He put such fierce emphasis on the last word that Wentworth knew they never would be.

Traveling through the countryside between Topeka and Lawrence, he saw and heard evidence of the cruel nature of the intermittent guerrilla warfare that had dominated the life of every one. The prejudices of the participants were impressed on their farm animals, he noted, as he heard references to an "antislavery cow," that was taken away, or a "proslavery colt," plucked from a band of raiders. Even that symbol of the peaceful countryside, the grain mill, was considered fair game, and at one rural village he saw the burned-out ruins of one that had been built by a Pennsylvanian named Straub. Near the ruins was a handsome girl of about twenty who rose and faced them defiantly as Higginson and two companions approached. One from Topeka called her by name, and her face then softened at once. She was the miller's daughter, and she apologized for her seeming discourtesy, "Why, I thought you were Missourians, and I was resolved you should hear the truth," she declared.

Wentworth understood her courage in thus standing and facing (as she had thought) three hostile strangers when he heard the story of her plucky behavior at the time of the burning of the mill by the invaders. She had walked into the group of mounted marauders and called upon one of them to give up her favorite horse. This she did with such spirit that his own comrades compelled him to dismount and surrender the beast. She then mounted and rode away, but the man followed her and attempted to grab her halter. She held on. He took his Bowie knife and threatened to cut her hand off. She dared him to do it. He cut the rope close to her hand and got control of the horse. She was forced to dismount, defeated for the moment. Soon afterwards two of the raiders came back and gave her the horse once more.

When he arrived at the beleaguered city of Lawrence, the Reverend kept a promise of long standing to preach to the people there. The sanctuary of the day was a low chamber over a store, built of rough boards, lined with odds and ends of cloth tacked over the wood. The sacred desk was made of a large packing box draped with buffalo robes, while the Bible rested on a smaller box that was covered with a coarse blanket. He took for his text a verse that had been used by a Boston clergyman the Sunday after he had been engaged in the battle of Bunker Hill, "Be not afraid of them; remember the Lord, which is great and terrible, and fight for your brethren, your sons, and your daughters, your wives, and your houses."

A few days later he rode to Leavenworth, a town then under proslavery control, to see how an election was conducted by that faction. He found himself in a village of not more than two thousand inhabitants, provided with more than fifty liquor shops. The doors of the hotel were practically barricaded with whiskey casks. He was accosted several times and offered a vote and a drink almost in the same breath, as if the two belonged together. When he protested that he was only a traveler and did not live in Kansas, he was told it did not matter; people from Missouri came over to vote all day long.

On the steps of McCarty's Tavern, principal meeting place in the town, where he lingered before leaving, he overheard a conversation that began to seem somewhat personal.

"Tell you what," said one man who had just ridden in, "we've found out one thing: there's a preacher going about here preaching politics."

"Fact?" and "Is that so?" were indignantly muttered around.

"That's so," continued the new arrival, "and he fixes it this way.

First he has his text and preaches religion. Then he drops that and pitches into politics; and then he drops that too, and begins about the sufferin' niggers, [this last with dripping contempt] and what's more, he's here in Leavenworth now."

"What's his name?" several eagerly called out.

"Just what I don't know," was the sorrowful reply, "and I shouldn't know him if I saw him; but he's here boys, and in a day or two there'll be some gentlemen here that'll know him."

"Won't our boys enjoy running him out of town," was the last remark Higginson heard as he casually sauntered away from the group.

XIX

"NEGROES WANTED—AND FOR SALE"

WHEN HE FINALLY REACHED St. Louis, after four days aboard a steamer loaded with two groups that seemed about to attack each other, Higginson felt a most curious sensation. He realized that for the first time in six weeks the proper thing to do, if he were conscious of any danger, was to look about meekly for a policeman instead of reaching for his revolver.

His Kansas experience had convinced him that the conflict of arms would have to be nationwide unless there were some drastic change in the tendency of events. But it gave him optimism, or rather restored his optimism. Though his disposition had always been to look for the best, he had begun to get discouraged at the Washington policy of retreat and surrender before the demands of the slave states.

"I found a great deal in Kansas," he told one meeting he addressed on his return, "but I did not go there even to see an underground railroad, for I had seen that in Massachusetts. I wanted to see something above ground. All my life I had seen my fellow-citizens retreating and retreating before the Slave Power, and I heard that there was one town, a thousand miles west, where men had made their stand and said to slavery, 'Thus far and no farther.' I went the thousand miles to see it. I saw there the American Revolution and every great Revolution of bygone days in still living progress. I was tired of reading of LaFayette; I wanted to see him. I saw in Kansas the history of the past, clothed in living flesh before me."

While he was still in St. Louis, he had an opportunity to learn something more about his fellow countrymen. He had been in other slave states before. His longest single visit had been at the plantation that his mother had visited before he was born, where she was told by the seemingly contented coachman, "Ah, Missis, free breath is good." Now he was to have some new experiences.

The first thing that struck him on arriving at this northern-type city in a slave state was the surprising absence of Negroes. There were a thousand people drawn to the levee while he was debarking, because of a fire on a nearby steamboat, and hardly any black faces to be seen. For explanation he was told that the colored people were all uptown. They were not permitted even to walk in the business district of the city.

Glancing through the local newspaper, he noticed an announcement by a Mr. Corbin Thompson. "Negroes wanted and for sale," advertised Thompson, "of all kinds, at my office No. 67 Locust Street; Have a good and safe yard to board and sell Negroes. Buy and sell on commission as low as any other house in the city." Higginson resolved to respond to the invitation and to pay a call on Mr. Thompson.

As he approached Number 67, he observed that from the outside the structure looked like a Boston livery stable, with a doorway that was also a passageway to a yard and an office that was entered from the passageway. Corbin Thompson was a large, lounging, good-natured-looking man, not unlike a reputable stable keeper in appearance and manner. The stock could be seen through the passageway, and Thompson readily agreed to permit the stranger to have a closer look.

There was a dark little room behind the office, and beyond that a tiny kitchen that opened into a dirty and not very large yard. The yard was surrounded by high brick walls reaching an average height of twenty feet and reinforced near the top with iron plates. The place was crowded with Negroes in various conditions of clothing and cleanliness. There were perhaps two dozen in all, most of them children under fourteen. Many had small paper fans they were using vigorously because of the heat. One was cooking, two or three were washing in a tub, and two playing cards with a pack unbelievably worn and filthy. The sun shone down, intensely hot, and the merchandise sat, lounged, or lay about, with only the children restless.

Higginson attempted to talk a little with them to find out something of their history. Some were quiet and said little; some seemed to respond with a mixture of humbleness and impudence. Thompson kept interrupting and trying to answer the questions for his "stock." The "niggers" came mostly from the immediate neighborhood, in Missouri, he said, although a good many came from Virginia, where people seemed to have a hard time keeping them these days. "Buy and sell when I can, that's my way, and never ask no questions, except about the merchandise. At this season we get a good many from travelers."

This last puzzled Higginson, and he asked why that should be so. The answer was so simple he should have thought of it himself. At this time of year, many families went north to spend the hot summer months at lake and mountain resorts. Not having much ready cash, they brought with them a sound and healthy Negro boy or girl to sell to pay for the expense of the vacation. As Wentworth strolled back to the office he reflected that the next time he saw a southern belle at a Newport ball, he would ask her for the name of the likely boy or girl sold to pay for the trip and the splendid clothing in which she shone.

He waited in the office for a few minutes, hoping to see a customer come in and do business. There was a clatter of hoofs outside and a rather handsome two-horse carriage pulled up. Out stepped a small, delicate-looking man, with languid movements. Higginson exchanged pleasantries with the newcomer while they waited for the dealer to enter from the yard. The stranger yawned after a while and then said angrily, "Well, it is all bad enough, housekeeping, marketing and all, but I'll be dadblasted if buying servants ain't the worst nuisance." Other than that he seemed the pleasantest type of southerner—courteous, kind, simple, if a little imperious—a man of property who lived a little way out of town and was a member of the city government.

Thompson came in and greeted him. "Got a good article of a small girl?" asked the gentleman. "Need one to wait on my wife."

Soon afterwards the dealer ushered in three good articles, aged eleven, nine, and seven. They were wearing nice little pink frocks, and were fairly clean except for their bare feet. They had not been too badly cared for and seemed to be sisters. They were arranged in a line before the customer.

The customer fixed his eyes on the youngest and there was heard a whispered "four hundred and fifty dollars," as he looked at her while she stood, unflinching, a black marble statue. Nothing could have been kinder and gentler than the customer's manner in addressing her, "Would you like to come and live with me and have some girls to play with?"

There was a moment's pause. The child neither smiled nor responded in any other way at first. "Speak up, child," said the merchant, rather roughly. But she neither spoke nor looked up. Slowly her little face went down until the chin rested on the breast of the neat pink frock. Down came one big tear, and then another over the black marble cheeks. Then the little item of merchandise turned away to the wall and burst into a flood of tears. And all, thought Higginson, because she had an offer from the very kindest man who ever chewed tobacco in the streets of Missouri.

The purchaser looked delicately annoyed and turned away. The dealer gave the child an ominous look, then quickly turned and almost bowed in deference to the impatient customer.

"Beg pardon, sir, they only came from Virginia yesterday and haven't learned how to treat gentlemen yet."

After an embarassed pause, the customer returned to the subject of his visit. He turned and looked at the eldest sister, the eleven year old, a bright, winsome girl. Her appearance was marred slightly by a pale streak across her cheek that could have been an old scar.

"What's that on her cheek," asked the gentleman, bringing an embarrassed grin from the girl.

"Somebody's whacked her chops, most likely," answered the slave trader with a cool and natural air.

The gentleman pulled the child over to him, felt the muscles of her arm, and asked her a question or two, which she answered softly. At this point a price was quickly whispered, "Seven hundred dollars."

"Well, Martha," said the customer in his most winning way, "wouldn't you like to go with me and have a pleasant home?"

The smile suddenly left the child's face, but she did not cry. "Please, sir," she said, "I wish to stay with my mother."

"Confound the girls," said the gentleman, turning to Wentworth as if he were appealing to him. "They must be sold to somebody, you know. Of course I can't buy all three of them and the mother too!"

Of course not, thought the abolitionist minister to himself, and that is the story of slavery in a nutshell.

"Nonsense, gals," said the dealer, "your mother will come up to visit you someday." He turned to the customer and the minister. "She ain't even here and may never come for all I know. She's still in Virginia, and they haven't made up their mind they'll sell her off. These gals, though," and he leaned forward and lowered his voice, "I've got to sell 'em in a day or two, and if I don't it won't pay to keep 'em. There's an agent going south who'll take the lot at a wholesale price."

At this point Wentworth realized that the best to hope for in the interest of the girls was that the present customer would buy at least one. Even if the mother was to be sold, the chances were slim that she'd pass through Thompson's hands. As if to help convince the visitor that it wouldn't be so bad the customer took him to one side and said, "I mean to bring her up well. She'll be a help to my wife and a pet for the children—and while I live I shan't sell her—that is, as long as I can help it."

No, thought Higginson to himself, they never sell them unless they can't "help" it.

Turning to the dealer the gentleman said, "I'll take her. She's sound, I suppose."

"Absolutely, of wind and limb," responded the trader. "You're entitled to strip her and examine every inch of her. We never hold back anything from our customers."

Higginson had seen enough and soon took his leave. He thought of one of the incidents of his stay at Fayal and remembered his last look at the wreck of a vessel at sea floating off into the darkness and how sad the moment seemed. It was sadder still, he reflected, to think of that little wreck of babyhood floating off into the dark ocean of the South's barbaric institution.

Just before leaving he asked Mr. Thompson if any of the dozen or more children in his yard had their parents with them. "Not one," answered the trader as if surprised at the question. "I take 'em as they come, in lots. Hardly ever have a family. Folks generally don't sell off more'n one or two at a time, unless they're really hard up."

"Wouldn't you rather keep a family together?"

"Yes, I suppose so. Can't think much about that, though. Have to shut up shop pretty quick if I did. Have to take 'em as they come, in assorted lots."

Walking through the streets to the hotel, the Reverend noticed what a very religious city it was. Inscriptions abounded on the houses of worship in all languages. He saw "Jehovah," in Hebrew lettering, "Deo uno et Trino," and in English and French the same phrase, "My House shall be called the house of prayer."

AN IMPORTANT UNDERTAKING

DANIEL WEBSTER HAD REMARKED, in his Seventh of March speech in favor of the Compromise of 1850, on the "strange enthusiasm" of the abolitionists. What was strange to Webster and men like him was that others should risk property, honor, and life, itself, in the seemingly futile crusade against slavery and the racialism that was its fruit and its root. The central idea of the abolitionists' belief was strange for their day, even extreme. It was that a Negro was a human being and deserved to be treated like one. This was the great fanaticism of the abolitionists; whatever their sect or their creed, it came down to that simple proposition.

To Wentworth Higginson after his return from Kansas and Missouri the future looked difficult. He was more certain than ever of the justice of his cause and more fearful that it would not be attained by peaceful methods. The abolitionists had spoken and written against slavery for twenty-five years, and the prospects for its abolition did not seem much closer. Men had been murdered by mobs, printing presses thrown into the river, homes burned. And all for what? Slavery and the race prejudice that accompanied it seemed indestructible.

On leaving Kansas Higginson wrote to a friend, "I am sure the disease is too deep for cure without amputation." He meant to put into practical effect the idea of the tiny group of Disunionist Abolitionists: if slavery could not be talked out of the union, then the union had to be purified by casting out the slave states.

In January of 1857 a call was issued for a Massachusetts state Disunion Convention to urge the separation of the free and the slave states. Higginson's name led the signatures. The slave states had repeatedly talked "secession" to blackmail the businessmen and politicians of the rest of the country to submit to their never-satisfied demands. They had done this most recently to influence the outcome of the 1856 presidential campaign. Now Higginson proposed to take the secessionists at their word.

He denied, when his disunion plan was criticized by such associates as Theodore Parker, that it would mean abandoning the slaves. On the contrary, he hoped it would mean that after disunion ten slaves would be able to escape for each one that had previously, since forcible recapture of fugitive slaves would no longer be national policy. After the Worcester meeting a National Disunion Convention was called for July. During the spring of 1857 there was a financial panic and depression that forced cancellation of the July meeting, and the northern disunion movement fizzled out.

Early in 1858 Higginson received a communication that was postmarked at Rochester, New York, a city that had almost as fine a radical reputation as Worcester, itself. It was there that Frederick Douglass, Negro abolitionist leader, edited his own newspaper. The writer of the letter said he was only in Rochester temporarily, that he had been told that the minister was "both a true man and a true abolitionist," and invited him to a small conference. The purpose of the conference was to raise funds, he wrote, "for the perfecting of by far the most important undertaking of my life." The letter was signed "John Brown."

This was the man who had become almost legendary as leader of the guerrilla freedom fighters of Kansas. Higginson had never met Brown so far as he remembered, but he had begun to hear about him at the time of the Kansas troubles. He knew Brown had never been a member, or even a supporter, of the organized abolitionist movement. Brown's first practical experience with the movement had been at a meeting at Syracuse on his way to join his sons in Kansas in 1855, when he saw the usefulness of an organization that could hold meetings where appeals for funds could be made.

Higginson had heard the story of Brown's early life from George L. Stearns, a wealthy friend who lived in Medford, Massachusetts. Brown had written it for the benefit of Stearns' twelve-year-old son. When Brown was about twelve he had become friends with a Negro boy of his own age during a trip to Kentucky. He saw there how, at the whim of the owner, who was kindhearted and generous to Brown, himself, the Negro (who "was fully if not more than his equal") was cruelly mistreated. Young John Brown had been especially appalled that the young slave had had no father or mother to stand by him, and asked himself, "Is God their Father?" It was then, he wrote young Stearns, that he had vowed to himself, "Eternal War with Slavery." Wentworth could not help but think, when he heard this story, of the fatherless, motherless young girls he had seen for sale in St. Louis.

Higginson was naturally interested in Brown's project, whatever it might be and answered his letter with a request for further information. The Kansas struggle had been all but won; the intervention of Governor Geary, which he had mistrusted, had succeeded in insuring slavery's defeat. He asked whether the "important undertaking" that Brown had mentioned in his first letter had anything to do with the Underground Railroad, the system of loosely organized routes by which slaves were helped to escape to the North and Canada. Brown wrote in answer that "Rail-Road business on a somewhat extended scale is the identical object for which I am trying to get means." The letter was followed by a meeting between the two at a Boston hotel in March of 1858.

As they sat down together in Brown's room, Higginson saw before him a clean-shaven man with a thin, worn, resolute face. He reflected that in the man's eyes there were signs of a fiery determi-

John Brown as Higginson saw him. From a Boston photograph, 1857.

nation that might burn him out, but his conversation was calm, persuasive, and coherent. In a quiet, resolute tone, Brown unfolded his undertaking.

The Allegheny Mountains, he said, had been created by God as a place of refuge for fugitive slaves. He had taken many journeys through those mountains in his youth as a surveyor, and he had seen points that could be held by a hundred men against a thousand. He brought with him and showed Higginson rough charts and plans of connected mountain fortresses he had devised. Higginson's religious doctrine was not the same as Brown's, and he did not believe in a divine origin of the mountain range that ran from the Carolinas north through the free states, but the talk he heard made sense to him as a plan of operations.

His idea, said Brown, was to penetrate Virginia with a small body of chosen men and to attempt to get together bands of slaves who would be willing to take the risk involved in fleeing their masters and retreating to the mountains. There he would be guided by events as they developed. It was his hope that word would spread of the initial attack and that increasingly large groups would find their way to the mountain retreat. Perhaps it could be established permanently in the mountain fastnesses, like the colonies of runaway slaves in Jamaica or Surinam of whom Wentworth had read. If conditions made it impossible to build up and defend one or more strong points, they would make a break, from time to time, to take parties of fugitive freed families to Canada by the mountain routes. In either case he hoped for such a blow to slavery, such a continual drain that would destroy the value of slave property, and cause the whole system to topple.

Higginson agreed to join the others who supported and were helping to raise funds for Brown's project. There were six in the principal group. (They were later called The Secret Six, though they never thought of themselves as such.) Included were Theodore Parker, Dr. Samuel G. Howe, who had fought abroad for Greece's independence, George L. Stearns, Gerrit Smith, Frank Sanborn and Higginson. They not only raised money for the project. Their Kansas aid connections made it possible for Brown to secure control of some of the guns that had been cached in the Midwest after the Kansas fight.

Difficulties and delays were many, including a postponement that followed a threat of exposure. This had come from an Englishman who had fought with Garibaldi for Italy's freedom and had been invited to help train Brown's small and devoted band. Higginson had opposed the postponement, and after a time he began to doubt that the project was going to materialize. "Those who were so easily disheartened last spring may be deterred now," he wrote to Brown at one point. "If I followed my own inclination, without thinking of other ties, I should join you in person, if I could not in purse."

Wentworth lost track of Brown after hearing during the summer of 1859 that he had set out on his expedition. Then one October morning Wentworth went into a Worcester newspaper shop and heard the casual remark, "Old Brown has got himself into a tight spot at last." He grasped eagerly at the morning paper and read the story. Brown had set out with a number of his men, Negro and white together, to enter Virginia, but instead of proceeding to the mountains as his supporters expected, he had stopped to attack the United States Government arsenal at Harpers Ferry. There arms and ammunition could be procured for the slaves who were expected to join the raiders in the mountains. The town was captured without difficulty, but Brown delayed too long. The place was surrounded by Virginia militia, and United States forces under the command of Colonel Robert E. Lee killed or captured most of the band and seized Brown himself.

Higginson's first reaction was to regret that men such as he who had given Brown money and arms were not at his side. Though the plan as originally outlined to him did not include direct and frontal attack on the United States Government, he felt a sense of responsibility. He read in the paper that the raid had proved a total failure. Slaves had not been liberated and there was no evidence that any had risen to assist those who were seeking to free them. Of the twenty-two men, in all, who composed Brown's force, ten were killed, seven including Brown were made prisoners, and five had escaped.

What were Higginson and the others to do now? For himself, he resolved it was his duty to stand his ground, to give, if called upon, moral support from the witness stand, and practical support in a jailbreak. Theodore Parker, sick and dying, had sailed to Europe months before; others of The Secret Six fled to Canada or went into hiding.

Wentworth was in no danger of being informed against by the prisoner. When Brown surrendered, his captors ignored his raised hands and rushed in to inflict saber and bayonet wounds on his head and body. Cut and bleeding in his bonds, Brown was interrogated within a day after he was taken. He denied that he had any object except to free the slaves and told his inquisitors, "You may dispose of me very easily,—I am nearly disposed of now; but this question is still to be settled,—this Negro question, I mean; the end of that is not yet."

When pressed for information as to who had sent him, who had provided the means, Brown answered, "I will answer freely and faithfully about what concerns myself,—I will answer anything I can with honor,—but not about others."

Fear of exposure did not deter Higginson from going to the assistance of the man he had backed. He heard that the Virginia authorities were determined to rush Brown to trial without waiting for so much as a partial recovery from his wounds. His first effort was to help raise funds for the defense. The publicity that attended this effort brought him, among other messages, one from Alabama warning him that if the writer could get hold of him and his friends, "we will burn every mother's son of you."

His efforts to aid Brown were not confined to the law. He was too much of a realist to expect that legal defenses could avail in a slavery-dominated society and too much of a revolutionist to refrain from radical methods. The immediate difficulty was that Brown himself, after receiving a visit from a Massachusetts sympathizer, sent a message north absolutely prohibiting a rescue attempt. He seems perceptively to have sensed that the initial public reaction to his raid was one of timorous disapproval that would turn to sympathy only if he were executed.

Higginson received Brown's message at Worcester but did not accept it as final. He felt that if Brown's wife could be taken to visit him she might persuade him to cooperate in a rescue attempt, for which there were available men like Higginson and trusty comrades from the Kansas wars. The minister proceeded at once to the Adirondack Mountains of New York. There, at the remote hamlet of North Elba, Brown had settled with his family some years before on a tremendous tract of farmland that Gerrit Smith had offered on easy terms for the settlement of fugitive slaves and free Negroes.

After the roughest of trips on wild mountain roads, and then across tangled fields, and half a mile of forest at the end of the road, Higginson came to a clearing. There was a little unpainted frame house on a high hillside almost engulfed in forest and mountain. Outside the house was an old, mossy, time-worn tombstone that obviously had been used elsewhere. It bore the name of Captain John Brown, who had died in the revolution against Britain eighty-three years before, and was waiting to be placed on the grave of his grandson; it already bore the name of a great grandson, Frederick Brown, who had been killed and buried in Kansas.

It was the first of November when Wentworth arrived at the door of that humble cottage. Snow was already on the ground and likely to remain for five months. He hesitated at the latch-string. There were two widows of Brown's sons who had been killed at Harpers Ferry together with the woman whose husband was about to be sentenced to death in what seemed the utter failure of his twenty-year-old plan to bring about the end of the "sum of all villainies."

Higginson had lived, as he put it, in the best society all his life, that of abolitionists and fugitive slaves. He had seen the most eminent persons of the age: men on whose heads a price of thousands had been set; a black woman, Harriet Tubman, who escaped slavery herself and repeatedly returned to bring out people, some of whom she had never seen before. He had known one white man who had been twice stripped of all his property by court-imposed fines, and when penniless and taunted by a southern judge he had said, "Friend, if thee knows any poor fugitive in need of a breakfast, send him to Thomas Garrett's door." Knowing all these, Higginson felt that to have known the Browns was greatest of all. He traced in his mind the sons and sons-in-law who died for freedom at Harpers Ferry, a veritable genealogy of sacrifice and sorrow. One son who was about to die had written his wife from Harpers Ferry, "If I can do a single good action, my life will not have been all a failure."

After he had entered the Brown home and been warmly received, the family questioned him about events in Virginia and the probable outcome of the trial. When he was through, there was but one question that the two young widows and the older widow-to-be could ask, "Does it seem as if freedom were to gain or lose by this?"

In conversation with the visitor, the surviving son and daughters described their father and his home life. He was, they said, a person of absolute rectitude, thoughtful kindness, unfailing foresight, and inexhaustible activity. On his brief visits to the farm every moment was used. The sons had sometimes stood in awe of Brown but, said the oldest daughter, "we girls never did." When the question of her husband's alleged insanity came up Mrs. Brown expressed surprise and declared that if he were insane, he had at least been consistent in his insanity from the first moment she knew him.

In the face of the quiet dignity of the widow-to-be, Wentworth felt regret at having raised the question. His intentions had been of the best, much as had those of Brown's Ohio friends. They had sent to the Virginia court a sheaf of affidavits—some wholly concocted—declaring that Brown's relatives had shown signs of mental illness. Brown derided the affidavits and rejected the attempts of his lawyers to use them. "I will add, if the Court allow me," he said, "that I look upon it as a miserable artifice and pretext of those who ought to take a different course in regard of me. I view it with contempt."

Wentworth realized, as he changed the subject, that he should have been satisfied with the words of Frederick Douglass. CAPT.

JOHN BROWN NOT INSANE, had read the headline in Douglass' newspaper. He said "Are heroism and insanity synonyms in our American dictionary? Heaven help us when our loftiest types of patriotism, our sublimest historic ideal of philanthropy, come to be treated as evidence of moon-struck madness."

Governor Wise of Virginia agreed with Douglass. The Governor had repeatedly interviewed Brown and had had constant reports from the jail. "I know he was sane, remarkably sane," he announced, "if quick and clear perception, if assumed rational premises and consecutive reasoning from them, if cautious tact in avoiding disclosures, if memory and conception and practical common sense, and if composure and self-possession are evidence of a sound state of mind."

XXI

TRAVELERS AND OUTLAWS

WENTWORTH WAS SUCCESSFUL in inducing Mrs. Brown to agree to go south to try to persuade her husband to permit a rescue attempt. The first leg of the journey was to the railhead at Burlington by old-fashioned buckboard. In the solitude of the long ride Higginson came to know and understand her better. She evoked in him a recollection of the classical education he had loved. He saw in her an example of what he had learned to imagine a Roman matron was like, the elements of pride and bravery softened, in her case, with the even finer qualities of true Christianity.

As they talked during the long journey over the primitive roads of northern New York and Vermont, she began to confide in him. She told him that she had known that Brown's determination to attack slavery by force had occupied his thoughts and prayers for more than twenty years. She quickly added, "It wasn't only that *he* believed himself an instrument in the hands of Providence to free the slaves; I believed it too. I had always prayed that he would be killed in a fight when the time came, rather than to fall into the hands of the slaveholders. I do not regret his position now, in view of the noble words of freedom which it has been his privilege to utter."

It took all of a day's journey to reach Burlington, where they would be able to get a train for Boston the next morning. After they had boarded the train Wentworth excused himself and walked to the rear of the car. He beckoned to the conductor and whispered the name of his traveling companion. The conductor promptly called over the trainman, and gave orders, "No one is to ask that lady for a ticket between here and Boston."

From Boston Mrs. Brown was to go on to New York, where she would be met and guided to still another train to Philadelphia. There were a few hours layover between trains, and Wentworth took a hotel room so she could relax in the interlude. Word of her presence had been passed among some of the abolitionist stalwarts, and one by one they called on her as a mark of respect for the man of action whose deed had at first alarmed and repelled them. Each visitor had a gift—a packet of handkerchiefs, a pair of slippers, gloves, money, a picnic basket for the New York leg of the trip, which included a combination of train and steamer travel.

As Wentworth was walking with Mrs. Brown to the South Boston station for the New York train, a friend approached them. He had a look of concern, but did not speak. Wentworth sensed that something was amiss and after he had put Mrs. Brown aboard the car, he found an excuse to walk off with his friend. The latter said nothing, but thrust a newspaper into his hands. TO BE HANGED were the words at the head of one of the columns, and the fatal news, though fully expected, sent a chill through the minister. He had no choice, however, but to pass on the information, and he walked back to where Mrs. Brown was seated. He quietly handed her the paper with the story of the signing of her husband's death warrant. She did not say a word; she simply bent her head forward for a few moments and rested it on the back of the seat before them. Then she raised her head with quiet dignity and pointed to another headline: BROWN ADDRESSES COURT.

Together they read John Brown's answer when asked by the Virginia judge whether there was any reason why the sentence of death should not be passed on him. The words he spoke had been politely addressed to the court, but really directed to all of his countrymen, North, South, East, and West:

. . . I deny everything but what I have all along admitted: of a design on my part to free slaves. . . . Had I interfered in the manner which I admit, and which I admit has been fairly proved—for I admire the truthfulness and candor of the greater portion of the witnesses who have testified in this case—had I so interfered in behalf of the rich, the powerful, the intelligent, the so-called great, . . . every man in this Court would have deemed it an act worthy of reward rather than punishment. This Court acknowledges, too, as I suppose, the validity of the law of God. I see a book kissed, which I suppose to be a bible, or at least the New Testament, which teaches me that all things whatsoever I would that men should do to me, I should do even so to them. It teaches me further to remember them that are in bonds as bound with them. I endeavored to act up to that instruction. . . . Now if it is deemed necessary that I should forfeit my life for the furtherance of the ends of justice, and mingle my blood further with the blood of my children and with the blood of millions in this slave country whose rights are disregarded by wicked, cruel, and unjust enactments, I say, let it be done. . . .

Mrs. Brown and Wentworth sat in silence for a few minutes after reading Brown's address to the Virginia Court; then they heard the conductor's warning call, and he left the train. He was to return to Worcester. Mrs. Brown's route had been carefully and well worked out: she was to be met by loyal abolitionists in the cities en route to Virginia, and all that remained was a signal from her to make possible a rescue attempt.

This was not to be. The morning after he returned to Mary and his home in Worcester, Wentworth received a telegram. It was from a trusted friend who had visited the prisoner the day before. As he read the words, he knew that Brown's decision was final—and that it would have to be respected: MR. BROWN SAYS FOR GOD'S SAKE DON'T LET MRS. BROWN COME. SEND HER WORD BY TELEGRAPH WHEREVER SHE IS.

There was no choice but to obey. Higginson knew the itinerary and sent telegrams at once, one of which reached Mrs. Brown at Baltimore just as she was to take the train to Virginia on the last lap of her pilgrimage. She took the news with the same calm and resolute spirit with which she had endured all that had gone before. As for Higginson, he was to receive from Brown himself a few days later a letter closing with words he would always remember "I can certainly judge better in this matter than any one else." Wentworth knew that Brown was repeating what he had said to visitors to his cell. "I am worth now infinitely more to die than to live."

Brown's telegram and letter ended all thought of rescuing him by direct action dependent on the prisoner's cooperation. There was talk for a brief period, begun by another Boston abolitionist, of a scheme even more daring. Higginson and several others began exchanging letters discussing the idea of fitting out a small steamboat that would take a small body of picked men to a point in Virginia. The plan was then to steal into Richmond by night, kidnap Governor Wise, and hold him hostage at sea until Brown should be released. It was fortunate for the plotters that they were prevented from throwing their lives away in this mad scheme. They lacked the money needed to hire the pirate steamboat.

December 2, the day on which Brown had been condemned to die drew near. It had been only six weeks since the raid, when the initial public reaction in the North and West was hostile to Brown. His speech to the court, his conduct when interviewed, the activity of the abolitionists in his behalf, had succeeded in that short time in winning for him the sympathy of many of the most moderate. "I know of nothing so miraculous in our history," said Henry David Thoreau. "Years were not required for a revolution of public opinion; days, nay hours, produced marked changes in this case. The man this country was about to hang appeared the greatest and best in it."

At the moment of Brown's execution the London *News* published a letter from Victor Hugo, most popular writer on the Continent, imploring clemency in the name of the freedom America then symbolized to Europe:

> *A single State ought not to have the power to dishonor all the rest, and in this case federal intervention is a clear right. Otherwise by hesitating to interfere when it might prevent a crime, the Union becomes an accomplice.*

All such protest was in vain. The troops massed at Brown's execution were there to insure that there would be no interference. Among them, in his country's uniform, was the American who was later to inflict on his country one of the greatest blows in its history, John Wilkes Booth. Brown handed a prophetic note to one of his jailers, as he was led out to be hanged, with the farewell message, "I, John Brown, am now quite certain that the crimes of this guilty land will never be purged away, but with blood."

Wentworth sat at his desk in his minister's study six hundred miles away, looking at Brown's last letter to him. It closed with the words, "I am getting much better of my wounds; but am yet rather lame. Am very cheerful and trust I may continue so 'to the end.' My love to all dear friends. Yours for God and the right; John Brown."

There was something he could do to carry on John Brown's fight. Not as a minister, heard only by a radical congregation in a single town, but as a writer. Although Brown's death had won him widespread sympathy, there were too many who rejected his objective or thought it impractical or insisted that Brown had been proved wrong because the slaves had not risen to join him.

If Brown and his purpose were to be vindicated, it could only be by the lessons of history. Higginson had heard vaguely of slave revolts earlier in the century, especially in South Carolina and Virginia, and had known of the Africans of the British West Indies and Dutch territory in South America who had risen to free themselves. He determined to seek out the stories of these slave revolts and to retell them to a skeptical nation whose conscience was dulled by the belief that men of African descent deserved or desired freedom less than others.

Those who had condemned Brown and the biracial band that followed him into Virginia did not understand or believe him when he described his plan. The idea of a mountain retreat, a chain of strong points to which the slaves would flee, impregnable to outside attack, was incomprehensible to them. They could think, therefore, only that Brown was insane or that he and his men had sought to bring about a bloody slave insurrection, a head-on fight that would have been doomed to fail.

To answer this charge and to help make clear the sanity of Brown's basic scheme—if not of his method of executing it—Higginson retrieved from obscurity the stories of the Maroons of Jamaica and Surinam.

The very name "maroon" (which has come to mean abandon on a desolate shore) was derived from a West Indian word for mountain top and was first applied to fugitive slaves who guarded their liberty by living in the lonely hills. The Maroons of Jamaica, whose history Wentworth researched and retold, had been brought from Africa and enslaved by the Spaniards. They took advantage of the conquest of the isle by the British to strike out for their own freedom. "The Spaniards were readily subdued by the British; the Negroes remained unsubdued."

They made their way to the mountains and successfully held off the new masters of the island for many decades. Seventy years after they took to the hills, they won from the English a treaty granting them a tract of land for their exclusive use. Their peace and independence were not lost after military defeat, but as a result of treachery by the royal commanders. Hostilities had been renewed when the colonists became dissatisfied at the number of newly imported slaves who fled to make their way to the Maroon camp; during a truce, the leaders of the Maroons were rounded up and deported.

On the north coast of South America there had been a colony, until recently known as Dutch Guiana, that was referred to more often in Higginson's day as Surinam. There, too, a seventeenth century change in the occupying power (in this case from English to Dutch) provided the opportunity for fugitive slaves to begin to establish themselves in the woods. They too seemed capable of holding out indefinitely, and their numbers grew as more and more Negroes left their plantations to join them. Life in the mountainous jungles was not easy, but whatever the difficulties, it was preferred to slavery. After long periods of uneasy truce, broken from time to time by the sending of fresh Dutch troops against the refugees, the Dutch finally admitted they could not conquer the gallant Negroes. "If martial virtues be virtues," wrote Higginson, "such were theirs. Not a rebel ever turned traitor or informer, ever flinched in battle or under torture, ever violated a treaty or even a private promise."

Having made his point as to the practicability of Brown's plans in the articles about the Maroons, Higginson wanted next to prove the capabilities of the very Americans of African ancestry whom Brown had sought to enlist. It was said by many that the Brown expedition, in failing to attract to its support the many Negro slaves in the vicinity of Harper's Ferry, had shown they were contented or lazy, simple-minded folk, unwilling to fight for their freedom.

Higginson knew from his firsthand relationship with the northern Negroes in the abolitionist movement how false this was. Knowledge like his was rare indeed, for the opportunities to gain it were limited. Again he addressed his audience in *The Atlantic Monthly*, with the aid of history.

It was not easy to dig up the stories of the leading American slave revolts. Even as they argued that their subjects were neither fit nor anxious for freedom, American slaveowners took great pains to repress information that might prove the opposite. In 1856, as the conflict between slavery and freedom was rising to its last climax before the Civil War, one correspondent reported to a New York paper that "important facts" about small scale insurrections of that period were "suppressed in order to check the spread of the contagion and prevent the true condition of affairs from being understood elsewhere." Reconstructing the events of the past was immensely more difficult.

In the course of searching for the facts about the leaders whose names had not been effaced because of the breadth of the conspiracies for freedom they headed—Denmark Vesey of 1822 and Nat Turner of 1831—Higginson unearthed the story of an even broader, forgotten, plot for freedom. Led by a slave named Gabriel, it had been planned in 1800 and so vast was its reach and daring its conception that it might have been a disaster for slavery had not an unprecendented storm and flood destroyed the possibility of communication on the appointed day.

Higginson told the stories of Gabriel, Denmark Vesey, and Nat Turner with emphasis on their significance. "Wherever there was a black population, slave or emancipated, men's startled consciences made cowards of them all," he wrote of the public reaction in Gabriel's day, "and recognized the Negro as a dangerous man, because an injured one." Concerning Denmark Vesey's South Carolina plot of 1822, he stressed that the most trusted slaves were deepest in the plot," so much so that "the owners could not be convinced, till the fellows confessed themselves." His moral was that all men have an innate love of personal freedom for which no amount of indulgence by slaveholders could be an acceptable substitute. He stressed their courage and integrity, too, when he told about the execution of Vesey and others, including his chief lieutenant Peter Poyas. Poyas cried to his companions as he was pressed to give the names of men who had promised to join their uprising "Do not open your lips: die silent, as you shall see me do."

Sketching the setting of Nat Turner's rebellion, Higginson observed that known facts about the leader's personal life were rare, and he used those few facts to illuminate the whole institution of slavery:

> . . . *we know that Nat Turner's young wife was a slave; we know that she belonged to a different master from him-*

> *self; we know little more than this, but this is much. For this is equivalent to saying that, by day or by night, her husband had no more power to protect her than the man who lies bound upon a plundered vessel's deck has power to protect his wife on board the pirate schooner disappearing in the horizon. She may be well treated; she may be outraged; it is in the powerlessness that the agony lies.*

Concluding the story of the repression and widespread hysteria that followed the defeat of the revolt of 1831, he stressed a curious feature that has recurred throughout our history.

> *While these things were going on, the enthusiasm for the Polish Revolution was rising to its height. The nation was ringing with a peal of joy, on hearing the Poles had killed 14,000 Russians. The* Southern Religious Telegraph *was publishing an impassioned address to Kosciuszko; standards were being consecrated for Poland in the larger cities. . . .*

XXII

A WALK TO THE POST OFFICE

ON AN APRIL MORNING in 1862 that began like any other, Wentworth Higginson strolled down to the Worcester post office to see what the day's mail had brought. When he had given up the ministry for the full-time work his writing had become, he missed most of all the communicativeness of a congregation. Now he looked forward eagerly to response by mail to what he had put into print. He always liked to receive some kind of a reaction to what he had said. Whether the mail brought praise or abuse, criticism or crackpot letters, it was important above all that there should be *some* letters.

As he shuffled through the little handful of envelopes that the postal clerk had handed him, his attention was caught by one postmark "Amherst, Mass." There was, curiously enough, no other return address. The handwriting drew his attention, too; it was more difficult to read than his own, which was saying a great deal. As he looked at it, the irregular scratchmarks and the postmark suggested to him the museum he had visited in the little Connecticut Valley college town, where he had seen a case of stones containing, as it was thought, fossilized prehistoric bird tracks.

When he opened the envelope and read the opening sentence, he was even more intrigued, especially by the writer's style:

Mr. Higginson—Are you too deeply occupied to say if my verse is alive?

He glanced at the foot of the single sheet of paper, but saw no signature. Inside the envelope were four smaller sheets, each with a few lines of the same scrawl, but still no name. There was also inside the envelope a still smaller one, which he opened. It contained a card with a penciled identification: "Emily Dickinson."

He had expected a variety of responses to that month's leading article in *The Atlantic*. It had been entitled "A Letter to a Young Contributor," and its content was the fruit of his own years of experience with editors. He had learned, as an increasingly skilled and versatile essayist, many of the rules and some of the pitfalls of the writing craft. Much of what he had learned in a few years eludes would-be writers all their lives. In his usual polished prose he shared it with his readers:

No editor can ever afford the rejection of a good thing, and no author the publication of a bad one. . . . Look to the physical aspect of your manuscript and prepare your page so neatly that it shall allure instead of repelling. . . . There may be years of crowded passion in a word and half a lifetime in a sentence. Such being the majesty of the art you practise, you can at least take time and deliberation before dishonoring it. . . . Do not waste a minute, not a second, in trying to demonstrate to others the merit of your own performance. If your work does not vindicate itself, you cannot vindicate it.

It was not this portion of his essay that he expected to produce intriguing responses. Besides the general advice to writers, he had incorporated a kind of special message, seemingly intended for a very limited group of his readers. He defied the prevalent prejudices of the day by addressing his opening sentence to "My dear young gentleman *or young lady*." He defined his special target in

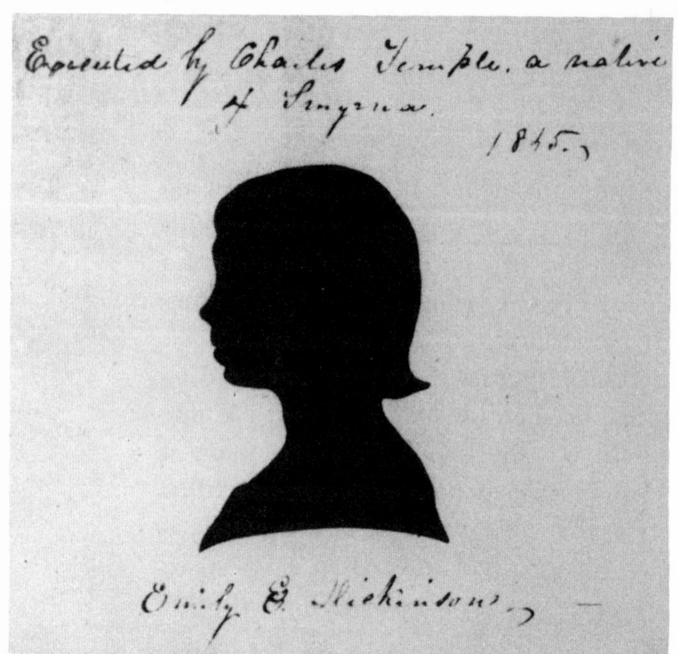

Earliest known likeness of Emily Dickinson, 1845.

a phrase declaring it to be the ambition of every editor "to take the lead in bringing forth a new genius." He made it very clear that the "new genius" need not be constricted by the customs or conventions of the past. The audience would have to adjust itself to the artist, "Remember how many great writers have created the taste by which they were enjoyed." All this seemed carefully intended to draw the attention of persons like this new correspondent who now asked if he thought her poetry breathed.

The enclosures seemed interesting, so much so that he put off looking at the rest of the mail and walked over to the high writing desk by the window. Each of the short sheets contained a poem written in a style that resembled nothing he had ever seen before. He sensed that he held in his hand the product of a wholly new and original poetic genius. "A Letter to a Young Contributor" had reached the desired destination.

When the April, 1862, *Atlantic* had reached the large and well-furnished Dickinson home in Amherst, the oldest daughter was not unprepared for Higginson's article. Miss Emily had come to a point in her life where she needed badly the friendship of a person with Higginson's depth of sympathy for the problems of the unappreciated artist.

She had grown up with warm, bright, lively ways, a great need for communication, and a great hunger for love. She had been rebuffed or disappointed, perhaps more than once, and gradually found that she was more comfortable alone with her imagination. There were few that she met or knew who could respond to her efforts to draw them out, to exchange ideas and reactions to the world of reality and imagination.

Her need to express herself found an outlet in gay or whimsical letters to relatives and friends of the family. She did not want to send or receive news or gossip. She wanted to put emotions into words, to have the pleasure of choosing among words and using them as the means of painting pictures. She was writing for the sheer joy of it, not to communicate with the particular person who might get the letter. Once she wrote to her brother, "I am writing an answer to the letter I haven't had." At another time she wrote a note to friends of her father saying, "I love to write to you—it gives my heart a holiday and sets the bells to ringing."

She had written an occasional poem in her youth, as almost every one does. She must have recognized, as the many letters poured from her pen, that they contained turns of phrase and images that were genuinely poetic. She came to discover for herself in her late twenties that writing poems gave her even greater joy than writing and sending letters. The poems she began to write were not quite like anything that had ever been published in English before—and not at all to the taste of a quiet, conservative Massachusetts college town. One or two of her poems were published, but they were unappreciated; many she strewed among her acquaintances, but their beauty remained unrecognized.

Only a month or so before she read "Letter to a Young Contributor" she wrote some friends a letter in which she included a story, whose full significance they might not have discerned:

I found a bird, this morning, down—down—on a little bush at the foot of the garden, and wherefore sing, I said, since

nobody hears? *One sob in the throat, one flutter of bosom—*
"My *business is to* sing"*—and away she rose!*

Miss Dickinson was not so resigned to nonrecognition as this anecdote suggests. She was endowed with genius and must have had a sense of her own capabilities. As a craftsman with pride in her work she spent many hours working over and revising what she did. One poem began with an expression of her brave and lonely self-confidence:

This is my letter to the world
That never wrote to me. . . .

And yet, her pride in her poetry, her joy in producing it, her probable satisfaction with its high merit were not enough.

This quiet and increasingly withdrawn and lonely lady had a desperate need for an audience with the taste to appreciate her work. It need not be much of an audience—one person if it were the right person—would be quite sufficient. It may be that she had had her eye on Thomas Wentworth Higginson long before she read his invitation in the April *Atlantic Monthly*.

In her world Wentworth was as conspicuous as she was hidden, bold as she was shy. He was an outstanding rebel of the day—a rebel with many causes. Emily Dickinson was not at all unsympathetic with the radical aims for which he fought. Once, after one of her father's conservative associates warned her that the ideas of Theodore Parker (who had been such a great inspiration to Higginson) were like poison, she blithely wrote to a friend, "Then I like poison very well."

She had followed *The Atlantic,* known all over New England as the new magazine, during its first four years of publication. She must have come to know Wentworth as both a writer and as a radical, a man whose every essay, on a broad variety of subjects, showed a wealth of learning and a broad background as a student of world literature. If her audience were to be limited to one, why should it not be one who was not only endowed with the best of all the learning of the past but at the same time identified, by the causes for which he fought, with the world of the future?

We do not know whether Wentworth ever guessed this. Certainly no such thought could have crossed his mind as he stood at the post-office writing counter, immensely impressed with the quality of the verse he had read. It was immediately evident that the poet had a capacity to compress into a few lines thoughts that others might require volumes to express. Her talent, as one of the enclosures showed, could convey a picture that excited the reader's imagination:

The nearest dream recedes, unrealized.
The heaven we chase
Like the June bee
Before the schoolboy
Invites the race,
Stoops to an easy clover—
Dips—evades—teases—deploys;
Then to the royal clouds
Lifts his light pinnace
Heedless of the boy
Staring, bewildered, at the mocking sky.

The verses were as nonconformist, as revolutionary for their day as they were beautiful. These first poems of Emily Dickinson presented Higginson with a problem he was not to solve easily: where would she fit in, in the literary scene, present and future? "The bee himself did not evade the schoolboy more than she evaded me," he confessed forty years later, "even at this day I still stand somewhat bewildered, like the boy."

He took the letter and its enclosures home and showed them to Mary. She did not think the work more impressive than the many other writings, ranging from mediocre to ridiculous, that had arrived in the weeks since publication of "Young Contributor" in *The Atlantic*. In fact, she said later, it seemed to her that the writer of such poetry might be "half mad." Wentworth was sufficiently impressed, despite Mary's discouragement, to seek out more information about his new correspondent. He wrote to Miss Dickinson almost at once, plying her with questions as to her interests and background. He managed to locate in Worcester an uncle of his Amherst correspondent, but her uncle was as abrupt in his speech as she had been in her poetry and lacked sympathy or understanding for his niece.

Emily Dickinson's second letter to Thomas Wentworth Higginson tells much about her and her early life that is unrecorded elsewhere. (Although she did not save his letters, Wentworth patiently and carefully saved hers, as he did almost every scrap of paper that might be of interest some day.) She gave hints about the episodes and encounters that had caused her to tend to withdraw from people and details of her family life and background, ". . . my mother does not care for thought and father, too busy with his briefs to notice what we do. . . ." The very extent to which she confided in the Worcester radical whom she had never met indicated how closely she must have followed his activities and his writings and her warm approval of all he represented. She had read his articles in *The Atlantic* (which by then had included not only his nature essays and the summons to the physical fitness revival, but a record of his visit to John Brown's household and his tales of slave rebellions), and she wrote that she had "experienced honor" for him. "I was sure you would not reject a confiding question."

With her letter (now signed, as an indication of the warmth of his first response, "your friend") were a few more of her verses. Her style continued to show a defiance of the forms dictated by the conventions of the day. Her talent, Wentworth saw, included not only an ability to comment on society and its false standards, but also a capacity to express a rare and delicate sympathy with the life of nature. This quality was important to him, representing something that he, frustrated poet, had been able to convey only in his own nature essays. He liked particularly one that began:

A bird came down the walk;
He did not know I saw;
He bit an angle-worm in halves
And ate the fellow raw.

And then he drank a dew
From a convenient grass,
And then hopped sidewise to a wall,
To let a beetle pass.

He promptly wrote to her again, and this time must have expressed warm praise and encouragement, which more than compensated for the criticisms expressed in his first letter. These criticisms had prompted her to respond, "Thank you for the surgery; it was not so painful as I had supposed." Responding now to his praise she wrote "Your letter gave no drunkenness, because I tasted rum before . . . yet I have had few pleasures so deep as your opinion, and if I tried to thank you, my tears would block my tongue." She brushed aside his comments on the doubt and difficulty of publishing work as revolutionary as hers with a pungent comment, "If fame belonged to me, I could not escape her; if she did not, the longest day would pass me on the chase. . . ."

In still another letter, Wentworth wrote to ask for her picture. It would help, he thought, to give a clearer impression of his enigmatic correspondent. To this there came the following reply in July of 1862:

Could you believe me without? I had no portrait, now, but am small, like the wren; and my hair is bold, like the chestnut bur; and my eyes, like the sherry in the glass, that the guest leaves. Would this do just as well?

"I am happy to be your scholar," she continued, apparently acknowledging his affirmative answer to her request in the previous letter that he be her preceptor. In the continuing correspondence, always marked with the transmittal of poems (that were not to see the light of day, in print, until after her death, thirty years later) she signed her letters "your scholar" "your pupil," or even "your gnome." It was not that he tried or that she would have accepted guidance into the rigidities of the conventional verse forms of the period. But there was much that he had to offer her in her loneliness and isolation. He provided the audience she needed as well as a means of communication with the intellectual life of her day. She would not seek it out, even under his urging. Responding to one suggestion on that subject she wrote, "Of 'shunning men and women,' they talk of hallowed things aloud, and embarrass my dog."

His correspondence with her was interrupted by the Civil War, and never resumed at the same pitch as the first half-dozen letters. Their importance in the literary history of the United States was recorded by Miss Dickinson herself in a letter she wrote him afterwards, "Of our greatest acts we are ignorant. You were not aware that you saved my life. To thank you in person has since then been one of my few requests."

XXIII

LEARN THE ALPHABET?

EMILY DICKINSON was among the few American women of the 1850's to have had as much as a year of higher education. There were only three institutions in the United States where a girl could get instruction beyond a high school level. One was Mount Holyoke, which Emily had attended with Wentworth's Worcester Underground Railroad coworker, Abby Kelley Foster. Each of these ladies, mild and gentle in appearance, had surprises to offer: Miss Emily in her poetry and Mrs. Foster in her platform appearances. Hecklers had stoned Abby Kelley more than once while on the platform, but this never discouraged the fiery fury of her antislavery addresses.

When arguing as an abolitionist against the evils of slavery, Wentworth Higginson was often told that most plantation owners were mild and generous, and really loved their slaves, their people, as proslavery northerners called them. In answer he would say that the greatest evil was the very power that one man had over another, even if, for a time, or in a particular place, that power was used mildly. The same argument was met again and again in the women's rights revolution. Most men loved their wives, were gentle to them, and so on—and it had to be met with the same answer.

Emancipation from the condition of subjection in marriage was not the only object of the movement. Just as it was argued in defense of slavery that the Negro was inferior, that it was impossible for him to benefit from education, that he was happiest as he was, it was said that woman's place was in the home, that she could not compete outside of it, and that an education was wasted on her. Business and the professions excluded her, and where she was allowed outside the home, such as in the teaching field, she might be paid one-fourth of the salary given to men.

Men like Thomas Wentworth Higginson saw the leaders in the women's rights movement, while fighting to improve their own condition, unselfishly give the greater part of their energy to the abolitionist crusade. Lucy Stone, Elizabeth Cady Stanton, and Susan B. Anthony fought on two fronts with a courage and persistence and ingenuity that disproved the myth of feminine inferiority as much as the eloquence and militance of Negro abolitionists demonstrated their own right to be free and equal before the law. Lady orators faced hostile audiences unflinchingly, talked down hecklers, and even shamed the more violently inclined opponents of their movement. Higginson was on a platform with Lucy Stone at one disrupted meeting when the audience began to flee and the mob pushed its way to the foot of the speakers' platform. She urged the men on the platform with her to retire quickly from the hall through the back door, saying she would stay to try to calm what remained of the audience as it left.

"Who will protect you?" asked Wentworth.

"This gentleman will protect me," she said sweetly, taking the arm of the ringleader of the mob as he sprang on the platform. After one look at her face and upon hearing these words, the leader of the attacking force said "Yes I will," took her arm, and piloted her safely out of the hall, which was rapidly becoming a shambles.

They all knew these mobs were not the most important opposition. Their task was to convert community sentiment, and they slowly moved in that direction during the 1850's. The most significant and hard core resistance came from sober-minded and serious leaders of community thought and action, the business leaders and many clergymen. They stood, stiff-necked and stolid, against the threat to their petty dictatorships and argued or preached that women, like Negroes, were inferior by nature, that God meant them to be held in subjugation because Eve had led Adam into temptation (even as some sympathizers of the slaveholders seriously contended that the Negro was the descendant of the biblical Ham, son of Noah, and doomed to be a servant because the curse of Ham had fallen on the Negro people). Nice women shouldn't even want to vote, said the leaders of press and pulpit, and it wasn't ladylike for women to fight for human rights for themselves.

It was such opponents as these that Thomas Wentworth Higginson was best fitted to answer. He denounced the leaders of the newly formed Republican Party of 1856, who had united to gain political power on a platform resisting the extension of slavery. If they had any manliness, he said, they would support the women. At the Seventh National Women's Rights Convention, of which he was vice-president and a member of the business committee he gave one good reason:

> *When I was invited to Vermont, to address the legislature, in support of an appropriation of funds to help finance the Kansas freedom fighters, the meeting was postponed on the ground that the short notice would not give time for the women to fill the galleries and influence the legislature. We waited a bit, filled the galleries, and got the $20,000.00*

There was a round of applause, and even the hecklers were quiet. He continued:

> *No man could go to Kansas and see what women had done there and then come back and see the little men who squeal and shout on platforms in behalf of Kansas and then turn to deride and despise women, without a feeling of disgust. I would like to place some of these parlor orators and dainty platform speakers where the women of Kansas had stood and suffered and acted.*

Higginson was present in a leading role at almost every one of the annual conventions of the 1850's. He spoke, he inspired them in their fight, he made practical suggestions for the agitation that should take place during the forthcoming year.

At an early convention he had declared, "If it be unwomanly for a girl to have a whole education, why is it not unwomanly for her to have even a half one." The logic of this idea haunted him, as he saw the continued lack of opportunities for education beyond high school for all but the merest handful of girls. After his early essays in *The Atlantic Monthly* gained acceptance and prestige for him as a writer, he determined to use his newly won standing in a major effort to aid this aspect of one of his two great causes. The magazine had become so successful, so widely read by those whose opinions counted, that his access to it offered him a fine opportunity. Not by preaching of that which was right could he persuade these readers, nor by the bitter denunciation of what was wrong. He had to make his assault by the use of irony, wit, and the store of historical materials he was so adept at unlocking.

"Ought Women to Learn the Alphabet?" he asked. That was the title and the recurrent theme of one of his most influential essays. His starting point was the proposal of a satirist of Napoleonic France of 1801 who suggested a law forbidding women to read. The earlier writer had given examples based on the prejudices of more primitive times when it was thought that knowledge rarely made men attractive, and females never. Higginson wrote:

> *It would seem that the brilliant Frenchman touched the root of the matter. Ought women to learn the alphabet? There the whole question lies. . . . Resistance must be made here or nowhere. . . . Woman must be a subject or an equal: there is no middle ground.*

He paid his respects to the great names of the bench and bar of the period, lawyers, jurists, and scholars whose opinions he ridiculed. He topped off the series of quotations with the solemn finding of a lord high justice who declared "The wife is only the *servant* of the husband" in the eyes of the law.

Wentworth needed no argument to answer this. He simply quoted a barbaric four-thousand-year-old Oriental doctrine that had been recently excavated, "A man, both day and night, must keep his wife so much in subjection that she by no means be mistress of her own actions. If the wife have her own free will, notwithstanding she be of a superior caste, she will behave amiss."

He reviewed the consistently increasing amount of published work by women of the eighteenth and nineteenth centuries. There was special interest in the highlights of their forgotten tracts and appeals, in all languages, arguing the case for their freedom and proving their right to equality of opportunity. Male predecessors in the fight were not neglected. The implication of the continued debate was summed up, "Ancient or modern, nothing in any of these discussions is so valuable as the fact of the discussion itself. There is no discussion where there is no wrong."

A brief glance at the other side of the question brought the appraisal:

> *The obstacle to woman's sharing the alphabet, or indeed any other privilege, has been thought by some to be the fear of impairing her delicacy, or of destroying her domesticity, or of confounding the distinction between the sexes. These may have plausible excuses. They may have even been genuine, though minor, anxieties. But the whole thing, I take it, had always one simple, intelligible basis—sheer contempt for the supposed intellectual inferiority of woman.*

This was the issue he wanted to meet. In the first place, he said, "it obviously does a good deal towards explaining the facts it assumes. If contempt does not originally cause failure, it perpetuates it." In the second place, he pointed out, "Women being denied, not merely the training which prepares for great deeds, but the praise and compensation which follow them, have been weakened in both directions. . . . Single, she works with half-preparation and half-pay; married, she puts name and wages into the keeping of her husband. . . ." When given equal opportunities and training, he proved with ancient and modern examples, woman will make her contribution, ". . . great achievements imply great preparations and favorable conditions." Who knows of what the world has been deprived by its prejudices, ". . . how many mute, inglorious Minervas may have perished unenlightened, while Margaret Fuller Ossoli and Elizabeth Barrett Browning were being educated 'like boys'. . . . Give an equal chance and let genius and industry do the rest."

The stock contentions of critics of the women's rights movement were answered with wit, ingenuity, and examples from history. He returned again and again to his theme, "woman must be a subject or an equal; there is no middle ground. . . . It is an alarming feature of this discussion, that it has reversed, very generally, the traditional positions of the sexes: the women have had all the logic; and the most intelligent men, when they have attempted the other side, have limited themselves to satire and gossip."

He closed on a note of good-humored optimism:

> *In how many towns was the current of popular prejudice against female orators reversed by one winning speech from Lucy Stone! Where no logic can prevail, success silences. First give woman, if you dare, the alphabet, then summon her to her career; and though men, ignorant and prejudiced, may oppose its beginnings, they will at last fling around her conquering footsteps more lavish praises than ever greeted the opera's idol,—more perfumed flowers than ever wooed, with intoxicating fragrance, the fairest butterfly of the ball-room.*

When he submitted "Woman and the Alphabet" to Atlantic editor James Russell Lowell, there was much grumbling and shaking of the head. Abolitionist though he was, Lowell thought the ideas Wentworth put forward on freedom for half the population a little too radical. It did not take long to win him over, and when published, the article was given place of honor. Reprinted often, it probably had a wider circulation and greater effect than any other single article Wentworth had written. Not only were bastions of prejudice toppled in many circles but there was a very practical effect: at least two women's colleges, one of them Smith, were founded as a direct answer to the question, "Ought women to learn the alphabet?"

AND THE WAR CAME

"There are difficulties," Wentworth Higginson once wrote, "which law cannot adjust." Early in 1857, at the twenty-fifth anniversary celebration of the founding of the Massachusetts Anti-Slavery Society, he shared with his fellow crusaders the joy of having survived violent disfavor and attempts at repression. Though tempered by the fact that they were nowhere near a majority in any free state, the pleasure of the occasion was enhanced by their knowledge that the slavery issue had become the central issue of national politics. Higginson, in a flash of foresight, warned the celebrants:

> *Tomorrow may call us to some work so stern that the joys of this evening will seem years away. Tomorrow may make this evening only the revelry by night before Waterloo.*

Within two months after the celebration the hope that the antislavery cause could ever peacefully overcome seemed more distant than ever. The federal administration, as Higginson himself had observed, was "largely in the hands of able men from the Southern states, as it had been for most of the years since 1789," and the Supreme Court of the United States was no exception. Suddenly, by its decision in the Dred Scott case in March of 1857, the Court delivered to the slaveowning interests one more of those victories that were, in the further awakening of the conscience of the North, to insure their final defeat and overthrow.

Dred Scott was a slave who attempted to establish in court that one who had lived in free territory had thereby gained his freedom. If the states had the right to make slavery lawful, he claimed, they also had the right to make it unlawful and to confer freedom on a slave who entered their borders. His case was lost, and Chief Justice Taney of the Supreme Court went beyond the issues in the lawsuit to declare that a Negro, even when free, could not claim to be a citizen of the United States. Not only that, the Justice added it was unconstitutional for Congress to outlaw the extension of slavery to new territories. One result that particularly shocked Higginson was that northern Negroes who had been born free could not even secure passports, since they were not citizens.

He and the militant abolitionists saw even more clearly than their moderate allies that the Dred Scott Decision struck at the very foundations of lawful opposition to slavery. The moderate antislavery men, working with those who disliked Negroes as much as they detested slavery, had hoped to put through a legislative program forbidding further extension of bondage to the territories. The hope was that, unable to expand, slavery was doomed to rot and die. The seeming frustration of his hope created the setting for a new national mood.

Among the abolitionists Wentworth pushed for wider interest in the idea of disunion as means to their end: to eliminate the influence of slaveowners at Washington by permitting them to secede as they had so often threatened, and thereby, too, to multiply by many times the effectiveness of the escape routes of the Underground Railroad. The idea never took hold, and the more popular view was voiced by men like Senator Seward of New York, who declared that the United States must and would "sooner or later become entirely a slaveholding nation or entirely a free-labor nation." The whole antislavery contest, said this senator, was "an irrepressible conflict between opposing and enduring forces." While his listeners at the East nodded their head in agreement, an unknown candidate for United States senator in Illinois named Abraham Lincoln said in a political debate "A house divided against itself cannot stand." The extreme abolitionists (many of them for the additional reason that the sisterhood of reforms had made them pacifists) preferred to separate peacefully from the South in the hope that that would be the strongest blow they could strike against slavery. The moderates refused to flinch at the idea of conflict with the slave South and perhaps helped bring on the war.

Musing on this difference in attitude, Wentworth Higginson observed later:

> *It was doubtless well that the march of events proved too strong for us, and that the union feeling itself was finally aroused to do a work which the antislavery purpose alone could not have accomplished; yet we acted at the time according to our light, and we know from the testimony of Lincoln himself that it was the New England Abolitionists from whom he learned that love of liberty which at last made him turn the scale.*

It was to take an act of aggression preceded and followed by long agony and vacillation before the union feeling could be sufficiently aroused and directed to the antislavery purpose. The first step in the process was the extraordinary election of 1860. Lincoln did not win so much because of his popularity or that of the moderate antislavery cause as because the violently proslavery politicians split the opposition to his candidacy. It was their inflexible purpose to rule or ruin, by maneuvering to bring about the secession they had often threatened. They had stamped out freedom of speech and press on the subject of abolition in their own region and were now determined that their intolerance should be national policy.

Wentworth Higginson listened attentively as he heard a first-hand report from John Andrew, later to become wartime governor of his state, about a conversation with Senator James Mason of Virginia, who had told Andrew, "We will not live in political society with people who hold the opinions entertained by the people of the eastern states while the principle of majority government prevails."

Wentworth was neither pleased nor wholly satisfied with Abraham Lincoln as a presidential candidate. He saw, as most abolitionists did, that the comparative stranger from Illinois was against slavery, but that he seemed to be very far from being *for* abolition. Nevertheless Higginson voted for Lincoln in the hope that his election would prove to be the first step toward the eventual abolition of slavery. Many northern Negroes supported Lincoln for the same reason, and the abolitionist poet, John G. Whittier, Higginson's friend from the early Newburyport days, hailed Lincoln's election as "the triumph of our principles—so long delayed."

Lincoln received only 1.8 million out of 4.6 million votes and as a minority president he would not have been able to put into effect even the mild free-soil platform of his party, which recognized "the right of each state . . . to control its own domestic institutions." Extremist advocates of slavery nevertheless forced the issue. In the fashionable resort of Beaufort, South Carolina, located on the lovely and remote Sea Islands that ranged around Port Royal Sound off its coastline, representatives of the great slaveholding families had met and planned the action they now took—the calling of a secession convention. When the first news of this swept the North, one abolitionist wrote that it would be the "oddest Revolution that history has yet seen, a Revolution for the greater security of Injustice and the firmer establishment of Tyranny."

The immediate effect of the announcement that South Carolina would secede, and that other Deep South states planned secession conventions, was to justify Higginson's hopes for the election of Lincoln. Just as he had argued for a disunionist disposition when the Dred Scott Decision had seemed to make a lawful solution of the slavery problem impossible, he now agreed with the words of William Lloyd Garrison, "Let the South go." The departure of the slave states would mean that those remaining would no longer have to live under a constitution that pledged the national government to protect slavery. Nonabolitionist free-soil editors seemed at first to agree, and Wentworth wrote his sister Louisa that if the crisis "simply ends in Disunion, even with a state of temporary war, I should be glad—for I think that is a mere question of time and it might as well come now."

As the weeks passed, however, a chorus of new voices were heard. The merchants and the bankers of the great northern cities had always been hostile to abolitionist agitation on the basis of a simple principle. Anything so radical as to threaten the property rights of others might later turn and threaten their own. There was also the general belief that Negroes would not work except under compulsion and the whip, and that cotton-growing, valuable to some northern industry and commerce, could not be carried on if there were emancipation of the slaves.

These bugaboos now were accompanied by more practical fears. Business and commerce is based on credit, that is, shipping goods to those who might not pay until a good part of the price had been paid them by their own customers. Merchants of Boston and Philadelphia and New York had many millions of dollars of uncollected debts, which the Charleston newspapers threatened with repudiation. Many northern bankers held mortgages on large plantations, and the security of these mortgages depended on the maintenance of the value of slaves. If, as men like Higginson were publicly advocating, secession would open the door for multiplying by ten times the operations of the Underground Railroad, it would threaten the security of their loans even if the new Confederacy were to pledge to honor them. Another kind of railroad, overground, played its part. Stockbrokers and investors were heavily involved in the growing national railroad industry. Now on the eve of railroad's greatest expansion, railroad stocks fell in value in the face of the threat of secession, which would create a foreign border at the most strategic part of some of the existing or planned rail lines.

These economic pressures brought about a slackening of the Republican zeal of men whose interest in the free-soil movement had not extended to the abolition idea. There was an upsurge of a new type of agitation: for conciliation and compromise. Conservative elements that had not supported Lincoln now said, in effect, "I-told-you-so," as it became evident how great was the threat to business and credit from the secessionist movement. Others decided it was desirable to show the slave South that radical antislavery men were discredited in their home states. The Democratic and conservative press, which had from time to time attacked the abolitionists, was now joined by many Republicans in a widespread increase in inflammatory attack on the men who had stood fast against slavery in the South and race prejudice in the North.

Having endured thirty years of unpopularity and abuse, of violence and repression, in single-minded, fiercely devoted pursuit of their ideals, the abolitionists could not have been expected to slip quietly off the stage and out of sight merely because of these new threats. Not only did they resist becoming a sacrifice to the slaveowners, they decided it was their duty to agitate against compromise, and agitate they did. The response of the northern "gentlemen of property and standing" whose financial interests lay southward led to a season of mob violence that was worse than in any period since the early years of the abolitionist movement.

Thirty years of mellowing of the character of the country, at least on the eastern seaboard, had somewhat changed the character of the northern antiabolitionist mobs. They no longer grabbed men and dragged them through the streets with ropes around their necks. They did not invade and break up women's prayer meetings. Tar and feathers were taboo, and eggs and bricks were rare. The 1860 fashion was to force your way into the hall and break up the meetings, if you could, with laughing, stomping, cheering, and interrupting.

Boston abolitionists were determined that there should be neither martyrs nor disrupted meetings. They turned to men like Thomas Wentworth Higginson, who had shown in the days of the Vigilance Committee and the Kansas troubles, that their physical courage matched their moral fervor. Fair warning of the need for protection had been given when a meeting called to commemorate the anniversary of John Brown's death was invaded by a combination of north-end roughs and Beacon Street aristocrats, working as a team. The invaders were aided by the police who, observers noted, stopped the disturbance by arresting and ejecting the quiet people and leaving the rioters in possession of the hall. Resolutions were then passed urging concessions to the slaveowners "in the interests of commerce, manufacturers, and agriculture."

Wentworth missed that one but he was to spend his week ends in Boston for the balance of the great secession winter. He received an urgent invitation to go to Boston to organize a body of guards for a series of Sunday meetings at which Wendell Phillips was to lecture. The addresses were to be given at Theodore Parker's Music Hall, which had been silent since the death of the social-action preacher. A secret preparatory meeting was held at a German Turnhall, a physical-education-society meeting house. A guard of forty men was formed, twenty of whom were native Americans, and twenty German immigrants, refugees who had failed in their own revolution for freedom in 1848. "The Germans were inconveniently full of fight," Wentworth reported, "and the Americans hardly awakened to the possibility of it."

The difficulties of disciplinary control of a democratic guard were experienced by the leader. Higginson would post his men at the various doors of the Music Hall and would find on a tour of inspection half an hour later that the Americans had taken seats inside the hall and were applauding the speakers, while the Germans, instead of guarding their posts, had gotten into heated political arguments in the corridors. Once he complained to one of his nominal lieutenants, an American, that one of his orders had been disregarded by his squad.

"Oh, that was an order, was it?" said the lieutenant calmly. "I had viewed it in the light of a suggestion."

Following the series of Sunday meetings, Wentworth's squad was called upon to stand guard at the annual convention of the Massachusetts Anti-Slavery Society to be held at a larger hall. The meeting began on a Thursday, and despite the efforts of the security guard, which was able to screen the delegates on the main floor of the Tremont meeting hall, the gallery had been packed. The hostile group there was formed largely of young men reputably employed in the business quarter of the city. State Street, which was much the same as New York's Wall Street, had given them a holiday with the specific intention of having them break up the meeting.

With songs and shouts and jests these young men tried to disrupt the proceedings at the convention. They did not succeed. During an afternoon session they attempted more violent methods. There was a sudden movement at the doors, and a body of men came pressing toward the platform along each of the aisles. Wentworth reached for his revolver and signaled his lieutenant to bring up a squad to protect the speakers. The invaders then stopped and revealed in their midst the antiabolitionist Mayor of Boston with several police. He had come, said the Mayor, to dissolve the meeting at the request of the trustees of the building. The trustees, who were present, denied that they had invited the intruders and the meeting went on. As the mob scuffled and made his remarks inaudible to most of the audience, Wendell Phillips turned to the press section, near the platform, and said to the reporters, "When I speak to these pencils, I speak to a million of men. My voice is beaten by their outcry, but they cannot beat the typesetters and the presses. All honor to the inventors of type, for they have made mobs ineffectual."

If they were of any effect at all, the mobs undoubtedly aided the abolitionist cause by attracting public attention and sympathy to their arguments at a crucial hour. "Every sentence that Mr. Phillips utters is read as never before," wrote W. L. Garrison, Jr., "The *Tribune* scatters his speeches throughout the North, and the *Herald* prints them likewise to send South."

Later, on the day the Tremont Temple meeting was disrupted,

Higginson heard that a portion of the mob, bent on mischief, had set off in search of trouble, in the Negro sector of the City. Higginson followed, wishing to stand by his friends of the Fugitive Slave Law days. Lewis Hayden, Negro community leader told him afterward his excursion had been unwise and unnecessary: the Negroes of Boston were now armed and would have shot from their houses if they had been molested.

Signs of the coming storm were multiplying; men were beginning to use firearms more frequently, even in peaceful New England. Wentworth read military books, took notes on fortifications, strategy, and the principles of attack and defense. There seemed to be a lull, and then on the day Fort Sumter was fired upon the storm burst and the whole northern community awakened. Political differences were forgotten. Abolitionists were absolutely astounded. Every village and town had its war meeting; a movement to support the government swept spontaneously across the North and West. Higginson was at the Worcester meeting. Men who had avoided him in past months walked over to press his hand as if to say, "You were right all along."

He walked home after the meeting, his mind full of a thousand thoughts. He sat down and wrote his sister Louisa at Brattleboro:

Tonight we have more than enthusiasm, we have unanimity. . . . Never before since I lived here (or anywhere else) has there been such absolute unanimity on a single subject.

XXV

ENTERING THE RANKS

"WAR," HIGGINSON HAD WRITTEN in one of his *Atlantic* essays, "is brutal and disgusting." Some of his fellow abolitionists were opposed to international war and militarism. They believed in and practiced nonresistance, a philosophy not too different from the nonviolent teachings of today. When the War came, however, most realized, sooner or later, that they could not turn their backs. Long before the firing on Fort Sumter, when it appeared that hostilities might break out, Wentworth had written to his mother, "The only way for anti-slavery men to share in the control is to share in the sacrifices."

Frederick Douglass echoed Wentworth's words of a few months before in an appeal to the ultra-pacifists among the abolitionists to close ranks, "He who faithfully works to put down a rebellion undertaken and carried on for the extension and perpetuation of slavery, performs an anti-slavery work."

The beginning of the conflict found the United States totally unprepared for effective military action. Elements of the army and, especially, many officers had deserted to the rebels. Most of the soldiers who remained loyal were stationed at isolated outposts on the western frontier. Washington, the capital city, was in an isolated and exposed position, facing disloyal Virginia across the Potomac and with doubtful Maryland at her back.

Many Massachusetts men were gravely concerned about the

danger to the capital. Higginson, who had followed every development with the keenest interest, originated an idea for the defense of Washington based on his knowledge of the battle readiness of the men of Kansas, veterans of the border troubles there, and on his more recent plotting to save John Brown. Until the free states could equip and send new regiments, why not defend the Union by guerrilla warfare? He went to several leading Worcester citizens with his project, and they promptly gave him a letter of recommendation to Governor Andrew.

Wentworth hastened to Boston and outlined his plan to the Governor, who was intrigued at the idea of summoning Colonel Montgomery and his surviving Kansas freedom fighters to the mountainous Pennsylvania region that was within striking distance of Virginia. "We'll have a company of picked men, with John Brown, Jr., among them," said Wentworth. "I want most of all to just get the name of John Brown rumored on the border. It will kindle a backfire of alarm and draw any rebel forces away from Washington."

"The idea is a good one," said the Governor, "but I have no appropriation or contingent fund to finance it. If your friends can raise the money to do the job, I'll give you a letter of recommendation to the Governor of Pennsylvania."

No time was wasted. Wentworth and his friend Sam Howe raised pledges of several thousand dollars, enough to re-equip the Kansans and bring them east. Then Wentworth journeyed to Harrisburg to see Governor Curtin of Pennsylvania. Meanwhile Governor Andrew of Massachusetts had sober second thoughts about the idea of free-lance defense of the Union and wrote to the Pennsylvania Governor advising caution. Concerning Higginson he said:

He is a man capable of facing great perils, of gallant and ardent spirit, and one whose plans I would not endorse in blank or in advance. You may find on enquiry that he proposes some scheme not only courageous but wise.

Events at Washington had not gone as badly as Higginson and his friends in Massachusetts had feared. The Confederates failed to strike the threatened blow, and scouts reported that no great forces were massed in the vicinity of the capital. The Pennsylvania governor listened attentively to Wentworth and decided the time was not ripe for border warfare. If Higginson were to enter western Virginia with the kind of troops he proposed to enlist, he wrote Governor Andrew, "it would not only destroy the loyal sentiment of that part of the State, but would influence the people of Kentucky, Tennessee and Missouri."

Wentworth took the news philosophically. He had hoped to serve his cause and country in the emergency. He would have liked to do it in an adventurous way, to reap the dividend he described in one *Atlantic* essay, "the relish of peril and the luxury of daring deeds." It was just as well, he reflected, on the train trip back from Harrisburg to Worcester. The war was on and the danger continued, but he was not so certain that it was his place to rush in.

He was, after all, thirty-eight years of age, too old to be a private, and not being a professional military man, he was not needed at once as an officer. The enthusiasm he had noted after Fort Sumter was filling the ranks with young volunteers, even some of the broadcloth rowdies, the young State Street gentlemen whom employers had given time off to attack abolitionist meetings. It began to seem that the Confederacy was not prepared or disposed to undertake offensive actions. Victory for secession would consist, its leaders felt, in holding intact the territory and property stolen from the United States, and in receiving recognition of nationhood from foreign countries. This, the Confederates hoped, would be followed by peace overtures from the free United States, which would need and want cotton, restoration of trade, and the opening of the Mississippi River badly enough to submit to coexistence with a slave nation or to reunite on the slaveholders' terms.

Because race prejudice was so widespread in the North there was enough division of opinion in the free states on the slavery issue to give rebel leaders hope of such an outcome. The war might have started as one to perpetuate slavery on the part of the seceders; it did not begin as a fight *against* slavery by the loyal states. Wentworth feared that public opinion and the character of the Union military leaders was such that officers in the Union Army would drive fugitive slaves back from their lines and even return them to their masters. And this was true at first. In such circumstances, it might be more important for him to remain a civilian and to continue to agitate, as the rest of the abolitionists did, for a transformation of the character of the war into an antislavery conflict.

Events of the first few months of the war were to justify his fears. President Lincoln, believing that he must maintain the fullest possible support of his government, permitted the war to follow a conservative course. When the Negroes of Cincinnatti tried to recruit a home guard to help defend the city, which was quite vulnerable to secessionist territory, police interfered and told them "We want you damned niggers to keep out of this, it is a white man's war." News reports began to drift in about the forcible return of fugitive slaves to their masters.

In addition to his doubts about the government's policy and his desire to agitate against it, there was Mary's illness to think about. She had never been able to regain her health, and she passed from being homebound to being bedridden or confined to a wheelchair. She had always been a wonderful companion—her mind sharp, her wit brittle. Her presence and her capacity for criticism were valuable to Wentworth as a writer. Their and Margaret Fuller's niece Gretchen still lived with them and was now eighteen. She made possible Wentworth's many journeys of a few days or weeks for lecturing or agitation. But to depart for months under military discipline was another question.

When he returned to Worcester, Higginson was offered a commission as major of a battalion of infantry that was being called into federal service. Despite the compliment and the temptation the offer presented, he felt obliged to decline. Aside from his doubts about his place at that stage of the war, he would not have thought himself, only recently a minister, qualified for such a command. He continued to study military tactics. He resumed his fencing lessons, and transformed some of his physical-culture activity into teaching groups of civilians the elements of drill and marching and the manual of arms and perfecting his own knowledge while teaching others. He felt that his work as a freedom writer was more important than soldiering, especially in view of the government's vacillating policy.

He continued the series of "Travellers and Outlaws" articles, stories of slaves in rebellion and their capacity to fight that he had begun after John Brown was hanged. He completed during this period his studies of the Denmark Vesey and Nat Turner slave insurrections. The point these articles made had become more pressing.

Wentworth joined more directly in day-to-day political agitation. A skeptical and prejudiced North was a long way from being convinced that slavery was the real cause and central issue of the war. The enemy had no illusions. Their vice-president, Alexander Stephens, had attacked his fellow southerner, Thomas Jefferson, for believing that men were created equal. "Our new government," said this leading Confederate, "is founded upon exactly the opposite idea; its foundations are laid, its cornerstone rests on the great truth that the negro is not equal to the white man." Higginson was among those who swiftly recognized the utility of this statement, who repeated it again and again for the benefit of the laggards and doubters of the North:

> *It is impossible to blink the fact that Slavery is the root of the rebellion. Either slavery is essential to a community or it must be fatal to it,—there is no middle ground; and the Secessionists have taken one horn of the dilemma with so delightful a frankness as to leave us no possible escape from taking the other. Never, in modern days, has there been a conflict in which the contending principles were so*

> *clearly antagonistic. The most bigoted royal house in Europe never dreamed of throwing down the gauntlet for the actual ownership of man by man.*

He joined Frederick Douglass, Wendell Phillips, and his other comrades in the movement to stress that slavery was itself a source of military strength to the Confederacy and could be converted into a weakness by a proclamation of emancipation.

Talk and agitation were important, but for Wentworth Higginson they could not permanently replace action. Early in August he reported to his mother on his reaction as he observed a fresh Worcester regiment leave for the field, with the song "John Brown's Body" resounding through the streets. "I never heard anything more impressive," he wrote, "and it seemed a wonderful piece of popular justice to make *his* name the War song." Soon afterwards he was to return to his earlier theme that it was "of the greatest importance that men of Anti-Slavery principle should take their full share in the War," and that "a great many antislavery men, all over the state are holding aloof, and can only be brought in by leaders in whom they have confidence."

He was really trying to persuade himself to reverse his initial decision to refrain from volunteering. One week he would write in his diary, "I have thoroughly made up my mind that my present duty lies at home." Then, a few days later, he would waver and enter the remark, "This war I shall certainly enter if I can." He observed with satisfaction that the Congress—the same Congress that before the firing on Fort Sumter had proposed a Thirteenth Amendment, making slavery inviolable in an effort at compromise—had reacted to defeat at Bull Run by passing a law emancipating all slaves used in the rebellion. His mother knew of Wentworth's initial decision to abstain because of the government's vacillation on slavery, and it seemed as if he were writing to prepare her for a change when he reported:

> *I am satisfied that we are gravitating toward a bolder antislavery policy, and it was foreseen that several defeats would*

be needed to bring us to that. The desideratum is to approach a policy of emancipation by stages so clear and irresistible as to retain for that end an united public sentiment.

Finally he could hold off no more and there came the decision:

I have made up my mind to take part in the affair, hoping to aid in settling it the quicker. Mary has, of course taken this with her usual courage, seeing it not to be a fever of the blood but a conviction of duty.

His first attempt to take part in the war was frustrated. He secured authority from the Governor to help to raise a Massachusetts regiment on condition that the colonel to be put in command should be satisfactory to him. This unusual arrangement was based on the expectation that many young men, loyal in spirit to Higginson or acquainted with his work in physical culture, would be tempted to enlist in a regiment with which he was connected. He hoped that the colonel would prove to be Rufus Saxton, an abolitionist army career officer with whom he was acquainted. But by the time Wentworth had signed up enough men to fill several companies, recruiting throughout the state was suspended, and the companies were disbanded. Shortly after this, in his period of involuntary leisure, Wentworth wrote "Letter to a Young Contributor," the article that evoked Emily Dickinson's first letter to him, and its final paragraphs reflected his disappointment in giving up plans for the new regiment.

His spirits could never remain depressed for long. He was soon to congratulate himself and feel satisfaction with having escaped a monotonous winter's drill at what he sarcastically called "the seat of peace—the Potomac." In this he was giving expression to the sentiments of many who were weary with the procrastination and lack of aggressiveness of the eastern Union generals. There followed the exciting news of the beginning of Grant's successful campaigns in the West—heading South. As Wentworth studied maps and realized that some of Grant's gunboats had penetrated the Tennessee River as far as Florence, Alabama, he shared the rising spirits of the people of the North who were as yet unused to victory.

When the chance to recruit companies for a new regiment came his way again later in 1862, he could not resist. The young men who had drilled or boated or played football under his leadership flocked to the banners, and Higginson soon had captaincy of a company of volunteers. At thirty-eight he was older by far than many of the raw officers of his rank, so it was not unusual for the parents of a new enlistee to seek him out and ask him to promise to be a father to their boy.

By early September he had his official commission, and within a month he was satisfied that his company was in acceptable condition. On one occasion he had a drill in the streets of Worcester so he could give Mary the pleasure of viewing the company under his command from the windows of the home to which she was now confined. Later that month, on the pressing invitation of the family of one of his recruits, he marched the company to the little country village of Auburn, three miles from town. There they found the whole community—fifty men, women, and children—waiting for them in an orchard under a great American flag stretched between the two highest apple trees. On tables underneath were the makings of a wholesome New England autumn picnic: cheeses, apples, cider, doughnuts, and pickles. As they marched back from the Auburn picnic he knew this was one type of expedition he would not repeat. How, he asked himself, could a commander order into battle young men whom he had seen in their peaceful, rural home surroundings?

Just as the organization of the Fifty-First Massachusetts Regiment was complete and soon after marching orders had been received, Wentworth sat down to dinner with his company's lieutenants. He was handed a letter postmarked, Beaufort, South Carolina, and signed, Rufus Saxton, Brigadier-General, Commanding. The letter read:

My dear Sir—I am organizing the First Regiment of South Carolina volunteers, with every prospect of success. Your name has been spoken of, in connection with the command of this regiment, by some friends in whose judgment I have confidence. I take great pleasure in offering you the position of Colonel in it, and hope that you may be induced to accept. I shall not fill the place until I hear from you, or sufficient time shall have passed for me to receive your reply. Should you accept, I enclose a pass for Port Royal, of which I trust you will feel disposed to avail yourself at once.

THE SABLE ARM

THE OFFER WENTWORTH had received from Rufus Saxton took his breath away. Fulfilling a wish that he had never really expected to be granted, it was like a dream come true. "First South Carolina Volunteers"—those four words meant that after eighteen months of Civil War the loyal men in the seceding states would be permitted to fight for their country and freedom. If he found he could accept the conditions, he would be a pioneer in initiating a daring experiment in a doubly dangerous area.

Until that November day Wentworth had always hoped for the arming of the blacks, had agitated and argued for it, but he knew that the prevalent tone of public sentiment was still opposed to it. The government of Abraham Lincoln never went very far ahead of public sentiment, and it seemed impossible that the time had come when the abilities of Negro soldiery could be fairly tried.

It was a national lapse of memory that contributed to the public sentiment against permitting black men to defend their country. Negroes had fought bravely and well during the first American Revolution. They had responded once more when their nation was endangered in the War of 1812, the Second War of Independence, as it was sometimes called. In a message to the Negro battalions who helped him save New Orleans from the British, Major General Andrew Jackson saluted them:

TO THE MEN OF COLOR—*Soldiers! From the shores of Mobile I collected you to arms,—I invited you to share in the perils and to divide the glory of your white countrymen. I expected much from you. . . . But you surpass my hopes.*

Twenty years later, when Jackson was president, he seemed to have forgotten these words. He denounced the abolitionist movement as "wicked and unconstitutional" in its objectives. By the time the Civil War arrived, the deeds of the Negro soldier had been obliterated from the pages of history and so were Andrew Jackson's words of 1814.

When the Civil War began there was not a single Negro in the United States Army. The Union Army was to add to its strength mostly by raising regiments of militia from the free states. Volunteers were funneled into the rapidly growing national forces via the state administrations. Even Massachusetts had excluded Negroes, by law, from the state militia. These barriers did not discourage Negroes of the northern states from attempting to volunteer. Patiently and persistently, beginning even before the actual start of hostilities, they offered to help their country.

Shortly after Fort Sumter was attacked, when the capital city was in such peril that Higginson sought sponsorship for a guerrilla force in defense, Jacob Dodson made an offer to the Secretary of War. Dodson was a man of experience and ability. He had traversed the Rockies three times with explorers of the frontier, but now could find employment only as an attendant in the Senate chamber. He offered three hundred Negro volunteers from his people's community in the District to help defend the capital. Despite the emergency, the response to this offer was a cold, "This Department has no intention at present to call into the service of the Government any colored soldiers."

This and similar rebuffs did not discourage attempts to volunteer. They spurred on what was to become a fight for the right to fight. It was not merely loyalty to the country that inspired these offers. There was a quick and instinctive grasp of the probable future course of events, should the Negro be permitted to prove his courage and manhood. The average Negro sensed (as most whites, except for the abolitionists, did not) that the character of the conflict would change, that slavery was doomed, and that the nation would be committed to recognition of full citizenship and equal rights for men who were willing to die to defend it—if only they were permitted to do so.

White as well as Negro abolitionists criticized repeated refusals of the Lincoln administration to accept the Negro as a soldier, the attitude that the rebellion was a white man's war. They denounced the idea that it was necessary to keep the Negro out to keep the border states in. They secured evidence that slave labor was freeing southern whites from factory and field to fill the rebel armies. They stressed in their agitation the cases in which Confederates had used slaves and even free colored men to build fortifications and trenches. They resorted to history to prove their point and published pamphlets reviving the record of the services of Americans of African ancestry in the wars of 1776 and 1812. The words of Andrew Jackson of Tennessee made especially good propaganda.

Their primary argument was that of their ablest orator and editor, Frederick Douglass:

> *One black regiment would be the full equal of two white ones. The very fact of color in this case would be more terrible than powder and balls. The slaves would learn more as to the nature of the conflict from the presence of one such regiment, than from a thousand preachers.*

This, however, was precisely what moderate pro-Union (but hardly antislavery) northern business interests feared. They still hoped for a peace based on compromise in which property rights of *all* kinds would be respected and protected. For such men the very thought, hinted at by Douglass, of slaves rising in revolt in response to the approach of black fighting men was frightening. You could not encourage or incite one kind of lawfully protected property to take a gun in hand and liberate itself without raising a question as to the standing of other property. In April of 1861 the *New York Times,* main spokesman for the moderates, decried a southern accusation that the Lincoln administration planned to arm "the free blacks of the North to aid insurgent Negroes in the South." A few days later the *Times* deplored talk of the stirring up of slave insurrections, "Whatever may be the course or issue of the war that seems to be impending, we trust it will not be accompanied by the unutterable horrors of a servile insurrection."

Campaigns of the war began on this note. General George B. McClellan, leading the first Union offensive into Virginia, directed his colonels, "Preserve the strictest discipline. See that the rights and property of the people are respected, and repress all attempts at Negro insurrection." Some of the abolitionists muttered to each other that the Union soldiers seemed to be doing more to protect the institution of human slavery than they were to put down the Confederacy.

There were any number of events that began to change that state of affairs and to help the abolitionists who constantly propagandized against it. There was the inability of proslavery generals like McCellan to make progress in the field. The defeat Union forces sustained at the battle of Bull Run produced compensating advantages. It caused many loyal Americans who did not agree with the abolitionist position to question the course the war was taking. In a way this was like those apparent victories for slavery that Higginson had seen during the 1850's, each of which helped to bring its end nearer.

A law was passed in Congress emancipating and declaring forever free any slaves whose labor was used directly in support of the armies of the rebellion. The border states that wanted slavery and yet supported the Union did not desert. In midsummer, 1861, Thaddeus Stevens, abolitionist congressman from Pennsylvania, rose to say at the capitol that there would be a time when "every bondman in the South . . . shall be called upon to aid us in war against their masters and to restore the Union." Hardly a month later, Higginson wrote his mother about a speech delivered at Worcester by General Benjamin Butler, whose prewar politics had been proslavery and who in the first weeks of the war had offered to put down slave revolts. Wentworth liked especially the part of Butler's speech that showed how the war had educated him. Butler reflected a growing mood of free-state opinion when he said "wherever our armies go they must carry Freedom with them, since it is absurd to fight to give the benefit of our institutions to those who *do not* desire them (masters) and not to those who *do* (slaves)."

Examples of Negro heroism helped as much as the floundering and failures of proslavery generals. In June of 1861 a Negro steward aboard a Yankee schooner electrified the country with one of the war's first cases of spectacular gallantry. His ship was captured by a rebel raider, which took off some of the men and put a prize crew aboard to sail the Yankee schooner triumphantly into Charleston harbor. The steward, William Tillman, proceeded to liberate the ship singlehanded. He seized an opportunity to kill the Confederate captain and mate, and then, with the aid of the mate's revolver, to drive the rebel crew below decks. He freed his white fellow crewmen from irons and successfully piloted the ship back to New York Harbor. "To this colored man," wrote the New York *Tribune* in describing the acclaim Tillman had won, "was the nation indebted for the first vindication of its honor at sea."

Another spectacular sea exploit by a heroic Negro, this time a southern slave, drew the nation's attention in the direction of the precise place where the experiment of arming the slaves was to begin. Robert Smalls had thought long and hard about freedom since news of the words and deeds of Frederick Douglass was first whispered to him. He was employed, when the war came, as assistant pilot on a side-wheeled Charleston steamer that had been used to ply about the harbor and to ferry cotton from some of the great island plantations in the vicinity. This ship, the *Planter,* was converted to service as a Confederate gunboat and utility vessel, with Smalls continuing to serve aboard her with his younger brother John.

The paths of Robert Smalls and Thomas Wentworth Higginson were to cross after a series of events that began early in the war. One of President Lincoln's first acts of grand strategy was to declare a blockade of the Confederate coastline. To forbid shipping that would carry cotton out and war supplies in was one thing; to enforce it was another. Ships of that era could not patrol the entire southern coast from northern bases. It was essential that harbors be used on the South Atlantic coastline that could provide anchorage and supply depots for patrol vessels. The most logical beachhead was South Carolina's Port Royal Harbor, around which clustered the islets noted for the valuable Carolina Sea Island plantations. The town of Beaufort, better known as a plantation-owners' resort, than as a seaport (since it was not used commercially) would make a base astride Port Royal Sound from which both Charleston and Savannah could be choked off. Two military questions were presented: could it be seized by sea power and could it be held by land forces? Development of the answer to the second question was the key to the change in attitude that was to permit the slave to fight for his freedom.

Robert and John Smalls had seen with sorrow the lowering of the United States flag on Fort Sumter in Charleston Harbor. Like most Negroes of the South, they kept their thoughts to themselves. They were aroused when Charleston's forts were alerted, in November 1861, against the Union armada that Confederate agents reported was steaming down the coast from Hampton Roads, Virginia. It was a disappointment, at first, when it became evident that the fleet's objective was not Charleston. A few days later the great news came. The fleet massed outside the forts guarding the entrance to Port Royal Sound; the forts were pounded into submission; Beaufort was taken without the firing of a shot; and the slaveowners and the rest of the whites had left the islands.

But not their "property." Some ten thousand human beings, young and old, farmers and shell-fishermen, remained behind. The fall of Beaufort and the seizure of the Sea Islands took place too quickly for their masters to be able to evacuate them. Thirty miles from Savannah and fifty from Charleston the government that was not yet against slavery found itself with a problem whose only solution was freedom.

Robert Smalls and his brother performed their duties aboard the *Planter*, quietly awaiting their opportunity. They were impatient for every scrap of news that came from the islands they knew so well. In the slave country there was a remarkable ability to communicate, despite the many oppressive rules and laws, including the law that forbade teaching slaves to read. The mere interposition of a battle line did not change this. Word filtered through to them about the new life on the Sea Islands. Negroes on the plantations were being put back to work under government-appointed superintendents. They were receiving pay for their work. Teachers were beginning to arrive, young and old, white men and women, who did not fear the precarious condition of the beachhead on the Sea Islands. They had answered a call for volunteers to satisfy the hunger for education that the people on the islands had displayed.

Then came the word for which the Smalls brothers were waiting. A new general, David Hunter, had arrived to take over the island command in the spring of 1862. On May 9, two weeks after he took command, without waiting for authority from Washington, Hunter issued a proclamation declaring all the slaves in South Carolina, Florida, and Georgia to be free. Robert and John Smalls did not pause to learn the outcome of the debate that Hunter's proclamation produced in Washington or its cancellation by President Lincoln.

On Monday evening May 12, the *Planter* lay at its Charleston wharf, loaded with supplies and munitions for forts Ripley and Sumter. Delivery was scheduled for the next morning. The white officers gave orders for the night and went ashore as usual. Robert

Robert Smalls (pilot).
William Morrison (sailor). A. Gradine (engineer).
John Smalls (sailor).

A drawing from The Black Phalanx *by Joseph T. Wilson, Hartford, Connecticut, 1888.*

was his usual respectful and obedient self. Everything was made shipshape for the night. Later that evening the wives, children, and a few friends of the brothers went on board. Since the wives often brought meals to their husbands on the nights they were required to remain aboard, this caused no concern. Shortly after midnight the fires were built up below and steam was raised. Robert put into operation a plan he had long ago worked out in his mind.

The *Planter* backed slowly away from the wharf and blew her whistle in the usual signal. She steamed past Fort Sumter and saluted, with two routine blasts of the whistle, the heavy guns there that could have blown her out of the water. It was not unusual for the vessel to ply the harbor so early in the morning. The daring deception worked. The same strategem took her past the outer batteries of the harbor, since short coastal trips to Confederate territory were not rare.

Now came the most dangerous moment. Robert ordered a white flag hoisted and headed directly for the Union blockaders. As the union warship *Onward* watched tensely, with its crew at the battle stations to which they had been hastily summoned, the tiny *Planter* steamed nearer. There were no white faces to be seen on her deck, much to the astonishment of the Union lookout. As the *Planter* passed under the stern of the *Onward,* Robert Smalls called out to a curious officer, in words soon to be repeated on the front page of every northern newspaper, "Good morning, sir! I've brought you some of the old United States guns, sir!"

The heroic feat of Robert Smalls and his brother called the attention of the nation once more to the fact that the Negro could be no less brave, no less daring, no less valuable to his country than any other man. It was to have more far-reaching effects than the mere delivery of a fine little vessel laden with supplies to the national forces. After having turned over much valuable intelligence to the commander at Beaufort and having served as pilot in the tidal creeks and channels he knew so well, Smalls was invited to Washington during the summer. There he was given a hero's reception and brought to meet government officials, including the President.

A few weeks later the Secretary of War, while holding off on every other theater of conflict, gave orders to the commander of the Department of the South (as the Beaufort headquarters was styled) authorizing him "to arm, equip, and receive into the service of the United States such volunteers of African descent as you may deem expedient, not exceeding five thousand." He was allowed to assign officers to drill and instruct the men, and he was promised the regular rate of pay for officers and men.

The nation that had so long refused to employ its sable arm in its own assistance had decided to try an experiment. An answer was given to the Negro poet who had written in May:

Shall we arm them? Yes arm them! Give to each man
A rifle, a musket, a cutlass or sword;
Then on the charge let them war in the van,
Where each may confront with his merciless lord,
And purge from their race, in the eyes of the brave,
The stigma and scorn now attending the slave.

XXVII

BLACK REGIMENT MEETS WHITE COLONEL

GENERAL RUFUS SAXTON, military governor of the Sea Islands, was the first Union commander with full legal authority to place rifles in the hands of ex-slaves and admit them into the United States Army. He was not merely concerned with their immediate military mission: as a good antislavery man he sensed how important it was to the cause of freedom that Negroes be fully accepted into the fight. If the nation were to be indebted to them as soldiers, it could hardly continue to be unfair to them as men.

His task was complicated by a legacy of mistrust that hung over the islands as the result of the failure of an unauthorized venture by his predecessor, General Hunter. The latter had attempted to organize an ex-slave regiment on his own shortly after issuing the premature proclamation of freedom that had lured Robert Smalls and his brother from Charleston Harbor. Hunter had made a number of mistakes, the most serious of which was to employ a rough and ready form of the draft, which Congress had not yet even authorized for the northern states. Squads of soldiers were sent at random to the plantations to round up able-bodied men and force them to join. No people could render useful service when so impressed into the ranks, and the method revived rumors that slaveowners had previously spread (in an attempt to induce

Sea Islanders in Union uniform in front of former slave quarters. From an 1862 photograph by H. P. Moore.

COURTESY NEW YORK HISTORICAL SOCIETY

slaves to follow them off the islands) to the effect that the Yankees intended only to sell them to Cuba and the West Indies. Distrust, discontent, and desertion brought about the disbandment of most of Hunter's regiment. There remained a single company of volunteers, who had served bravely and well during the summer, though without technical legal status in the Army and hence without pay. This handful of men was to be the nucleus of the new regiment, the First South Carolina Volunteers.

In his plan to build a new black regiment, General Saxton made sure Hunter's mistakes would not be repeated. Recruiting was carried out with tact and persuasion by groups of junior officers who had themselves volunteered to transfer from their own outfits to the new regiment. The most important problem of all was to secure a commanding officer who could win the affection of the men as well as their respect, who could train them as well as inspire them. He would have to help, in the transition from slavery to manhood, men who had not been treated like human beings since their kidnapping from their African homeland or since they had been born in slavery.

James H. Fowler was a Massachusetts man and an abolitionist minister who had volunteered to serve as chaplain with the new body of troops. General Saxton discussed his problem with Fowler, who looked up at the General and said, "Why not Thomas Wentworth Higginson of Worcester?"

Others of the civilian corps of missionaries, teachers, and social workers serving on the islands seconded the suggestion. Saxton, who knew Higginson by reputation, decided that his experience as a social action minister and militant abolitionist would be an advantage in working with the newly enlisted that would outweigh any disadvantage from his lack of military experience. Saxton dispatched the letter that was delivered to Wentworth at table with his officer-comrades in Worcester.

Shortly after the arrival of General Saxton's invitation to command, Wentworth received a follow-up letter from Chaplain Fowler, begging him to accept. "The success or failure of this regiment," wrote the man who had proposed him for the mission, "is to be a most important fact in the solution of the whole Negro question."

Wentworth was cautious and did not rush to accept General Saxton's offer. He was sufficiently skeptical about the proslavery influences that still abounded at Washington to wonder whether he was really going to lead a regiment—or a plantation guard in uniform. He secured a furlough from his Worcester captaincy so that he could travel to Beaufort to find out what was in store for him on the Sea Islands.

It did not take long after his arrival at Beaufort for Wentworth to be convinced that this was his place. He was almost won over at the first encounter with a contingent of the troops who were to serve under him. This took place soon after he saw the white tents gleaming through the trees as he gazed from the deck of the steamer *Arago* chugging up the Beaufort River.

While the ship was dropping anchor Wentworth saw a broad, low-decked, paddle-wheeler moored nearby. The silhouette was familiar from the dozens of newspaper sketches and drawings that had flooded the northern papers a few months before; he read with satisfaction the name *Planter* on her stern and looked forward to meeting Robert Smalls himself. Shortly after landing, Wentworth was escorted to report to General Saxton through the pretty little town of Beaufort, with its impressive old houses amid southern foliage.

Wentworth was introduced to General Saxton and exchanged the usual greetings. He wanted to make it plain that his purpose was to command a combat regiment that would not be treated differently because of the color of the men or their previous condition. He was wondering whether to explain to the General the source of his own confidence as to the courage and essential manhood of the blacks—his many experiences in fighting side-by-side in the abolitionist movement and the Underground Railroad—when General Saxton broke in on his thoughts.

"I have never had any doubts, Colonel, since my services in the Seminole Wars. There were many fugitive slaves among the Indians who fought us in the Everglades,—in fact I realized later that that was why we had been ordered to attack. The Negroes would stand and fight back, even with their bare hands, while at times the Indians would run at the first gunshot."

Just at this moment there was a providential interruption. An aide came near and whispered to the General. A group of black recruits was waiting to be marched to the headquarters area for their official mustering-in to United States Army service. One of the officers present explained to Wentworth that these men were a part of the regiment that, it was hoped, he would command. Some of them, in fact, had seen service already, at General Saxton's order. In one brief engagement enemy coastal salt works had been destroyed. In another, quantities of planking had been taken from a rebel sawmill and brought to the islands for the practical purpose of furnishing material for tent floors and storage sheds for all United States troops in the lumber-poor islands.

The ceremony began. Orders were read whereby the assembled black troops became an official part of the United States Army.

Wentworth looked them over and felt his doubts slipping away. He heard General Saxton address the men directly and unpretentiously. The new recruits gave close attention to the General's words, although they were so imperturbable that it was hard to tell what their reaction was. After the order, "At ease," was given, Wentworth circulated among the men, extending a greeting here, asking a question or two there. One man to whom he spoke carried his arm in a sling, swathed in blood-stained bandages. Higginson learned that he had been in the lumber raid.

"Did you think," asked the prospective new colonel, "that that was more than you bargained for?" and he pointed to the injured arm.

The answer came very promptly and firmly, "I been a'tinkin, mas'r, *Dat's jess what I went for!*"

This did very well, Wentworth thought, for his first exchange with his recruits. It was not long afterwards that the mail sacks aboard the *Arago,* on her return voyage to New York, carried back the resignation of a Massachusetts captaincy, and a letter that was read aloud to a family in Worcester.

"Will not Uncle Wentworth be in bliss!" exclaimed Gretchen, his niece, "A thousand men, every one as black as coal."

It was not quite bliss that he felt, but a heavy load of responsibility as he began his duties as colonel. He knew that on the performance of his regiment rested the prospect of lowering the barriers against Negro soldiers in other battlefields of the war. This, in turn, might decide the nature of the future history of the slavery-accursed land. As an abolitionist and follower of John Brown he could not resist a feeling of pride and joy at being in the position in which Brown had wished to be. Except for the technical legal distinction of wearing the United States Army uniform, Higginson's First South Carolina Volunteers were, from the point of view of the law of the state where they fought, conducting a slave insurrection.

The first need, however, was not to lead his men into battle, but to complete their transformation into soldiers. Discipline and drill

Colonel of the Black Regiment, 1862.

COURTESY MRS. WILLIAM HALLOWELL AND MRS. W. J. WOODIN

were required for the proper functioning of an army unit. In this particular instance, concentration on training was imperative for an additional reason. The men needed to be given the pride and self-respect that a slaveowning society had conspired to keep from them. Officers too, volunteers from a dozen states in a great variety of military outfits, were uneven in their training. It was essential to learn to work and serve together as a team.

The next period of almost unbroken training lasted for about two months. Higginson rarely left camp. Army camp life is always a strange sensation for amateur officers. Here, among eight hundred men suddenly transformed from slaves into soldiers, he carefully recorded these experiences.

Wentworth was not alone in recording the experiences of his regiment. He, his officers, and men lived for months in the glare of publicity. Sensation-seeking newspaper men observed the pioneer effort on the Atlantic Coast to arm the Negro. There was also a constant stream of visitors, both military and civilian. "I felt sometimes," he wrote, "as if we were a plant trying to take root, but constantly pulled up to see if we were growing. The slightest camp incidents sometimes came back to us, magnified and distorted, in letters of anxious inquiry from remote parts of the Union. It was no pleasant thing to live under such constant surveillance; but it guaranteed the honesty of any success, while fearfully multiplying the penalties had there been a failure."

While Higginson and his visitors observed the training of the First South Carolina Volunteers, one of his lieutenants, Abraham W. Jackson, made a careful chronicle of the performance of his colonel. He noted how, in the beginning, many of the officers (of whom some volunteered for transfer to get a quick promotion, others out of pure idealism) were skeptical about the possibility of making soldiers out of slaves. Wentworth's arrival, charged with optimism and self-confidence, infused fresh courage into these faint-hearted followers. His methods, which he persuaded his officers to emulate, were just what were needed to win the confidence of the ex-slaves themselves.

It was a new experience for most of the young officers to be associated with a man of culture and refinement. They responded with eagerness to his gestures of friendship, which included sending around books and magazines as a polite hint as to how the Colonel preferred his officers to pass their leisure time. They quickly learned that coarseness and profanity were not tolerated.

This extended to relations with the enlisted men. Once he encountered an officer swearing profusely at one of the Negroes. The Colonel asked gently if so much profanity was necessary and requested that the young officer come to his tent. After the interview, the offending captain swore violently with tears in his eyes that he would never swear again.

The enlisted men were held to strict obedience to orders, but were at all times treated as men. Degrading punishments were forbidden and "insulting epithets" were ruled intolerable. The word "nigger" was never to be used, even in private conversation among the officers. The "affection and reverence of his soldiers for their Colonel were beyond words," wrote Jackson.

The Lieutenant drew in his own diary a picture of his "stately Colonel" that he regretted being unable to transfer to canvas. A little, ragged, old Negress had approached Higginson to complain about some grievance. Wentworth stood with head bared, bending over attentively to hear her every word. "No grand lady," wrote Jackson, "could win a more responsive interest or a more royal courtesy."

XXVIII

LEAVES FROM AN OFFICER'S DIARY

WENTWORTH'S DIARY TELLS better than any one could retell the story of his days and nights with the Black Regiment in training—that crucial period during which, in Lieutenant Jackson's words, "He met a Slave; he made him a Man."

Thanksgiving Day, 1862:

It is a holiday wherever General Saxton's proclamation reaches. The chilly sunshine and the pale blue river seem like New England, but those alone. The air is full of noisy drumming, and of gunshots; for the prize-shooting is our great celebration of the day, and the drumming is chronic. My young barbarians are all at play. I look out from the broken windows of this forlorn plantation-house, through avenues of great live-oaks, with their hard, shining leaves, and their branches hung with a universal drapery of soft, long, moss, like fringe trees struck with greyness. Below, the sandy soil, scantily covered with coarse grass, bristles with sharp palmettoes and aloes; all the vegetation is stiff, shining, semi-tropical, with nothing soft or delicate in its texture. Numerous plantation-buildings totter around, all slov-

enly and unattractive, while the interspaces are filled with all manner of wreck and refuse, pigs, fowls, dogs, and the omnipresent Ethiopian infancy. All this is the universal Southern panorama; but five minutes' walk beyond the hovels and the live-oaks will bring one to something so un-Southern that the whole Southern coast at this moment trembles at the suggestion of such a thing,—the camp of a regiment of freed slaves.

It needs but a few days to show the absurdity of distrusting the military availability of these people. They have quite as much average comprehension as whites of the need of the thing, as much courage (I doubt not), as much previous knowledge of the gun, and, above all, a readiness of ear and of imitation, which for purposes of drill, counterbalances any defect of mental training. To learn the drill one does not want a set of college professors; one wants a squad of eager, active, pliant schoolboys; and the more childlike these pupils, the better. There is no trouble about the drill; they will surpass whites in that. As to camp life, they have little to sacrifice; they are better fed, housed, and clothed than ever in their lives before, and they appear to have few inconvenient vices.

A few days later, writing home:

I wish you could see how pretty our encampment looks, with its 250 tents glimmering white in the moonlight. . . . The white curlews hover and wail all night invisibly around us in the air, like vexed ghosts of departed slave-lords of the soil. . . . This was considered an especially severe plantation and there is a tree which was used as a whipping post, so that the marks of the lashes are still to be seen.

December 1, 1862:

How absurd is the impression bequeathed by Slavery in regard to these Southern Blacks, that they are sluggish and inefficient in labor! Last night, after a hard day's work (our guns and the remainder of our tents being just issued), an order came from Beaufort that we should be ready in the evening to unload a steamboat's cargo of boards, being some of those captured by them a few weeks since, and now assigned for their use. I wondered if the men would grumble at the night-work; but the steamboat arrived by seven, and it was bright moonlight when they went at it. Never have I beheld such a jolly scene of labor. Tugging these wet and heavy boards over a bridge of boats ashore, then across the slimy beach at low tide, then up a steep bank, and all in one great uproar of merriment for two hours. Running most of the time, chattering all the time, snatching the boards from each other's backs as if they were some coveted treasure, getting up eager rivalries between different companies, pouring great choruses of ridicule on the heads of all shirkers, they made the whole scene so enlivening that I gladly stayed out in the moonlight for the whole time to watch it. And all this without any urging or any promised reward, but simply as the most natural way of doing the thing. The steamboat captain declared that they unloaded the ten thousand feet of boards quicker than any white gang could have done it; and they felt it so little, that, when, later in the night, I reproached one whom I found sitting by a campfire, cooking a surreptitious opossum, telling him that he ought to be asleep after such a job of work, he answered with the broadest grin,—

"Oh no, Cunnel, da's no work at all, Cunnel; dat only jess enough for stretch we."

December 3, 1862:

A simple and lovable people, whose graces seem to come by nature, and whose vices by training. Some of the best superintendents confirm the first tales of innocence, and Dr. Zachos told me last night that on his plantation, a sequestered one, "they had absolutely no vices." Nor have these men of mine yet shown any worth mentioning; since I took command I have heard of no man intoxicated, and there has been but one small quarrel. I suppose that scarcely any white regiment in the army shows so little swearing. Take the "Progressive Friends" and put them in red trousers, and I verily believe they would fill a guard-house sooner than these men. If camp regulations are violated, it seems to be usually through heedlessness. . . .

I see that the pride which military life creates may cause the plantation trickeries to diminish. For instance, these men make the most admirable sentinels. It is far harder to pass the camp lines at night than in the camp from which I came; and I have seen none of that disposition to connive at the offenses of members of one's own company which is so troublesome among white soldiers. Nor are they lazy, either about work or drill; in all respects they seem better material for soldiers than I had dared to hope.

December 11, 1862:

Their love of the spelling-book is perfectly inexhaustible,—they stumbling on by themselves, or the blind leading the blind, with the same pathetic patience which they carry into everything. The chaplain [Rev. Fowler] *is getting up a schoolhouse, where he will soon teach them as regularly as he can. But the alphabet must always be a very incidental business in a camp.*

December 19, 1862:

Last night the water froze in the adjutant's tent, but not in mine. To-day has been mild and beautiful. The blacks say they do not feel the cold so much as the white officers do, and perhaps it is so, though their health evidently suffers more from dampness. On the other hand, while drilling on very warm days, they have seemed to suffer more from the heat than their officers. But they dearly love fire, and at night they will always have it, if possible, even on the minutest scale,—a mere handful of splinters, that seems hardly more efficacious than a friction-match. Probably this is a natural habit for the short-lived coolness of an outdoor country; and then there is something delightful in this rich pine, which burns like a tar barrel. It was, perhaps, encouraged by the masters, as the only cheap luxury the slaves had at hand.

As one grows more acquainted with the men, their individualities emerge; and I find, first their faces, then their characters, to be as distinct as those of whites. It is very interesting the desire they show to do their duty, and to improve as soldiers; they evidently think about it, and see the importance of the thing; they say to me that we white men cannot stay and be their leaders always and that they must learn to depend on themselves, or else relapse into their former condition.

January 12, 1863:

It is this capacity of honor and fidelity which gives me such entire faith in them as soldiers. Without it all their religious demonstrations would be mere sentimentality. For instance, every one who visits the camp is struck with their bearing as sentinels. They exhibit, in this capacity, not an upstart conceit, but a steady, conscientious devotion to duty. They would stop their idolized General Saxton, if he attempted to cross their beat contrary to orders; I have seen them. No feeble or incompetent race could do this.

January 14, 1863:

As to their availability for military drill and duty, the only question I ever hear debated among the officers is, whether they are equal or superior to whites. I have never heard it suggested that they were inferior, although I expected frequently to hear such complaints from hasty or unsuccessful officers.

Of one thing I am sure, that their best qualities will be wasted by merely keeping them for garrison duty. They seem peculiarly fitted for offensive operations, and especially for partisan warfare; they have so much dash and such abundant resources, combined with such an Indian-like knowledge of the country and its ways. These traits have been often illustrated in expeditions sent after deserters. [Here the Colonel sketched the details of an expedition in which a squad led by a black sergeant was more effective than one taken by a white lieutenant.] *This was managed by Sergeant Prince Rivers, our color-sergeant, who is provost-sergeant also, and has entire charge of the prisoners and the daily policing of the camp. He is a man of distinguished appearance, and in old times was the crack coachman of Beaufort, in which capacity he once drove Beauregard from this plantation to Charleston, I believe. They tell me that he was once allowed to present a petition to the Governor of South Carolina in behalf of slaves, for the redress of certain grievances; and that a placard, offering two thousand dollars for his recapture, is still to be seen by the wayside between here and Charleston. He was a sergeant in the old "Hunter Regiment," and was taken by General Hunter to New York last spring, where the* chevrons *on his arm brought a mob upon him in Broadway, whom he kept off till the police interfered. There is not a white officer in this regiment who has more administrative ability, or more absolute authority over the men; they do not love him, but his mere presence has controlling power over them. He writes well enough to prepare for me a daily report of his duties in the camp; if his education reached a higher point, I see no reason why he should not command the Army of the Potomac. He is jet-black, or, rather, I should say, wine-black; his complexion, like that of others of my darkest men, having a sort of rich, clear depth, without a trace of sootiness, and to my eye very handsome. His features are tolerably regular, and full of command, and his figure superior to that of any of our white officers,—being six feet high, perfectly proportioned, and of apparently inexhaustible strength and activity. His gait is like a panther's; I never saw such a tread. No antislavery novel has described a man of such marked ability. He makes Toussaint perfectly intelligible; and if there should ever be a black monarchy in South Carolina, he will be its king.*

In these and many other pages of his diary, Colonel Higginson put down with accuracy and care his day-to-day impressions as he carried on the most difficult task of his career: training as soldiers while educating as men the people whose immediate and unconditional emancipation, as a prospect, had frightened New England conservatives as much as it had worried southern aristocrats. To close this chapter it is best to turn backward a few pages to the entries for the holiday season.

Christmas, 1862:

"We'll fight for liberty
Till de Lord shall call us home;
We'll soon be free
Till de Lord shall call us home."

This is the hymn which the slaves of Georgetown, South Carolina, were whipped for singing when President Lincoln was elected. . . .

Last night, at dress parade, the adjutant read General Saxton's Proclamation for the New Year's celebration. I think they understood it, for there was cheering in all the company streets afterwards.

January 1, 1863 (evening):

A happy New Year to civilized people,—mere white folks. Our festival has come and gone, with perfect success, and our good general has been altogether satisfied. . . .

My first greeting to-day was from one of the most stylish sergeants, who approached me with the following little speech, evidently the result of some elaboration:—

"I tink myself happy, dis New Year's day, for salute my own Cunnel. Dis day las' year I was servant to a Cunnel ob Secesh; but now I hab de privilege for salute my own Cunnel."

That officer, with the utmost sincerity, reciprocated the sentiment.

About ten o'clock the people began to collect by land, and also by water, in steamers sent by General Saxton for the purpose; and from that time all the avenues of approach were thronged. The multitude were chiefly colored women, with gay handkerchiefs on their heads, and a sprinkling of men, with that peculiarly respectable look which these people always have on Sundays and holidays. There were many white visitors also,—ladies on horseback and in carriages, superintendents and teachers, officers and cavalrymen. Our companies were marched to the neighborhood of the platform, and allowed to sit or stand at the Sunday serv-

ices; the platform was occupied by ladies and dignitaries, and by the band of the Eighth Maine, which kindly volunteered for the occasion; the colored people filled up all the vacant openings in the beautiful grove around, and there was a cordon of mounted visitors beyond. Above, the great live-oak branches and their trailing moss; beyond the people, a glimpse of the blue river.

The services began at half-past eleven o'clock, with prayer by our chaplain, Mr. Fowler. . . . Then the President's Proclamation was read by Dr. W. H. Brisbane, a thing infinitely appropriate, a South Carolinian addressing South Carolinians; for he was reared among these very islands, and here long since emancipated his own slaves. Then the colors were presented to us by the Rev. Mr. French, a chaplain who brought them from the donors in New York. All this was according to the programme. Then followed an incident so simple, so touching, so utterly unexpected and startling, that I can scarcely believe it on recalling, though it gave the keynote to the whole day. The very moment the speaker had ceased, and just as I took and waved the flag, which now for the first time meant anything to these poor people, there suddenly arose, close beside the platform, a strong male voice (but rather cracked and elderly), into which two women's voices instantly blended, singing as if by an impulse that could no more be repressed than the morning note of the song-sparrow:—

> *My Country, 'tis of thee,*
> *Sweet land of liberty,*
> *Of thee I sing!*

People looked at each other, and then at us on the platform, to see whence came this interruption, not set down in the bills. Firmly and irrespressibly the quavering voices sang on, verse after verse; others of the colored people joined in; some whites on the platform began, but I motioned them to silence. I never saw anything so electric; it made all other words cheap; it seemed the choked voice of a race at last unloosed. Nothing could be more wonderfully unconscious; art could not have dreamed of a tribute to the day of jubilee that should be so affecting; history will not believe it; and when I came to speak of it after it ended, tears were everywhere.

XXIX

"WE CALLED HIM BOB"

HIGGINSON WAS IMPATIENT, during the two-month training period, for the day he could lead the men into action, and they were too. He could sense their restlessness and their growing mood of militancy. He particularly relished the complaint that was voiced by one husky black soldier who had, in proper military form, sought permission to address his colonel and then blurted out, "Ought to go to work, Sa,—don't believe in we lyin' in camp eatin' up de perwisions."

From time to time the Colonel would receive more specific suggestions from the men. They would come to his tent in the evening, and by the light of a flickering candle he would jot down notes of vulnerable points along the coast, charts of rivers, rumors of rebel outposts. As a writer and as an advocate of the cause of human equality he valued these conversations as much for what he learned of the men as human beings as for the information they gave him about the mysterious and threatening mainland.

One of the men in particular attracted his attention. This was Corporal Robert Sutton, a large, powerful black man who had escaped from Florida and made his way to the Sea Islands. Corporal Sutton had been engaged in lumbering and piloting along the St. Mary's River, which flowed between Georgia and Florida. He had escaped along the coast in a dugout canoe, and then returned, heedless of the danger, to bring away his wife and child.

"I wouldn't have leff my child, Cunnel," said Corporal Sutton to Colonel Higginson with a quiet firmness that was one of the Floridian's traits that intrigued the Massachusetts man. They were standing outside the Colonel's tent in the cool of the late evening at the end of one of their frequent talks that covered every subject under the sun.

The Corporal had not yet learned to read or write, but his mind was strong and lucid; and the Colonel had quickly sensed Sutton's hunger and thirst for intellectual companionship. He found a pleasure of his own in probing the man's character as he satisfied these intellectual appetites. History, geography, philosophy, anything at all that a well-read college man could talk about, there was no limit to the mental horizon of this man, whom a more superficial judge would have rejected as a lowly illiterate. On one subject Higginson found he did not have to instruct Robert Sutton; the uneducated corporal's comprehension of the social and economic aspects of slavery was more thorough than that of the average abolitionist.

Wisely selecting the need of the Union forces for lumber as the peg on which to hang his arguments, Sutton was successful in promoting his own plan for the initial expedition of the First South Carolina Volunteers. He convinced his commander, and through him the Colonel's superiors, that lumber in quantity could be secured by an expedition up the St. Mary's, the river on which he had toiled as lumberman and pilot while a slave. Higginson had convinced headquarters that the men were ready for action, and he secured orders authorizing him to travel down the coast on his own responsibility and to attack at discretion.

Three vessels under Higginson's command made up the flotilla that carried the first expeditionary force of black soldiery against the Confederate mainland. The Colonel took pride in the fact that one of the three was the *Planter* herself, the little ship that Robert Smalls had taken to freedom with his family. Another was a former East Boston ferryboat, a double-ender that seemed ideal for a river expedition aimed to secure lumber and to make off with human freight. It was unsettling to have his first combat command include naval responsibilities, but the former commodore of the Lake Quinsigamond boat clubs soon adjusted to the expanded duties he knew would be inevitable in attacks from island bases.

After a trip southward close to the coast, they had a rendezvous with a naval outpost near the mouth of the St. Mary's River. There they learned, from some of those Negroes loyal to their country (who could be found wherever Union armies penetrated), of a troop of rebel cavalry encamped near a landing fifteen miles upriver. Corporal Sutton told his commander that there was a back road from the nearest boat landing to the spot where the enemy was encamped. He knew this because it was a lumber route he had himself traversed as a slave. The Colonel decided that the time had arrived for something even more important to his men than foraging for lumber: contact with the enemy. Before the full employment of Negro troops to win their freedom could begin, their capacity had to be proved to the hundreds of thousands of Americans at home.

With the aid of a Negro guide who had come from one of the cabins at the river landing, whose enthusiasm to aid the invaders was increased when told of the preliminary September proclamation that would grant him freedom, they marched through the woods in the moonlight. The encounter with the enemy came sooner than they planned. A rebel cavalryman spotted the unfamiliar uniforms and even more unfamiliar wearers. His shot began the conflict. While some slipped through the woods to attack at the flank, the main body of the First South Carolina settled down in the grass as coolly as if they were at one of the turkey shoots that the New Englanders had introduced to the Sea Islands. Higginson's invaders stood their ground until the rebel cavalry broke and fled. The engagement was over. The first notch in the guns of the black infantry recorded the flight of the mounted members of the rebel guard.

The surgeon of the regiment, Dr. Rogers, made a report concerning the casualties the next morning. Better than a battle dispatch, the doctor's description showed what was possible when a leader with a compassionate understanding of the meaning of slavery is given a few weeks to work with men thought to be examples of its worst effect on its victims:

> *Braver men never lived. One man with two bullet-holes through the large muscles of the shoulders and not a murmur escaped his lips. Another, Robert Sutton, with three wounds,—one of which, being on the skull, may cost him his life,—would not report himself till compelled to do so by his officers. While dressing his wounds, he quietly talked of what they had done, and of what they yet could do. To-day I have had the Colonel* order *him to obey me. He is perfectly quiet and cool, but takes this whole affair with the religious bearing of a man who realizes that freedom is sweeter than life. Yet another soldier did not report himself at all, but remained all night on guard and possibly I should not have known of his having had a buck-shot in his shoulder, if some duty requiring a sound shoulder had not been required of him today.*

The expedition was resumed after a trip downriver to leave the wounded and to unload some lumber that had been acquired. Following a dangerous and exciting passage in the moonlight, between dark hills and meadows, the Boston ferry laden with most unsouthern passengers dropped anchor before the little town of Woodstock, Florida, Corporal Sutton's desired destination. It was not yet daybreak, and the advance parties of the black regiment were able to occupy the town without firing a shot.

Their demeanor toward the forlorn and ragged men and even the tumultuous women that they rounded up was quite correct and entirely self-disciplined. One soldier, as Higginson chuckled to overhear, when threatening to throw an old battle-ax into the river if she did not stop scratching and clawing at him, took care to address her respectfully as "madam."

As he landed at the town dock and surveyed the scene, the Colonel saw that the wealth of the wharves had not been exaggerated by the man who had urged the expedition. There was lumber enough to freight half a dozen steamers, and plenty of bricks to fill the orders he had for that valuable material. Along the river bank there was building after building crowded with costly furniture, crated and sent up from coastal towns that had been evacuated after the federal forces occupied the island beachheads. China, glassware, mahogany, pictures, many pianos, all the symbols of a life of comfort in the midnineteenth century were there. "And here were my men," as Higginson wrote later, remembering their grim and disciplined obedience to his orders directing self-restraint, "who knew that their own labor had earned for their masters these luxuries or such as these; their own wives and children were still sleeping on the floor, perhaps, at Beaufort or Fernandina; and yet they submitted, almost without a murmur to the enforced abstinence."

As Higginson turned away from the wharves the most impressive building he saw was the mansion of the owner of the lumber mills and warehouses, who had owned Corporal Robert Sutton as well. The Colonel, with a pair of junior officers and the Corporal himself, approached the big house to explain their presence and to describe the limited nature of the objectives of the expedition. They were received at the door by the lady of the house (who was now sole owner, her husband having died) with a stately, "To what am I indebted for the honor of this visit, Sir?"

After a few words of explanation and as if to present his credentials, the Colonel pointed out his dark-skinned companion, erect, handsome, and impassive, in his Army blues with stripes on his sleeve that portrayed his rank. "I believe you have been acquainted with Corporal Robert Sutton, ma'am?"

The effect for one with his sense of the dramatic was all that he could have desired. Inexpressible indignation came over the face of the hostess, as she recognized for the first time her former article of property standing with a rifle on his shoulder and a bayonet in his belt. She drew herself up haughtily and let the syllables of her answer drip from her lips like a kind of acid, drop by drop, "Ah, *we* called him BOB!"

The Corporal was not in the least abashed. He turned from the lady without rancor and without disrespect and touched his hat to his commander. Would the Colonel and staff like to see the plantation's private slave jail? It was almost as if he suspected that the dangerous community of interest of northern and southern upper-class might reawaken. If there had been any such danger (certainly not with Higginson) his was a master stroke.

When the doors of the edifice that Sutton had called the slave jail were thrown open, Higginson was glad his main interview with the proprietor had taken place before he had seen the interior. It would have been difficult to have been as courteous and proper to her after viewing the villainous edifice. It was a small building, not much larger than a northern cornbarn, but with as seemingly important a place among the buildings. Rusty chains and pegs hung on the door. There were also three pairs of stocks, one of them with smaller leg-holes, obviously intended for women or children's punitive detention. But these were not the worst.

In a building nearby Sutton pointed out a contraption far more complicated, one which was perfectly unintelligible to the Colonel and his companions until the Corporal explained its workings. It was a machine so contrived that a person who had been condemned to imprisonment within it could neither sit, stand, nor lie, but must support his body in a position half raised. For a while Wentworth was tempted to try to load it on his boat, and later he was to regret that he had not. He did bring away as trophies some of the chains and ankle-grips, together with the great, rusty keys to the door. As he stood outside that door after completing his inspection, he was filled with contempt and hatred. He had thought himself seasoned to any conceivable horrors of slavery. The visible presence of the infamous place he had just seen seemed to choke him. He would have burned it to the ground if it had not threatened the rest of the buildings to do so.

Newspaper artist's idea of Black Regiment river raid. From The Black Phalanx *by Joseph T. Wilson, Hartford, Connecticut, 1888.*

Although there were still some difficulties and dangers in store, the rest of the expedition was something of an anticlimax. The return trip was marked by the presence of white hostages aboard, as well as liberated slaves. The presence of the white prisoners did not save the converted ferry from repeated sniper attacks. More than one devastating hail of bullets came from behind a riverbank and during one of them the vessel's captain was killed. Though penned below decks, the men of the regiment never panicked; they repeatedly pleaded with their officers to be permitted to land and fight back. Their most earnest prayer, then and later, was for the opportunity for a fair fight against their former masters. They had no doubt of the outcome of a fair fight.

When the Colonel had finally seen to the disembarkation and return of his men to quarters, he could hardly wait to report to General Saxton. Upon his arrival at headquarters he placed before the General his written report on the good conduct of the men, and the keys and shackles of the Woodstock slave prison. It was, as the surgeon of the regiment remarked, a message from heaven—and one from hell.

The St. Mary's River expedition of the First South Carolina Volunteers does not loom large among the battles that have drawn the attention of Civil War buffs, and in terms of its actual military significance it was negligible, a puff of breeze in the midst of a mighty hurricane. The First South Carolina had greater achievements to come, such as the capture and holding of the city of Jacksonville side-by-side with another black and two white regiments.

In the perspective of history, the tiny conflict in the woods was its greatest victory. The newspapers of the day gave great attention to its successful return. The mass of pro-Union northerners were slowly learning the need for the destruction of slavery. They needed some evidence to persuade them of the essential fact that was at the heart of the abolitionist philosophy: that the Negro was a man and entitled to be treated as a brother. The example of the First South Carolina in its initial exploits was publicized widely enough to help break down much of the prejudice against arming the Negro elsewhere.

The St. Mary's expedition had come at a crucial time. The House of Representatives was debating a bill that had been introduced by Representative Thaddeus Stevens on January 12 calling for the enlistment of 150,000 Negro soldiers. Ten days after the St. Mary's expedition the bill passed by a vote of 83 to 54. At about the same time Governor John Andrew of Massachusetts obtained the authority he had persistently sought to raise colored troops from among the free Negroes in Higginson's home state. This was the initial step in the formation of the 54th Massachusetts Volunteers. The heroism of that outfit in a tragic battle at the outskirts of Charleston in July of 1863 was to help immensely in causing national public opinion to agree with the abolitionists that emancipation must mean freedom from prejudice as well as freedom from slavery.

NEGRO LIFE AND HISTORY

In General Saxton's position as military governor of the first area of any size to be liberated, he was plagued by paperwork. Hardly a week would pass without a long list of questions from some well-meaning philanthropic organization that had obtained clearance from Washington to investigate the condition of the ex-slaves. They were constantly inquiring, as Higginson recalled, into the "peculiar tastes, temptations, and perils" of the newly emancipated race. One day he saw the General's secretary arrive with still another catechism and heard his superior officer exclaim impatiently, "Draw a line across that whole list of questions about the freedmen, and write at the bottom, 'They are intensely human.' "

Higginson, the practicing abolitionist, knew this very well before he had come to the Sea Islands. His collaboration with the free Negroes of the North and the frequency of his contact with fugitive slaves from the South had instructed him in the essential humanity of the Negro. Years of propaganda from the slave states, echoed by their free-state sympathizers, had obstructed the vision of most northerners.

One of Higginson's chief aides, Lieutenant Colonel Trowbridge, enjoyed describing his first encounter with Private Sam Roberts, one of the youngest rookies in the regiment. When liberated with a group from another island plantation, Sam was seen anxiously scrutinizing the Yankee soldiers fore and aft. His father, who had been conversing on the beach with officers of the raiding party, called him to account, "Hi, Sammy, what you's doin' chile?"

"Daddy," answered the young teenager, "don't you know mas'r tell us Yankee hab tail? I don't see no tail daddy!"

This story reminded the Colonel that there were many whites whose beliefs about the Negro people were as accurate as the picture of the Yankees that Sam's master had given him. There was a great deal for the Colonel, himself, to learn about Negro life and history.

He admitted ruefully that "they all looked just alike," when he began living among five hundred men of sable complexion. As he grew more acquainted with them, their individualities emerged. He found their faces and then their characters to be as distinctive as that of any group. One thing they had in common was a constitutional distrust of all white people. This was a characteristic he understood in depth and coped with on a simple basis: when treated like human beings, they acted as such.

One of his discoveries was to help direct the attention of the nation to an outstanding contribution of the Negro to American culture. He would often stroll through the camp in the evening while the men were resting or engaged in recreational pursuits. He would mingle and banter with them freely when discipline was relaxed. Sometimes he would observe them at play or in conversation uninhibited by the presence of whites. Occasionally he would watch, unobserved, as they sat around a roaring campfire, telling one another tales of their escape to freedom. The ingenuity, the foresight, the caution, and the planning, the qualities of mind and character that they unconsciously revealed in their stories, all spiced with a rich, rare sense of humor, deepened his understanding. He wished he could convey the fullness of his knowledge to some of those who came to Port Royal as well-meaning idealists and saw only the mask of seemingly hopeless, impenetrable stupidity that bitter years of experience had taught the Negro to display to strangers.

It was not long before an unfamiliar type of activity caught the Colonel's attention. At twilight, when the chores and training tasks of the day were done, the air would be full of singing or chanting, sometimes accompanied by the clapping of hands in unison. The songs he heard were not, for the most part, carefree songs of joy. They varied in tempo from slow to quick but were almost always full of plaintive cadences. Many of them had a religious quality or words of seeming religious significance, yet they were not solemn or singsong dull like the hymns of New England Puritan churchgoers with which he was familiar,

One of the first he heard came from a group that was unaware of his presence at the edge of his tent:

We'll fight for liberty
Till de Lord shall call us home;
We'll soon be free
Till de Lord shall call us home.

A little black drummer boy sitting nearby responded to the Colonel's summons as the song closed and told him his own story of the part the song had played in his life not long before. The news that Abraham Lincoln had been elected president of the United States had come to the slaves in Georgetown, an inland city in South Carolina. Even though Lincoln had pledged himself not to interfere with slavery, these back-country people, forbidden to read and write, sensed that the outcome of the election was an event of great promise. Their masters heard them singing "We'll fight for liberty/Till de Lord shall call us home" and angrily rounded them up for a taste of the lash. The drummer boy grinned as he finished the story, his white teeth gleaming, "Dey tink 'de Lord' meant for say de Yankees."

Soon afterwards, when time for lights out arrived one evening and most of the camp had settled to rest, the Colonel was deeply moved to hear the strains of another song:

I know moon-rise, I know star-rise;
Lay dis body down.
I walk in de moonlight, I walk in de starlight,
To lay dis body down.
I'll walk in de graveyard, I'll walk through de graveyard,
To lay dis body down.
I'll lie in de grave and stretch out my arms;
Lay dis body down. . . .

He was overwhelmed by the mood the words conveyed of human spirit crushed by slavery, of a longing for rest after exhaustion by unutterable weariness. No white poet he had read had ever put such feelings into words so well.

The United States was then nearly a century old but no one knew what folk music was, nor did anyone realize that we had such an asset. Higginson's cultural background and his sensitivity qualified him to perform a unique service: he was to be the first American to recognize and report the great gift of the oppressed to the nation that had oppressed them.

There was a special pleasure in this for him. He had pioneered with the Transcendentalists in their initial effort to break loose and set a distinctively American style. He had always chafed at the dependence of American prose and poetry on European models.

In the 1830's the melodies of some of the slave songs—sorrow songs, as they were later called by W.E.B. Du Bois, Negro leader and historian—had come to public attention. It was not long before their origin was quite forgotten. Some were lifted, their words and music changed so that they could not be recognized, and they attained a certain currency as popular airs. Others were put into faster tempo, made into minstrel songs for comedians to sing on stage. There was no real appreciation of their character, their origin, or their significance until the northerner Higginson met the southern slave alone, face to face, on the Sea Islands with (as Du Bois put it) no slaveowner or overseer as a constraining witness to the meeting.

At the beginning of his encounter with the musical expression of the ex-slaves, Wentworth was reminded of the experience of Sir Walter Scott, whose writings helped him to enjoy and understand the Scotch ballads of love and war and tragedy on the border. He remembered how Sir Walter had tramped across the moors and through the heather to locate old people who knew the ballads, so that he could preserve them in writing. He had always envied Sir Walter the experience; now he suddenly found himself in the midst of a world of unwritten songs, simple and home grown, more plaintive, as quaint, and as poetic as the Scotch border ballads.

Wentworth was quite familiar with the literature of the antebellum South, and he knew that the region's published writers barely mentioned these songs. To admit that the oppressed were capable of creativity and poetic expression would not have been tolerated.

He had heard a couple of the songs that had been carried north before the war by refugees from South Carolina whom he met in the movement. The words and music had interested him, but that was all for the moment. Now that he was living among hundreds of ex-slaves from South Carolina, Georgia, and Florida, he began to experience the spirituals in depth. The realization that this was a national treasure concerning which nothing had been written or published made him think of the experience of Scott. He could now gather on their native soil (as his botanist's mind put it) these valuable plants that he had only observed uprooted and out of context.

The burden of his duties as officer in an unprecedented situation and the efforts he made to keep up with current literature and letters from home did not interfere with the pursuit of the new hobby. He would often stand within hearing distance of a campfire surrounded by his men and jot down the words as best he could in the darkness. Afterwards he would carry the scrap of paper to his tent ("like some captured bird or insect," he thought) and take it out of his pocket, lovingly examine it, and put it away. Sometimes he would interview a man whose special confidence he had gained. This supplied the missing words or lines of an elusive specimen or helped him to puzzle out its hidden meaning.

Some of the songs seemed at first to have only a religious significance or to express no more than weariness or longing. With the aid of his interpreters he saw that they also expressed bitterness or frustration or defiance. He understood how these songs helped those who sang them to survive by providing an outlet for release of their feelings. Some of the words were traceable, as were the rhythms of the music, to African origins, but the message of the songs was not primarily racial. It was the product of a group experience with oppression.

There was resistance and rebellion to be found as well as sadness and longing. He often detected a military ring in the words that was hidden behind the biblical passage from which they were derived. Jesus would be described as bravely enduring his suffering—"they nailed him to the cross but he never said a mumblin' word"—and at the same time as a figure ready to lead a fight at the right time:

Ride in, kind Saviour!
No man can hinder me,
O Jesus is a mighty man!
No man can hinder me.

The repeated references to wars, battles, swords, and armies in these songs was no coincidence. It preceded and prepared for the transition from slave to soldier. Although they had concealed it from their masters, the slaves had long been at war with slavery. When they sang:

My army cross over,
O Pharaoh's army drownded,
My army cross over,

Higginson knew that masters who believed the Negroes to be merely dumb, submissive brutes, were themselves victims of their own stupidity and self-inflicted prejudices.

Reviewing the words of the songs he had gathered and comparing them with the Bible, he was struck by the sources. Most of the slaves' songs were drawn from the books of Moses, with their story of liberation, and the book of the Apocalypse, with its chronicle of vengeance and destruction. Other chapters of the Bible were hardly significant to those in bondage.

Wentworth did not interest himself only in the words of the songs. As he came to know the men better he delighted to explore the mysteries of the craftsmanship that produced the spirituals. He never could get definite answers or explanations. He learned that folk music really isn't written by any one person or even group. He did get the thrill, one day, while he was being rowed between two islands, of coming upon a fresh trail. One of the oarsmen laid claim to having helped originate one spiritual in response to the cruelty of an overbearing taskmaster. But even this man confessed that most of the credit had to be shared among his fellows at the plantation, who had taken up the first two lines and sympathetically developed them together with the originator.

Spirituals and songs of protest had an effective military function, now that the men were free and fighting for the freedom of others. They were both sources of relaxation and stimuli to courage. There was one major difference, as far as he could see, between the singing propensities of his men and the average white regiment: never, among the First South Carolina Volunteers, was there a profane or vulgar ditty.

Based on his published letters home, and an article he prepared soon after the war for *The Atlantic Monthly,* there developed a growing interest in the spirituals. The Negro as the focus of attention in the war and the Negro soldier as an unexpected and reliable ally became the subject of thoughtful concern in the North and West. Higginson's reports of his army experiences were always interesting; his account of his experiences with Negro life and history as reflected in their folk singing became extraordinarily popular. He had the immediate distinction of having opened the door to the wider interest that developed as the spirituals were performed in concert style and the later credit—not always assigned to him—of having been the pioneer recorder of what many have called our greatest single artistic creation.

XXXI

EXIT FIGHTING FOR EQUAL PAY

RECOGNITION OF THE Negro American as a human being—which was to evaporate less than a decade after the war—did not come either easily or quickly. The deep-seated prejudices that delayed the entry into uniform of the man of African descent persisted to obstruct his contribution as a soldier. Colonel Higginson knew of the double disadvantage under which his men were obliged to perform their service to army and to nation. There was the inhumanity of the Confederates, who ordered that they be put to death on capture. There was the less understandable inhumanity of the Washington administration, which broke its promise to give them pay and allowances equal to those furnished white troops.

It was no great surprise to Wentworth to learn of the rebel reaction to the use of ex-slaves as soldiers in the United States Army. For decades, the masters of southern society had lived in constant fear of slave revolt, as he had learned in his researches into the stories of Denmark Vesey and Nat Turner. The prewar propaganda of slavocracy's closed society, that black men were contented because better off under bondage, was belied by that real and constant fear and the means of suppression that were widely employed.

Now they were faced with the reality of black men carrying guns and bayonets under the American flag. The rebel War Department issued an order, about which Wentworth learned as soon as he landed, that white officers leading such troops were to be treated as outlaws and that ex-slaves were to be denied the basic human rights guaranteed by international law to prisoners of war. They were to be hanged or sold back into slavery, as local authorities might decide. After some battles they were simply murdered on the spot. "We all felt," said Higginson, "that we fought with ropes around our necks."

It did not surprise the men of the black regiments that their ex-masters should treat them so, and they took grim satisfaction in the threat. But they were dismayed and their commander enraged when they learned, a few months after their enlistment, that the Washington War Department was as mean in its own way as its rebel counterpart was cruel. A ruling was made during 1863, based on a narrow interpretation of the law, that soldiers of African descent were to receive pay and allowances less than three-fifths of that of white soldiers of the same rank. Such mistreatment tended to discourage those who had not yet joined from volunteering. It gravely imperiled the morale of those who were serving.

The admiration and affection of the first South Carolina Volunteers for their "cunnel" prevented the threats and outbreaks of mutiny that arose in other regiments. A third of Higginson's men, with a fine sense of pride, protested by refusing to take any pay at all at the reduced price. "We'se gib our sogering to de Guv'ment, Cunnel," they said, "but we won't 'spise ourselves so much for take de seben dollar." (White privates were then receiving thirteen dollars per month, and the effect of the new order was to reduce colored men of the same rank to seven dollars.) They even made an improvised folk ballad on the subject, of which the Colonel once heard a verse:

"Ten dollar a month!
Tree ob dat for clothin'
Go to Washington
Fight for Linkum's darter."

Lincoln's daughter, he learned, stood for the Goddess of Liberty, who had made her appearance on poster and handbill. They would be true to her, they were saying, but they would not take reduced wages. A more extreme reaction came from a noncommissioned officer in the Third South Carolina, who had led his men in stacking rifles in front of his Captain's tent. This symbolized the fact that as the government had broken its contract, the men felt released from their end of the bargain. For this Sergeant William Walker was court-martialed and shot.

Higginson's fellow guerrilla fighter from Kansas, Colonel Montgomery, had come to the Sea Islands to form and lead a Negro regiment of his own. He found it difficult now to induce Negroes to enlist. Somehow he wangled the authority to resort to the draft. He found the reluctance of the Negro to volunteer completely understandable. He wrote to Mrs. Stearns, wife of another of John Brown's Secret Six:

> *The Negroes re-indicate their claim to humanity by shirking the draft in every possible way; acting exactly as white men under similar circumstances. Hence, I conclude, they are undoubtedly human. The only difference that I notice is, the Negro, after being drafted, does not* desert; *but, once dressed in the uniform of a soldier, with arms in his hands, he feels himself a man; and acts like one.*

"Outrageous Fraud" declared Higginson, denouncing the unequal pay ruling. Rolling up his sleeves he began a fight that did not slacken. It was not so much the thought that discriminatory treatment was the product of northern race prejudice that spurred him on in his campaign. He remembered from his early days in Massachusetts and his travels elsewhere as a lecturer how cruel and widespread that prejudice was. He had seen, in Cambridge, within sight of George Washington's elm tree of revolutionary fame, the ejection of Negro passengers from stagecoaches.

Breaking a solemn promise was quite another thing. The precise words of Secretary of War Stanton to General Saxton were that his Negro recruits were to "be entitled to, and receive, the same pay and rations as are allowed by law, to volunteers in the service." It was too humiliating to be the representative of a race and class that could break such a solemn pledge.

He was not alone in this fight. Nor was it only among the abolitionists and their staunch congressional supporters, like Senator Charles Sumner, that voices of protest were heard. The Governor of Massachusetts, who had personally taken the lead in recruiting two black regiments that bore the name of his state, hastened to Washington to demand justice. There he found that Higginson's friend, George Stearns, under prodding from Frederick Douglass as well as his own associates, had requested President Lincoln to receive Douglass and listen to his protest. The President, too concerned with maintaining a consensus among the people of the loyal states, replied in words that he was later to regret. There was still a great deal of popular opposition in the North, said Lincoln, to the very use of colored troops. It was "a necessary concession to smooth the way to their employment at all as soldiers," he declared, to tolerate discrimination in pay. He did promise to ask Congress for equal treatment later in the year.

For those who were disappointed in his gradualism, the President tried to make up by paying tribute to the achievements of Negro soldiers during the few months they had been allowed to fight. "Some of the commanders of our armies in the field who have given us our most important successes," he announced, "believe the emancipation policy and the use of colored troops constitute the heaviest blow yet dealt to the rebellion. To those who say they will not fight to free Negroes, I say that some of them seem willing to fight for you."

True to Lincoln's promise, the Secretary of War called upon Congress in December of 1863 to right the government's wrong and equalize the situation of Negro and white soldiers. Opposition was stiff, but through the efforts of Higginson and the abolitionists, public opinion had gradually been built up in favor of the change. One of the dramatic events that helped was the dignified answer of the Massachusetts black regiments to a stopgap measure that their own governor had secured for them.

Governor Andrew had called a special session of the Bay State legislature during the autumn when he saw that Washington would not act until the beginning of 1864. He had asked for a special appropriation of state funds to make up the difference in pay between what Washington had promised and what it had decided to give. When the appropriation was made and the Massachusetts paymasters went to the Sea Islands to arrange distribution of the difference to the men, the brave black regiments electrified the nation by their response.

"Imagine our surprise and disappointment," one of them wrote in a letter that was published in the Boston *Journal,* "to find a proposition to pay this regiment the difference between what the United States Government offers us and what they are legally bound to pay us. This, in effect, advertises us to the world as holding out for *money* and not from *principle,*—that we sink our manhood in consideration of a few more dollars. How has this come about? What false friend has been misrepresenting us to the Governor, to make him think that our necessities outweigh our self-respect?"

When Congress began to dawdle over the bill for equal pay, Wentworth Higginson went into action with his pen once more. In January 1864 he wrote a letter to the New York *Tribune,* from Beaufort, South Carolina, beginning, "No one can overstate the intense anxiety with which the officers of colored regiments in this Department are awaiting action from Congress in regard to arrears of pay of their men." The very fact that officers were paid fully and promptly made it more difficult. "How are we to explain to the men the mystery that Government can afford us a hundred or two dollars a month, and yet must keep back six of the poor thirteen which it promised them? Does it not naturally suggest the most cruel suspicions in regard to us?"

He addressed himself particularly to the fact that Congress

seemed likely to pass a bill limited to making pay rates equal for the future for the men who had been cheated. "The public seems to suppose that all required justice will be done by the passage of a bill equalizing the pay of all soldiers for the future. . . . Should it be so, it will be a repudiation more ungenerous than any which Jefferson Davis advocated or Sydney Smith denounced. It will sully with dishonor all the nobleness of this opening page of history, and fix upon the North a brand of meanness worse than either Southerners or Englishmen have dared yet to impute."

Higginson's letter, an extraordinary document to appear in print over the signature of a colonel still commanding, received a warm reception. Civilian comrades of the abolitionist movement back home were not content to risk its being seen merely as a letter to the editor. It was reprinted as a leaflet and sent to every member of Congress and distributed among all the papers of the North. The Chicago *Tribune,* for one, reacted energetically. The technical ruling that made an appeal to Congress necessary was itself a product of racialism, the great Midwestern paper said. "The fact is, the chief disability of the black race lies in prejudice, not in law."

Neither General Saxton nor any other superior officer rebuked Wentworth for his outspoken agitation. He turned to the *New York Times,* and its pages burned with his indignation:

> *We presume too much on the supposed ignorance of these men. I have never yet found a man in my regiment so stupid as not to know when he was cheated. If fraud proceeds from the government itself, so much the worse, for this strikes at the foundation of all rectitude, all honor, all obligation.*

Nor was this all. He kept up a ceaseless flow of letters to friends, to friends of friends, and to senators and congressmen. The fruit was not quite victory at first. A law was passed that did provide for equal pay, but that only went back to January 1, 1864. By one of those perverse and unjust compromises that Congress is accustomed to making, arrears prior to that date could be paid only to those "persons of color who were free on the 19th of April, 1861," the day the war began.

This was a multiplication of injustice: Frank Sanborn, another of the John Brown Six, denounced it as a travesty, an admission of the legality of the idea of property in man. "The Government says to the rebels—'Some of these men are free; some of them were once *your slaves. We* discriminate between the two grades, what do you intend to do about it?' Let Fort Pillow tell of the effect of these bloody instructions of pro-slavery prejudice and meanness." (Fort Pillow was a reference to a battle that had been followed by a brutal and savage slaughter of captured Negro troops by merciless Confederate cavalrymen.)

Thomas Wentworth Higginson was now colonel in name only. He had been injured during the third upriver raid of the previous summer, when a cannonball grazed his side. The after-effects left him a partial invalid for a period of time. He had insisted, after taking sick leave in the North, on returning to duty with his troops during the winter of 1863-4 and the spring of 1864. Finally he was obliged to ask for sick leave again in May of 1864, and ultimately to resign in October. During this period of terminal leave and convalescence, his pen began to burn again with outrage at the discrimination between black soldiers who had been slaves and those who had been free.

"No one can possibly be so weary of reading of the wrongs done by Government toward the colored soldiers as am I of writing about them." So began another letter to the editor of the *Tribune*. "This is my only excuse for intruding on your columns again." He wrote to Massachusetts' senior senator, Charles Sumner, that he must redouble his efforts in the struggle for full justice for his men. Failure to secure equality of treatment, he wrote Sumner, "will be the greatest blow ever struck at successful emancipation in the Department of the South, for it will destroy all confidence in the honesty of the government."

To one friend he wrote that he would carry on the fight for equal pay, full equal pay, back to the date that military service began, for the rest of his life if necessary. To the next session of Congress he submitted a petition, now signed "Late Col. 1st S.C. Vols. (now 33d U.S.C. Vols.)" for legislation to fulfill the thirty-

Henry Williams, sergeant of the Black Regiment.

COURTESY MRS. WILLIAM HALLOWELL AND MRS. W. J. WOODIN

month old pledge. "Until this is done the nation is still disgraced," he wrote to the New York *Tribune.* The stubborn persistence of Higginson and his fellow abolitionists was finally rewarded, although not until the war was practically over, by the passage of an Act of Congress on March 3, 1865, that remedied the wrong.

This was not the least of the wartime achievements that he could recall with pride as he faced the period of adjustment to a new life in a new nation. He left the service with the satisfaction of having been a pioneer in what became the most revolutionary feature of the war. He expressed in a few words, soon afterwards the full significance of the contribution of the Negro soldier to his country and his people:

> *We had touched the pivot of the war. . . . Till the blacks were armed, there was no guaranty of their freedom. It was their demeanor under arms that shamed the nation into recognizing them as men.*

With these words he put the finishing touches on his finest book, *Army Life in a Black Regiment,* the personal chronicle of his own experiences with the first contingent of American slaves that were permitted to fight for their own freedom.

But it was not only in the larger political sense in the opening of the door to the full breadth of the fight for freedom, that the Colonel had been of service. His officers appreciated his leadership and his men the enthusiasm with which he gave recognition to their own humanity. The formal tribute of the officers he received from a reunion four decades later, which addressed him in a memorial:

> *In those brave days you were not alone our commander; you were our standard also of what is noble in character. We were young and untutored; we saw in you a model of what, deep in our hearts, we aspired to be.*

This the Colonel treasured less than a letter from one of his privates:

I meet manny of the old Soldiers I Spoke of you—all hailed your name with that emotion (that become you) of the Soul when hearing of one who when in darkness burst light on their pathway.

XXXII

NEW HOME IN OLD PORT

WHILE WENTWORTH WAS OFF to war, Mary had moved from Worcester to Newport. Since her purpose was to seek relief for her afflictions in its highly regarded year-round climate, the absent soldier could hardly object. Its advantages to one whose terminal leave from the service was to be as a convalescent helped diminish his displeasure at ceasing to be a Massachusetts man. He was soon to find in the old Rhode Island seaport a setting that was not altogether unpleasant in which to live and work.

The Newport of the 1860's was not yet dominated by the summer homes of the tremendously wealthy nor its harbor by the trappings of a major naval base. There were resort hotels and fashionable summer people and the shops and servants that went with them. But these were still on a relatively modest scale. There were the queer streets, quaint old houses, wooded paths for solitary walks that would lead either to a placid countryside or to rocky cliffsides with entrancing views of blue sea, snowy sails, and floating gulls.

There were wharves to explore along the waterfront that might be decked in summertime with floating seaweed and studded with an armor of shells—and surrounded in winter with a smooth coating of ice with detached piles standing white and gleaming like the walls of a snow maiden's palace in a Russian fairy tale. Among the wharves he explored was one, long unused, that gave a graphic picture of Yankee complicity in the sins of the South. It adjoined an abandoned distillery and bore in its upper story the remains of slave quarters. They told a silent tale of triangular trade; rum that was distilled of molasses imported from West Indies plantations, and shipped to Africa to be traded there for the kidnaped slaves-to-be.

When Wentworth joined Mary in Newport he was slow to pick up the threads of the many extracurricular agitational interests that had filled and colored his prewar life. His sense of duty to her was now enhanced by a feeling of guilt at having left her as an invalid in the care of others for more than two years. He was mindful of his own convalescence as well.

The favorite outdoor pastime of the fashionables during the Newport season was riding about in a carriage. It was always amusing to Wentworth to watch the vehicles that moved so slowly, as part of the ritual, that they could have been photographed even by the primitive cameras of the day. It was difficult to restrain his merriment when he saw the faces of those intent on participating in the solemn rite of observing and being observed. They "wore a dismal expression" that seemed to him to convey "the renunciation of all human joy."

The monotonous procession of the stylish would be interrupted by donkey and goat carts and basket wagons driven by pretty girls. To add spice and variety to Mary's life so that she might feel less left out of things, he procured a carriage with a removable side and contrived, with the aid of planks, to wheel her chair directly in.

During most of the early Newport years, the Higginsons did not set up housekeeping in a home of their own. Instead they took rooms in a boarding house, one maintained by a gentle Quaker lady, Mrs. Dame. Here Wentworth would begin the day with an early breakfast, then go out and saw wood for half an hour. After he read a little it would be time to join Mary at her own late breakfast. He would then work at his writing desk from ten until

Thomas Wentworth Higginson,
Newport citizen, 1865.

COURTESY MRS. WILLIAM HALLOWELL AND MRS. W. J. WOODIN

about two in the room to which she was confined in a wheel chair. She might have an open book before her on a reading stand, or she might receive a caller or even a group of friends. Regardless of the distraction, Wentworth was able to go on with his work, the writing that was again the principal source of their livelihood.

As a writer he lacked neither subjects nor markets. *The Atlantic* had changed editors, but the new management respected his reputation and welcomed his work. In addition to writing essays, he began to review books for this and other publications. One of his first assignments was the posthumously published *The Maine Woods,* written by his friend Thoreau, who had died at a tragically early age while Wentworth was off to war. In his review, which was a tribute and friend's farewell, Wentworth flatly declared ". . . the world repaid him with lifelong obscurity and will yet repay him with permanent renown." These words were published decades before most American critics and editors recognized the greatness of Thoreau's genius.

During this quiet beginning of his Newport years there were activities and distractions that appeased what remained at the age of forty-two of his prewar appetite for activity. There were opportunities abounding for him to sail, row, and swim. He could ease the continued frustration of childlessness by taking the children of friends and neighbors on fishing expeditions. Hikes along the beaches and in the woods refreshed him in mind and body.

The chief attraction was the nearby complex of bays, coves, and inlets. Sometimes he would row about in a wherry, at others in a clipper ship dory, the only craft of its kind in the harbor that was used for private recreation. "What is a good day for rowing?" he asked in one essay. "Almost any day that is good for living." Since his work was now almost entirely sedentary and his life domestic, it was increasingly necessary for him to seek space and time to dream out of doors or to continue his nature studies. His one-man boating expeditions served both purposes.

Within a year after his arrival in Newport he received an offer for local public service that was tendered in recognition of his reputation as a writer and minor war hero. He was asked to serve as a member of the seaport city's School Committee. This was to provide an opportunity for as fine a civilian conflict as he had had all his life. It would lead him back to the path of action as radical reformer.

The invitation was preceded by a rebuff that he found "delicious," that symbolized the issue on which he was to take on and overcome the local opposition. One stubborn and ignorant member of the School Committee, on hearing Higginson's name proposed as prospective member, began to shower profanity on the man who suggested it. Assured that the Colonel, whom he had never seen, had all the necessary qualifications, the objector snarled, "Don't know anything about that, but I am not going to sit on the same committee with a *black man.*"

Only after being reassured that the famed black regiment had been led by a white colonel did the bitterly prejudiced Rhode Islander withdraw his opposition.

One leading businessman in town was especially pleased to learn of the appointment of Higginson to the school board. He lost no time in seeking him out to talk about old times and the new times to come. This was George T. Downing, successful restaurant operator, who had invested his profits wisely to become a prominent real-estate owner as well.

Downing had long been a militant abolitionist. He had stood not far from Wentworth during the unsuccessful attack on the Boston courthouse a decade before and he had later operated Newport's station on the Underground Railroad. It was only recently that he had successfully resisted the dissolution of the Massachusetts Anti-Slavery Society, contending that mere freedom meant little without equality. Later, Mr. Downing was to accompany Frederick Douglass on a delegation that sought, without success, to persuade Andrew Johnson that justice for all depended on votes for all.

Mr. Downing was a Negro. He had never, merely because he had become wealthy, lost interest in the fight for his people's rights. He could have had his children well educated at expensive private boarding schools. He preferred to fight to have them educated at local public schools. Most of the Negroes of Newport had tired of open protest at the maintenance of segregated schools. Even the unprejudiced among the white community leaders assumed that the Negroes were content and that all was well. Downing was not the sort to leave injustice undisturbed. When his children reached school age, he began a campaign that had failed until he met with the ex-colonel who was now, once again, a school board member.

He had repeatedly attempted to have his children registered at the school nearest his house, a white school. "Up to that time our schools had been conducted in harmony," protested a white editor, "but from that time a scene of trouble has existed." The School Committee—local Board of Education—resisted Downing's efforts and he pushed the attack at the state legislature. There, too, he was rebuffed. The Newport legislators voted against integrating the school system, but that did not discourage George Downing, for a war that had begun to save the Union had gradually changed to a fight for the principles of freedom. He was determined that the people of Newport should not stand still while the nation's mood was changing. He was confident that Higginson would not let him down.

The persistent parent's first move, as the 1865-66 school year drew near, was to send a new application to the School Superintendent, making no reference to the past. The incumbent was newly appointed and went to the Downing house for the usual interview to determine the grade to which the child should be assigned. When he found that a Negro boy was involved he neither granted nor refused the request; he referred it to the School Committee.

There was one member of the committee who was not wholly unprepared for the new application, and Higginson had already lined up several allies on the board. A bitter debate ensued. The opponents relied on the age-old custom of the community and claimed that it was reinforced by Downing's recent series of defeats. The proponents insisted that the nation was changing and looked to their leader, who dramatized in his very war record the reason for the change.

Wentworth's strongest argument was derived from the wording of the state law on which the free-school system had been based: "No person shall be excluded from any Public School in the district to which such person belongs." If the Negro was a *person*, obedience to law would require granting the Downing application. A nation that had just been saved by white and black soldiers fighting side-by-side; in which a Negro lawyer had been admitted to practice by the Supreme Court; and in which, locally, the applicant himself was one of the most prosperous businessmen in town, could not deny that a Negro was a person. After a week end of more individual lobbying among the members who had been so bitterly divided in debate, Colonel Higginson carried the day. His resolution was passed by a vote of seven to three.

The community was startled by the news, but the opponents were more loud than numerous. An indignation meeting was called, but the call was then rescinded. It was hoped by the moderates in town that the token admission of the Downing boy would be the end of the matter. At first it seemed so, as only three more applications for transfer from the two colored schools were received during that semester. Two white children were withdrawn from the public schools in protest, while the town editor prayerfully hoped that the rest of the Negro community would "be satisfied to know that they have the *right* and let well enough alone."

By the beginning of the next semester an additional twenty applications were made and granted. During this period, according to the School Superintendent's annual report, "no disturbance has occurred among the scholars and the deportment of the white pupils toward the colored, with few and trifling exceptions, has been kind and courteous." Critical changes were occurring on the national scene between September, 1865, and February, 1866, that were to be reflected at the March, 1866, sitting of the Rhode Island State Legislature.

Congress had met at Washington in December, 1865, for the first time since President Lincoln had been assassinated. President Andrew Johnson had attempted to restore the governments of the seceded states to full equality in the national government without national protection of equality of rights for their inhabitants. Ex-Confederates and their sympathizers had seized control, with results that were disastrous to the southerners who had remained loyal during the war. Atrocities and repressive laws had moved public opinion in the free states in the direction of demanding national guarantees of protection to southern Negroes and pro-Union white southerners. By March of 1866, Congress had passed the very first civil rights law in an attempt to remedy the evils to which President Johnson had been indifferent. Rhode Islanders realized—sooner than some other northern states—that they could not tolerate at home what their representatives in Congress were forbidding at the South.

Wentworth's leadership in opening the battle contributed to a highly satisfactory outcome. The Rhode Island legislators passed laws forbidding the separation of children in schools by race and granting the right to vote to all their inhabitants. Within another year the segregated school system of Newport was ended entirely, when Negro parents transferred their children in such great numbers that it became uneconomic for the city to maintain the Negro school.

As School Committee member Wentworth lost no time in initiating another of the reforms with which he had been identified in Worcester. Regulations were introduced that provided for a physical fitness program in the Newport Schools. Calisthenic exercises were required for the first time in the city's history. He organized an association for the purpose of equipping and operating a gymnasium, another innovation for the city. This facility for providing adult physical education was in full operation by the end of November, 1865.

There was, nonetheless, a bit of a backlash at Higginson's leadership in putting an end to the indignity of separate schools in Newport. In the sixties, School Committee members were not yet elected by popular vote. They were appointed by the City Council. The Colonel's name was passed over by the dominant group, which feared that they would expose themselves to hostility if they reelected him.

Vindication ultimately came when the City Charter was

changed in 1873 to provide for democratic election of members of the School Committee. Not only was Wentworth sent back to membership on the board, but he returned side-by-side with a local Negro clergyman who integrated the School Committee itself.

XXXIII

THE NEGRO'S HOUR—AND WOMAN'S?

THE NEWPORT SCHOOL FIGHT had helped to draw Wentworth out of his seeming retirement. He began to feel that it did not help Mary for him to sacrifice completely the "mingled life of thought and action" that had been his youthful ideal. While demands for his services as a writer increased, he returned to the life of the agitator too. He resumed his career on the Lyceum lecture circuit, which was an important way of supplementing their income. At first he would decline, for Mary's sake, invitations to lecture that involved a trip requiring a night's absence. Gradually that rule came to be broken so often it was forgotten.

It is not recorded that Mary ever complained directly to Wentworth about his absences. She may have begun to regret her interest in James Freeman Clarke, the radical and outspoken minister on whom she had hoped Wentworth would model himself. On one occasion she let slip a plaintive note in a letter to his sisters at Brattleboro. Higginson's mother had died in 1864. "Wentworth has been away two days this week and going tonight to Washington to fight for women. I wish they had been fixed before we were born. . . ."

He was to spend the next forty-five years—the rest of his life—fighting for women, but Wentworth and most of his radical reformer associates had become more concerned just then about the need to complete (as they thought) the fight for the rights of the Negro. Even while he was still in South Carolina in command of his troops, he had written home about the need for changes in the conditions of life of the ex-slaves, changes that would go far beyond mere freedom. To make his point, he used the eloquent words of Sergeant Prince Rivers, one of the ablest of his black noncommissioned officers, "Every colored man will be a slave & feel himself a slave until he can raise him his own bale of cotton & put his own mark upon it & say *dis is mine.*"

Later, after joining Mary at Newport, he participated in the debate that was rising as the war came to a close, as to the terms on which the union should be rebuilt—"re-constructed" was the word that came into popular use then. President Lincoln had learned much during the last two years of the war about the inherent equality of the races; he had expressed in letters to General Saxton and others his gratitude for the great contribution of the Negro soldier to the nation's war effort. Nevertheless he had been reluctant to endorse national action to guarantee the right to vote to all regardless of color. A British professor who sympathized with the abolitionists wrote to Garrison's *Liberator* urging that presidential candidates in 1864 be required to support "total abandonment of your cardinal or ruinous national insanity—prejudice against color—or your national future may be lost forever."

Higginson endorsed the idea that the time to require the states to abandon discrimination based on color was when they would seek to return to participation in the making of national laws. He publicly urged that "if under any other circumstances we might excuse ourselves for delaying the recognition of the freeman's right to suffrage, yet it would be utterly disastrous to do so now, when two-thirds of the white population will remain disloyal, even when conquered." Wentworth felt that the failure of the public to unite on this point of view meant that the nation had been "sliding back" at war's end into a "mush of concessions."

Lincoln's assassination had shocked and aroused people but the tragedy was thought to have improved the chances for reconstruction based on justice. Unaware, like many others, that Lincoln had hoped to lead the nation gently but firmly on the road to full equality, Higginson declared that the assassination had "restored us to our senses" and united the North as it had not been since the firing on Fort Sumter.

As a convalescent soldier he had never ceased to follow with interest the issues that had attracted him before the war. During the Newport school fight he began to maintain a closer watch on the national scene and to keep in touch with the activities of the abolitionists. While some, like Wendell Phillips, recognized the evils of President Johnson's course, Wentworth stood to one side, hoping against hope that the new president would see the error of his ways. Finally, in October 1865, Higginson saw the need for an open break with Johnson and that public support had to be secured for the radicals in Congress who were uniting to resist the President. He put the issue into a few words:

> . . . *what most men mean today, by the "President's plan of Reconstruction" is the pardon of every rebel for the crime of rebellion, and the utter refusal to pardon a single black loyalist for the crime of being black.*

By the end of 1865 the nation had become a peacetime battle ground, not alone on sectional lines, as a result of the presidency of Andrew Johnson. His prejudices and his narrow views led him to adopt a policy that meant simply this: southern whites, even the ex-Confederates, were to be permitted to dominate the relations between the races in the former slave states. As long as they did not restore slavery in *name* they would be allowed to do what they wished to discipline and to control the private lives of the ex-slaves. For the property owners and the politicians who represented their interests in the South this seemed essential to restore the functioning of their economy. They could not or would not accept the idea of a biracial society in which all men alike could be given recognition according to individual worth. Before the war their institutions were protected by the theory that states' rights forbade federal interference with slavery; now Johnson and many northerners who sympathized with this claimed that states' rights required local control of interracial relationships. These men did not care how unjustly the white ruling group might treat those who had been loyal to the nation during the war.

The abolitionists and many whose moral sense had been awakened by the services of the Negro soldier refused such a settlement. They prepared to fight it. Higginson and his comrades were obliged to make a difficult choice. Should they concentrate their energies in behalf of the freedmen alone; or should they press, at the same time, for a great step forward in the women's rights revolution?

The break of Congress with Johnson and his vetoes of the first civil rights laws made it evident that the Constitution would have to be amended. The threat of resurgence of an anti-Negro majority made it necessary to protect for all time the human rights of the ex-slaves. The question arose: once the Constitution was amended, should it not also be changed to give women the emancipation for which the heiresses of Margaret Fuller and men like Thomas Wentworth Higginson and Frederick Douglass had been fighting?

Wendell Phillips had named the 1865-66 period "The Negro's Hour." By this he had meant two things: that public opinion in the states that had been loyal was now warmly sympathetic to human rights; and that the Constitution-amending process was controlled by the free-state congressmen who had exercised their undoubted right to exclude ex-Confederates.

Much could be said in favor of making this period the "woman's hour" as well. The war had not been about women or their rights or their mistreatment; yet it had had far-reaching effects on the lives of women and their part in American society. Women had contributed in their own way and in good measure to winning the war. Fittingly enough—since many of the abolitionists had been feminists, and most of the woman's rights leaders had been effective abolitionists—women had been important in the political fight on the homefront during the war. They had helped remold the war from a fight to save the Union to a battle to spread freedom.

When war came, American women were prepared by history to join as noncombatants to help on the road to victory. The experience of the pioneer woman, carrying a rough and heavy load in conquering the wilderness was a cherished tradition in the East and a very lively fact of life in the West. Women had become restless as a result of the agitation in their behalf, even though most did not openly support their movement. They had been more responsive than men to the moral issue presented by the abolitionist cause, especially because of the degrading effect of slavery on their sisters at the South, both white and black. All these factors combined to make many thousands of women eager and ready to meet the nation's needs.

As the panorama of Civil War unfolded, with manpower demands unprecedented in world history, it became imperative that women should serve. The places of white men in factory, dock, and workshop could be filled by the forced labor of slaves in the South. The gaps in the North were filled by the voluntary response of its women. They flocked also to schoolrooms and government offices, in order to release men for combat duty, and were there to stay by the war's end.

What Wentworth Higginson had been arguing all along as a matter of inner conviction and social theory was proved quite correct. Women were not inferior to men in courage or intellect, in enterprise or imagination. The laws and customs that Lucy Stone and he had denounced were shown to be unjustified by claimed differences between the sexes. Histories since then have been written for the most part by men and so the most "underrated aspect of the Civil War was the large role women played," the United States Civil War Centennial Commission recently declared.

While helping in their country's fight, women were willing,

for a brief moment, to shelve their own struggle for equality. No woman's rights convention was held for four years after the one that closed in February, 1861. The more militant among the ladies of their movement spurred the political fight for freedom and against slavery. Their most notable achievement was accomplished by a wartime organization formed and staffed by feminists: the Women's National Loyal League. Through this group there were secured four hundred thousand signatures on petitions asking Congress to rivet the Emancipation Proclamation into the Constitution as the Thirteenth Amendment. President Lincoln said in appreciation of this magnificent effort, "when the war is ended I will never forget the noble women of the North."

As the war drew to a close, women's rights leaders looked for more than words. Their demands had been deferred and they expected practical recognition of their performance. The death of Lincoln removed the President who had said he'd "never forget"; and the men they relied on to remind his successor disappointed them. They were diverted by the struggle into which they were forced, as President Johnson began the betrayal of the Negro soldier.

The more determined and militant of woman's rights leaders—Susan B. Anthony and Elizabeth Cady Stanton—could not accept the idea that they were to be put off. Mrs. Stanton argued that Negro suffrage and woman suffrage were based on identical principles of justice and that a combined campaign would aid both causes. Not so, said Wendell Phillips. The Negro was the key to the successful reconstruction of the South. Congressmen who saw no such practical political reason to vote for justice to women would vote for Negro suffrage even though still infected by race prejudice. "Causes have their crises," said Phillips. "That of the Negro has come; that of the woman's rights movement has not come."

Higginson, like most abolitionists, felt obliged to agree with Phillips. He saw that the problems created by Andrew Johnson's attempt to reconstitute a proslavery party in all but name were more pressing than the theoretical justice of the arguments of Mrs. Stanton and Miss Anthony. It was not that he was less willing to fight for theoretical justice—as he had in 1858 when Lucy Stone refused to pay taxes because she was unrepresented in the legislature that voted them. "I congratulate you," he wrote her then, "on doing what I have often wished to be a woman that I might do." The problem now was to win the fight that might be lost if coupled with the handicaps of the "woman question."

Miss Anthony, Miss Stanton, and their followers protested, "I would sooner cut off my right hand than ask for the ballot for the black man and not for the woman," said Miss Anthony. Not all suffragette leaders went that far. Lucy Stone, who yielded to none in eloquence and self-sacrifice for the woman's cause, declared, "I will be thankful in my soul if *any* body can get out of the terrible pit." Lydia Maria Child understood the emergency created by Andrew Johnson's alliance with the Confederates and their northern sympathizers. She and her husband wrote Phillips on New Year's, 1868:

> *To us the present crisis of the country seems more dangerous than that of '61. The insidiousness of oppressors is more to be feared than open violence. There can be no reasonable doubt that a murderous feeling toward the colored people prevails extensively at the South; and we are far from feeling very sure that a large party could not be rallied at the North in favor of restoring slavery.*

Higginson saw very well how difficult the situation was. He knew the laws protecting Civil Rights did not go far enough; that even a Constitutional amendment would not be sufficient protection. He remembered the words of his sergeant, Prince Rivers. Confiscation of land and its distribution to men who had enriched its owners as slaves "is an essential part of abolition," he declared. "To give these people only freedom, without the land, is to give them only the mockery of freedom which the English or the Irish peasant has. The time will come when the nation must recognize that even political power does not confer safety upon a race of landless men."

His forecast was to be proved more accurate than he was much later to admit. The concession of political power was no guarantee of safety, and in time the right to vote itself was taken away in violation of the Constitution and with the acquiescence of the people of the North and West. Postponement of the woman's hour may have seemed to have been in vain, yet it contributed to planting a pledge of equal rights for the Negro in the Constitution, if not in the hearts of his fellow Americans.

The split in the ranks of the woman's rights leaders was a more serious setback to their cause than the temporary desertion of male allies like Higginson. Miss Anthony, Mrs. Stanton, and their followers held stubbornly to their positions and opposed the ratification of the Fourteenth Amendment, and later the Fifteenth. The final break was postponed briefly as they united during a dual referendum in Kansas in 1867. One proposition that was offered to voters of the now free state was that the limitation to "male" be removed from the voting requirements; the other would have removed the "white." Women flocked to Kansas to fight—Lucy Stone for the group that agreed with Phillips and Higginson, and later Mrs. Stanton and Miss Anthony of the irreconcilables. Men stayed behind in the East for various reasons. Lucy sorrowfully noted the absence of Higginson in a letter to Miss Anthony.

> *I always thought that when this hour of our bitter need would come—the darkest hour before the dawn—Mr. Higginson would bring his beautiful soul and his fine clear intellect to draw all women to his side; but if it is possible for him to be satisfied at* such *an hour with writing the best literary essays, it is because the power to help us has gone from him.*

His friend had done him an injustice. She had overlooked his need to rely on his writing as a source of income and his determination to diminish his neglect of Mary. The time he could devote to causes was curtailed, but his capacity to assist was far from gone. The reverberations of his past writings, notably "Ought Woman to Learn the Alphabet," and "Woman and Her Wishes," furnished a persistently valuable source of propaganda. Lucy was herself to learn that both as writer and speaker he had much power to help left in him.

After a double defeat in Kansas, with woman suffrage beaten by a greater margin than Negro voting rights, Miss Anthony and Mrs. Stanton accepted the aid of an eccentric man of wealth whose virulent anti-Negro bias discredited them among many of the former abolitionists. Their new sponsor financed a newspaper to aid their cause at the price of advertising his own prejudices. In her zeal to support the paper and contribute to its circulation, Miss Anthony even went to President Johnson to sell a subscription, which she was able to do with the argument that the paper would break the radical party "into a thousand pieces unless we get our rights." This prospect pleased the bigoted president, but not Lucy Stone.

"I think we need two national associations for woman's suffrage so that those who do not oppose the Fifteenth Amendment nor take the tone of *The Revolution* (the Anthony-Stanton paper) may yet have an organization in which they can work in harmony," she wrote her friends, during the summer of 1869. Responding to her invitation, Higginson joined with the popular writer and lecturer George William Curtis, as well as such abolitionists as Garrison and Beecher in signing a call to a new association. Its first meeting was held in Cleveland in November, and the minutes record that announcement of Wentworth's name as president of the convention was "greeted with loud applause." To the new association he was faithfully to contribute his name as an official and his talents as a writer and speaker.

Ultimately, after twenty years, the two groups were to be reunited. Meanwhile Higginson constantly sought to help bridge the differences between the leaders. Mrs. Stanton rebuffed one of his bids for unity behind Lucy Stone but promised to refrain, at least, from recrimination during the division. "No word of mine shall ever wrong or detract from any woman, especially one who has done so good a work for woman as Lucy Stone."

Even while he was identified with the conservative organization, Higginson did occasionally assist the other. One case was the direct-action effort of Miss Anthony to attract support by walking in to a polling place, taking a ballot, and voting. For this she was arrested and prosecuted, and Higginson was one of the leaders of the committee formed to contribute moral and financial support for her defense. Years later he was to remark ruefully:

> *Reformers are not always alike capable of that strict combination, that firm concentration, which makes conservatism so powerful. . . . The force of reform is its individual enthusiasm, resulting from each person following out his own best view.*

THREE WOMEN

RALPH WALDO EMERSON had once written, "Better that the book should not be quite so good, and the book maker abler and better, and not himself often a ludicrous contrast to all that he has written." Wentworth Higginson was fond of quoting this to his friends. In his own life he had sacrificed time and energy that might have been devoted to his craft as a writer in order to give of himself to the causes he advocated.

This he was to demonstrate again in postwar private life. He preached nothing in his writings on the subject of woman's rights that he did not practice in individual acquaintanceships and friendships. He repeatedly extended himself to encourage women of promise and to draw out women of talent who might have been repressed by the rigorous prejudices of society. One breezy report to his Vermont audience announced, "Spring opens and business thrives. We have alder blossoms and snowdrops and six manuscript stories from three different young ladies with affectionate requests to read and criticize."

The Newport years were marked by three especially noteworthy friendships: two were the outcome of prewar associations, and one was entirely new. It was while living at Newport that his acquaintance with Julia Ward Howe developed into an intimate comradeship. From Newport he traveled to Amherst for his only meetings with Emily Dickinson. The long arm of coincidence brought to

Mrs. Dame's boarding house one day in 1866 a young widow who had been a girlhood neighbor of Miss Dickinson. Helen Hunt, the attractive woman in black, drew the Colonel's attention.

"There is a new boarder here with two dainty rooms upstairs arranged by herself—Mrs. Major Hunt, a young widow. . . ." he duly reported. "She is in deep mourning for husband and child, and I fancy has private depression to correspond with her high spirits in the family, which are so far invariable. She seems very bright and sociable and may prove an accession."

The public sociability that matched Mrs. Hunt's private depression led soon to an exchange of ideas and confidences. They had in common a sense of deprivation. Her widowhood and loss of two children were matched by his childlessness and the burden of Mary's invalidism. Each, moreover, loved children. Just as he could never meet a child without seeking to win its affection, she could not restrain herself from sharing a lively gift of story-telling with children she encountered. It did not take Higginson long to learn that she had an impulse to self-expression and talent that had been shown in poems written on the occasion of her bereavements.

Shortly after arriving at Newport Mrs. Hunt had bemoaned, in a letter, the loss to the world of her husband's abilities and added "I alone am left, who avail nothing." Within two months, under Higginson's encouragement, she had published a group of poems. With the stimulus of his prompting she set herself to learn her craft. She undertook travel reporting that summer when she left for the mountains during the hayfever season. Soon she began writing children's stories and novels as well. In the 1870's she was to be one of the most popular and successful of writers.

The one thing that Helen Hunt did not become, during those years of guidance and influence by Higginson, was what she would disparagingly have called a "woman with a mission." He could make a writer out of her, but not an agitator or a reformer. She could be a living example of the justice of the cause of woman's rights and at the same time reject his efforts to draw her into the movement.

Tolerant as he was of her refusal to participate in the fight for her sisters' rights, Wentworth was taken aback when she told him, one day, of a reportorial assignment she had received. "I'll travel to New York to attend the woman suffrage convention with you," she said, to his surprise. It was hard for him to restrain himself when she teasingly added "The New York *Tribune* has offered me a good sum for a satirical item about the session."

He reflected that the article she had been commissioned to do would be run by the antisuffrage press in any case and regretted that the formerly boldly progressive paper of Horace Greeley had fallen so far backward as to pander to conservative prejudices. Good manners and friendship prompted him to offer himself as Mrs. Hunt's escort, and he accompanied her into the hall, bravely risking the wrath that he might later incur from his comrades in the cause. The featured speaker of the first session was his old friend Lucy Stone whose marriage ceremony he had conducted fifteen years before.

Lucy was as persuasive and eloquent as ever. She did not learn until years later that her "sweet voice," as Wentworth always called it, had made a conquest if not a convert. She effectively neutralized the special correspondent of the *Tribune*, who sent a polite note to her editor asking to be excused for her failure to deliver the antisuffrage article she had agreed to write. "Do you suppose," she said to Wentworth, as she took his arm after the meeting, "that I could ever write against anything which that woman wishes to have done?"

Wentworth had induced another friend from Newport to be present at such a meeting and she was to prove to be a most valuable convert to the cause. This was Julia Ward Howe, lady of wit and culture, and wife of Samuel Gridley Howe. Her path had crossed his before but only as friendly neighbor. Dr. Howe had won world-wide fame as a physician pioneering in the remedial treatment of the blind. It was he who had been a fellow-militant in the abolitionist movement and a backer of John Brown, after having fought abroad for the ideals of the American Revolution.

Julia Ward had been a bright and lovely daughter of a New

Julia Ward Howe, from a portrait by John Elliott and William Cotten.

COURTESY OF THE SMITHSONIAN INSTITUTION NATIONAL COLLECTION OF FINE ARTS

York banker, one-time music student of Lorenzo da Ponte, Mozart's librettist, and had been Bostonized when she fell in love with Howe during a sightseeing visit to his institute for the blind. Her marriage to the restless romantic revolutionist-physician was the logical culmination of the life of a girl more interested in literature than wealthy playboy-suitors. Her attempts at self-expression during her youth and young womanhood were primarily in the field of poetry. This ranged from the "Battle Hymn," by which she will always be remembered best ("Mine Eyes Have Seen the Glory of the Coming of the Lord"), to the doggerel by which she amused her children and poked fun at their cause-loving, often-absent father:

Rero, rero, riddlety, rad:
This morning my baby caught sight of her Dad.
Quoth she, "O Daddy, where have you been?"
"With Mann and Sumner, a-putting down sin!"

Although she teased her husband about the time spent away from home, she came to envy his freedom to act in behalf of a commitment of conscience. Brought up to believe that such freedom should not be possessed or even desired by women, inclined to laugh at the woman's suffrage cause and its advocates, she was gently and skillfully guided by Higginson to reverse herself. Life had not been all work and agitation while he lived in Newport, and he had become part of a little band of summer residents, including several writers and artists. As a result he was often in Mrs. Howe's company. She was also the woman charter member of a Boston discussion group that Higginson, too, had attended from its first meeting, that was proud to call itself The Radical Club.

This developing comradeship of Mrs. Howe and Colonel Higginson made it possible for him to induce her to attend a suffrage meeting in 1868. Once she strayed into the hall, she was persuaded to remain when she saw on the platform, besides Wentworth, her husband's old companions-in-action, Garrison, Phillips, James Freeman Clarke. She saw Lucy Stone for the first time, with, as Mrs. Howe wrote later, "the light of her good life shining on every feature of her face." After hearing Lucy Stone speak with that same eloquence that had neutralized Helen Hunt, Mrs. Howe began to feel she had to join the revolution that was in the making. Higginson sent her a note asking her to come to the platform, and she looked up at him, nodding agreement. She rose and addressed the hall, saying only, "I am with you."

Higginson glowed with inward pleasure as he observed the change in Mrs. Howe's life that was brought about by her enlistment. "There was a visible change," he said, "it gave a new brightness to her face, a new cordiality in her manner, made her calmer, firmer; she found herself among new friends and could disregard old critics." She brought much to the cause that was to widen her own horizons. At first she added a highly desirable aura of prestige and propriety to those who had been scorned as disreputable extremists; second and more important to ultimate success was the effectiveness and strength of the newly founded woman's club organizations of which she was to become a lifelong leader.

Three years after Wentworth had helped free her from her prejudices against political action by women, Julia Ward Howe made a spirited attempt to organize women of all nations to unite for peace. Precipitated by the Franco-Prussian war of 1870-71, her efforts produced a world-wide appeal that is still eloquent and timely:

> *Again have the sacred questions of international justice been committed to the fatal mediation of military weapons. . . . Thus men have done. Thus men will do. . . . We, women of one country, will be too tender of those of another country, to allow our sons to be trained to injure theirs. From the bosom of the devastated earth a voice goes up with our own. It says: "Disarm, disarm!"*

While he could claim to have launched Helen Hunt's career as a writer and to have initiated Mrs. Howe's four decades as reformer-agitator, Wentworth could only claim to have saved Emily Dickinson's morale; as a poet she was self-made. He renewed in the Newport period the correspondence to which she owed the survival of her spirits during the deep intermittent depressions of her loneliness.

Emily Dickinson had obtained, even before they met, what she had sought from Thomas Wentworth Higginson when she wrote that first letter he had picked up in the Worcester post office seven years before. It was not instruction she had needed, though she had written, perhaps with tongue in cheek, "I am happy to be your scholar." She often addressed him as teacher, "preceptor," and he ruefully observed that she persistently attributed to him "a preceptorship which it is almost needless to say did not exist." Each of them expressed, after the war, a desire to see the other; yet for her it was evident that letters from one who read her own were enough. She put it in a phrase written shortly before they met, "A letter always feels to me like immortality because it is the mind alone without corporeal friend."

A meeting was arranged in mid-1870, when the death of one of his older brothers brought Wentworth to Deerfield, a little village near Amherst, where she spent her lonely life. Wentworth sent Emily a note asking if he could call on her. "I will be at home and Glad," was the response.

A walk from the inn brought him to a large brown brick country lawyer's house with great trees and a garden. In writing Mary afterwards to describe his sensations on meeting the woman she called his "half-cracked poetess," he reminded her of the novels, fashionable in that period, that described households in which a number of people live separate lives, unconcerned with each other. In Emily Dickinson's house Higginson saw no one except for the lady upon whom he came to call.

After a little delay in a dark, cool, parlor, during which he saw two of his books among the few around, he heard a faint and childlike pattering footstep. There glided in from the hall, almost noiselessly, a plain shy little person, with an undistinguished face, two smooth bands of reddish hair, immaculately white blouse, and blue net shawl. She put two day lilies into his hand and said, "These are my introduction." She added almost under her breath, "Forgive me if I am frightened. I never see strangers and hardly know what I say." When the amenities were ended and the conversation began she was never at a loss for words.

Many of the things she told him about her childhood and youth, her father's severity, a severity without harshness, helped to explain the introverted life she led. At one point she told how books other than the Bible had to be smuggled into the house. The very first was the book that first inspired him to write, Lydia Maria Child's *Letters from New York*. She described her ecstatic reaction. "This, then, is a book, and there are more of them."

Later in their talk she gave him this classical definition, "If I read a book and it makes my whole body so cold no fire can ever warm me, I know that is poetry. If I feel physically as if the top of

Emily Dickinson, from a daguerreotype taken about 1848.

my head were taken off, I know that is poetry. These are the only ways I know. Is there any other way?"

They talked of their mutual friend Helen Hunt, for Wentworth added in his letter to Mary, "Major Hunt interested her more than any man she ever saw." During the interview he did not introduce the subject of the publication of her poetry. While conscious of her genius, her "strange and wonderful power," as he called it, he was not sure the world was quite ready for it. Major Hunt's widow, when she had become Helen Jackson, wife of a man she had met in Colorado, disagreed. "You are a great poet," she wrote Miss Dickinson, "and it is a wrong to the day you live in, that you will not sing aloud. When you are what men call dead you will be sorry you were so stingy."

Helen Hunt had risen swiftly to contemporary success as a

writer of novels, travelogues, and children's stories, after a successful and sustained initial output of poetry. It seems odd now that this forgotten friend of Emily Dickinson won recognition by some as America's greatest woman poet. Her publications, during the ten-year period after Higginson helped to launch her work, had been far more prolific and successful than his. She freely and gladly conceded that she owed him "all my success as a writer." In one letter she declared, "I shall never write a sentence, so long as I live, without studying it over from the standpoint of whether you would think it could be bettered."

There was, ironically, nothing in her prose or verse that was to have a capacity to live until the third phase of her life. This began when she went to live in the West, far from Higginson's direct influence. There she was struck by a subject that shook her soul, aroused her fire and indignation, and caused her to become, in the

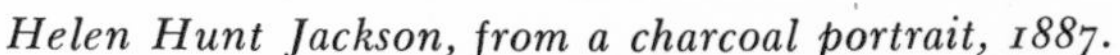
Helen Hunt Jackson, from a charcoal portrait, 1887.

last years of her life, an agitator as well as a writer. She wrote him in explanation:

> *I have now done what I had said I never would do, I have become what I said was odious, "a woman with a hobby." But I cannot help it. I think I feel as you must have felt in the old abolition days. I cannot think of anything else from night to morning. . . ."*

As she had studied the state of the American Indians in the West, she realized that their plight was almost more tragic than that of the slaves had been. They were practically outlaws, but not by choice, and few Americans took any notice of the injustices perpetrated against them. She began to work day and night on a study of the subject. She read books and records, interviewed survivors and refugees. The finished work, a book of nonfiction that is still recognized as a classic, summed up the history of the United States Government's morality in its title, *A Century of Dishonor*. She was so exhausted when she was finished that Higginson was left with the job of proofreading.

The book did not make quite the stir she hoped for, nor the impression it deserved. She remembered how Wentworth had told her that *Uncle Tom's Cabin,* by dramatizing its subject in compelling fiction, had done more for the abolitionists than two decades of speeches and meetings. After a visit to California she found her theme and her inspiration. Writing as if possessed, she turned out *Ramona,* a romance of the Indians living among the old Spanish missions that showed how they were mistreated. The novel achieved precisely what she hoped: a great sale and an aroused public opinion. Reforms were demanded, but she did not know that the sustained interest needed to insure true success was lacking. She died thinking she had won, after writing to Wentworth, "My 'Century of Dishonor' and 'Ramona' are the only things I have done of which I am glad now."

XXXV

HISTORY FOR YOUNG AND OLD

"Nothing gives to a calm observer," wrote Wentworth once, his tongue in cheek, "more respect for children than their apparent dislike for the study of history." The target of his shaft was the ponderous, dull, and statistic-laden history with which readers of his day were familiar. He had lived long enough, by the time he was fifty, to have learned that one could not understand or cope with the world unless one knew how it came to be the way it was. He was also convinced that the story of how things came to be the way they were—history—did not need to be dull but could be as interesting and as exciting as any fiction.

Few critics are given a chance to show what they can do at a job in which they have found the performance of others wanting. Even fewer succeed when given the opportunity. There came to Higginson one day in the early 1870's a veteran teacher and high school principal who had an idea. This was George B. Emerson, who had spent much of his educational career in Boston and knew Wentworth's reputation well. Why not, he asked, apply your literary skill to the production of a simple and entertaining history of the United States, one that it will be a pleasure for the teacher to use and an even greater pleasure for the boys and girls to read? Mr. Emerson was prepared to back his idea with an advance of one thousand dollars, enough to cover living expenses for Wentworth and Mary for the two years needed to do the research and write the book.

In the decade that had followed the war his position as a professional writer was firmly established. His first book—a collection of his prewar *Outdoor Papers* that had impressed his junior officers tremendously in 1863, the year of its publication—was joined by three new volumes. One was a novel, *Malbone*, that he wrote in the hope that this was the secret to permanent literary fame. This romance of life in Newport was moderately well received, but he soon knew that it would not endure.

His second postwar book still lives. He put together the separate chapters of his own story of the war, his unique personal history of his experience as leader of the First South Carolina Volunteers in *Army Life in a Black Regiment*. A third was a collection of additional *Atlantic* essays written over a period of ten years. He also edited a collection of biographies of young Harvard men who had been lost in the war, and translated the works of Epictetus, the Roman slave who became a philosopher.

He did not approach lightly the task of writing the book that was to become *The Young Folks' History of the United States*. He had mastered the craft of writing since the day he had given up the pulpit for the writing desk. On one of his lecture tours he was introduced to a university class as "the best living writer in the English language." He had made purposeful use of historical material as an abolitionist and feminist agitator and in several of *The Atlantic* essays.

The challenging new task was to address younger readers. It was the dull cataloging of events and names, dates, and battles, that he criticized in existing works. What he sought to achieve was a style that would be light and readable, that would attract the new student, and would make him want to read more. His animation of detail, the frequent telling of an anecdote that illuminated a whole scene, was his principal means to that end. Every historian has great freedom in the attention he will devote to one or another subject or period. Higginson insisted on breaking with tradition to give more space to the affairs of peace and less to the chronicles of war. He declared in the last words of the Introduction to the *Young Folks' History*:

> . . . *the true glory of a nation lies, after all, in orderly progress. Times of peace, the proverb says, have few historians; but this may be more the fault of the historians than of the times.*

His book was friendly, conversational, and is a colorful narrative at every stage. For example:

> *It has always seemed to me that the first explorers of North America were very much like a family of boys who have discovered a large pond in the woods, somewhere within reach of their dwelling house. The boys wish always to be on the water, and are constantly exploring. They have different objects: some to go merely for the fun of it; others, to catch fish; others, to look for black-birds' nests among the reeds; others, to find a shorter route to the village or to the school house. What wonderful stories they tell their little sisters about the things they have seen by the side of the lake!*

In telling the story of his nation's birth, he wanted to give his reader an intimate feeling of how it differed from the Old World. He gives us facts that may since have been forgotten:

> *There were great celebrations over all the country when the new Constitution went into effect, and the new nation began to exist. In Philadelphia, for instance, there was a procession of five thousand people, representing all trades and pursuits. Such a procession of trades was then quite a new thing . . . in Europe, at that time, all triumphal pro-*

cessions were almost wholly military in character. . . . The judges of the Supreme Court sat in a car, bearing the Constitution, framed, and fixed upon a staff, which was crowned with the cap of liberty, and was inscribed in gold letters "The People." . . . The clergy of the city walked in the procession; and the Jewish rabbi went between two Christian ministers to show that the new Republic was founded on principles of religious toleration.

Much as he had enjoyed the writing, it was a relief to Wentworth when the work was done. It had taken more time than he expected with little opportunity to keep up with his regular, free-lance, essay and review writing. "It will be pleasant to think," he mused, "that I have done something to make American history clear and attractive."

The book was to prove all that George Emerson and Higginson had hoped. It inaugurated a new era in the writing of history for school-age readers. Within a few weeks of publication it had become a solid success, a hit, and it was not long before it surpassed in sales all the rest of his works put together. There was more than initial popularity. A steady demand for the book developed and extended over many years. It was adopted as an official text by the public school system in the city of Boston, where just a quarter of a century previously the writer of the book had made history by battering down the courthouse door in his effort to rescue Anthony Burns. It was translated into French, Italian, and German, and then came the ultimate mark of success: a flock of imitations.

The financial reward that should have accompanied achievement was impaired by the business failure of the publishing firm. Nevertheless the *Young Folks' History* provided a steady supplement to the family income and made it possible to hire household help to permit Mary and Wentworth to resume housekeeping despite her invalid condition. This was a welcome change after years in and out of Newport boarding houses and summer homes.

His favorite endorsement of the book came from the young son of a Harvard professor who wrote him, "I like your history of the United States about as well as the Odyssey." A teacher in a North Carolina school wrote to him, "My class is intensely interested in it. The book has more in it to arouse the children's patriotism than any book I have ever seen. . . . The teaching profession is under many obligations to you."

The *Young Folks' History* was not to be the last of Higginson's contributions to the popularization of historical study and writing in the United States. He was asked by another publisher to write a popular American history for the general reader. The very first page of Wentworth's *Larger History of the United States* exhibited the personal touch that caught the attention of the reader and also shed light on the subject covered by the chapter:

> *It has happened to the writer more than once, during the American Civil War, to sail up some great Southern River that was to all appearances unvisited by the ships of man. It might well have been the entrance to a newly discovered continent. No light-house threw its hospitable gleam across the dangerous bar, no floating buoys marked the intricacies of the channel; the lights had been extinguished, the buoys removed, and the whole coast seemed to have gone back hundreds of years, reverting to its primeval and unexplored condition. There was commonly no sound except the light plash of waves or the ominous roll of heavy surf. . . . Amid such experiences I was for the first time enabled to picture to myself the American continent as its first European visitors saw it.*

Of course it was an advantage to one whose object was to write a book proving that history did not have to be dull to have lived a rich and varied life. It was a great help as well to have spent so much time reading the world's great literature. He had a wonderful memory for detail and the ability to select from his memory the right example or anecdote to illustrate a point. With these assets and his disciplined writing skill he was able to establish himself as the first of the American historical writers to humanize and popularize the past.

As the years went by another phase of his work was to make an even greater contribution to American history. For some time before the war, as abolitionist and feminist agitator, he had occasion to use historical research in writing essays that illuminated truths that would aid his cause. His skilled presentation in these essays brought him assignments to write biographical sketches of those with whom he had associated. As those of his own era began to die he would be called upon more frequently.

Based on his firsthand acquaintance he presented sketches that were more than mere dry summaries of the lives of the people involved. Personal interpretations and firsthand reminiscences enlivened the stories he wrote about these great figures. His articles were popular when published and even more so when collected and put into books. Best known of these works was called *Contemporaries,* sketches on those who had sought, in one way or another, to make the world over. Emerson, Bronson Alcott, Theodore Parker, and Whittier were remembered there, as were Lydia Maria Child and John Brown. The latter was seen through the eyes of his wife and family on Wentworth's futile trip to the Adirondacks to persuade Mrs. Brown to induce her husband to agree to an escape attempt. Charles Sumner, the abolitionist senator, was another subject as well as Dr. Samuel Gridley Howe, Wendell Phillips, and William Lloyd Garrison, of whom he wrote:

> *There passed away in him the living centre of a remarkable group of men and women who have had no equals among us, in certain moral attributes, since the Revolutionary period and perhaps not then.*

He described what he had seen with his own eyes as a young man in Boston and Cambridge. The witness he bore refutes the unfavorable estimate of Garrison's significance rendered by later writers:

> *In first looking in at any old time convention, any observing eye would promptly have selected Garrison as the leading figure on the platform. His firm and well-built person, his sonorous voice, and the grave and iron strength of his face would have at once indicated this. I never saw a countenance that could be compared to it in respect to moral strength and force; he seemed the visible embodiment of something deeper and more controlling than mere intellect.*

In his reports on his contemporaries in this and other volumes Higginson performed a valuable service to the historian and student of nineteenth century America. Again and again later writers have turned to his works, some without acknowledging their indebtedness, as a source of history for young and old that is being written even today.

XXXVI

WIDOWER, HUSBAND, FATHER

THE NEWPORT YEARS were dominated by the lingering presence of Mary's illness. It was like a long, dreary night in a storm, but with dawn somehow seeming further and further off. Slowly they realized, but would never admit to each other, that recovery would never come. Once, on a birthday, he confided in his diary:

> *I feel renewed gratitude for that wonderful cheerfulness and healthiness of nature I inherited from my mother. This birthday season always gives some feeling of loneliness to one of my temperament who is childless . . . and whose home is a hospital and who sees the only object of his care in tears of suffering daily.*

Wentworth's optimism and resilience made it possible for him to endure those years; Mary's make-up helped too. While her physical condition was an increasing burden, her spirit rarely faltered. He would have been loyal and devoted in any case, but her unfailing wit and lively tongue made it easier to bear his multitude of problems. She tried always to be a good companion, even to allow herself to be pushed to the beach in a wheelbarrow so that he could get in a daily swim during the frequent intervals that they were without household help. She was a good critic and audience as well.

Mary's sometimes waspish conversation is preserved in comments quoted in his essays, "why do the insane so cling to you?" or, referring specifically to Emily Dickinson, "your half-cracked poetess." There was so much worth recording that he based a character on her in his novel *Malbone* through whose conversation some of Mary's characteristic observations are preserved. This was Aunt Jane who might dispose of an acquaintance thus: "She always sends me her love. She has sent me enough love to rear a whole family on—more than I ever felt for anybody in all my life." Or as a mistress of compressed literary criticism, "I am reading a book so dry it makes me cough." Or to demolish one who displeased her, "There is an air of industrious nothingness about him, such as busy dogs have." As a general social commentary, "All the mischief in this world is done by lovable people. Thank heaven nobody ever dares to call me lovable."

Attributed to Aunt Jane in *Malbone* were some remarks that must have had a hauntingly tragic meaning to those friends of Mary and Wentworth who read the book. "What a short little thing summer is, and butterflies are caterpillars most of the time, after all." How Mary must have suffered in the late autumn and fogbound colder seasons in the old port on the ocean bay that her foolish physicians condemned her to, with her arthritic pains! "It is too late for me to change—at least anything about me but my countenance, and that changes the wrong way. Yet I feel so young and fresh; I look in my glass every morning to see if I have not a new face, but it never comes." Those who had seen Mary's face wither and wrinkle prematurely must have paused when they read that or the tragic exchange in the crisis chapter when Hope, a niece, encounters tragedy:

"I can see no way out," pursued Hope.

"Darling!" said Aunt Jane, with a voice full of womanly sweetness, "there is always a way out, or else the world would

have stopped long ago. Perhaps it would have been better if it had stopped, but you see it has not. All we can do is to live on and try our best."

The way out came suddenly for Mary in September, 1877, when she died after a week's illness at the age of 56. It was not entirely unexpected; she had weakened during the summer, as Emily Dickinson had sensed from Higginson's letters. Emily plucked a cape jasmin from her garden and mailed it to Mary during that last summer with a brief note saying, "Though it die in reaching you, you will know it lived, when it left my hand—"

And then, when she read of the death of Mary Channing Higginson, she wrote in condolence:

Dear Friend.
If I could help you?
Perhaps she does not go so far
As you who stay—suppose—
Perhaps comes closer, for the lapse
Of her corporeal clothes
Did she know she was leaving you? The
Wilderness is new—to you. Master, let me lead you.

For Wentworth, the wilderness was new but not in the sense intended by Emily, who had just lost her father. For him the end of the period of thirteen years of trying responsibility seemed strange at first. Perhaps he had guilt feelings at the sense of release and at the recollection of many trips away from Newport when he wrote in an overly sentimental poem:

O! I shrink from this untried freedom
In a world I do not know.
Give me back the long, long watching
And the pacing to and fro!

They will pass, these weak repinings;
And only one thought be hard,

That I know not which of God's angels
Is now at my post, on guard!

He had complained on his forty-fourth birthday, to the diary in which he could say what he would not to Mary, "I do not feel that I take root any more in Newport. . . . I gravitate towards my birthplace more and more." Now he was finished with Newport and his thoughts turned to the college town he had left three decades before. Cambridge called him back now but first a pair of journeys were to help him turn from the past to the future.

After a visit with his Virginia cousins and a quick dash southward to the scenes of the war, he headed for a long trip abroad that would give an opportunity for his soul to refresh itself entirely. The sights and sounds of England and the continent led to a variety of new impressions. After a full view of the trappings of monarchy in Queen Victoria's London he reflected:

I never find myself quite such a ruthless republican anywhere else as in England; and yet there is a certain historic satisfaction, after the long subordination of women, in thinking that the wealthiest monarchy of the world—and in some respects the foremost—takes its orders from a woman's hand.

His trip to Versailles impressed him with the power a people could produce when determined to free themselves. "I felt anew what a great landmark in history the French Revolution was and what strength it showed in the nation that could overthrow the old regime, with all its prestige about it." A certain national pride was evoked in Germany when he heard an Anglo-French lady say that for traveling up the Rhine "she needed no guidebook but Longfellow. As for Mark Twain, they all quote him before they have spoken with you fifteen minutes and always give him a place so much higher in literature than we do. I don't think any English prose writer's so universally read."

As he had long planned, Wentworth packed and moved his belongings to Cambridge on his return to the United States. In the nearby Boston suburb of Newtonville lived a young lady, Mary Thacher, who had been among the writers of her sex who had come to him at Newport with samples of their work. Since she had identified herself as a niece of Longfellow and had shown a friendly warmth that was more than the respect due him as a mentor, he paid her a visit.

This new Mary was more than twenty years younger but mature enough to be at ease and to talk with him in such a way that he did not feel the difference in their ages. He began to call upon her as a suitor when it became evident that her feeling for him was something more than mere admiration for a distinguished writer and war hero. An engagement was announced in December of 1878 and during that winter they were married. Cambridge was to be their home for good.

The many years of childless yearning came to an end in January, 1880, when a little daughter was born. She was named Louisa for Wentworth's mother. Tragedy struck within a few weeks. "Thus end our pride and our earthly hope," wrote the father after he had the news he feared, that the infant's attack of meningitis was fatal.

One niece said after the funeral of the babe, "I shall never forget Uncle Wentworth's beautiful, transfigured look when he said in a broken yet strong voice, 'The Lord gave, the Lord hath taken away.' "

In July of 1881 a second daughter arrived and was named Margaret, although not for Margaret Fuller as many who had followed Higginson's career thought at the time. This child brightened Wentworth's remaining years like a candle suddenly appearing at the end of a long dark corridor. Higginson was not terribly troubled about the age gap and confessed to a correspondent what few ever admit, "I am a truly happy man," and added with that incurable optimism that never left him, "Margaret gives me a new love of life, and I should like, at seventy-five, to go into company with her at eighteen."

The unusual intimacy of the friendship between the new father and Emily Dickinson, a friendship that save for two fleeting visits found fruition in letter-writing alone, is evident in a letter she wrote six months before Margaret was born. She had been recipient of a confidence that was rare in those Victorian days, "I am truly happy that you are happy—" she wrote, acknowledging the news. "Thank you for the whisper." The birth of the little girl was acknowledged: "I am very glad of the Little Life, and hope it may make no farther flight than it's Father's Arms—Home and Roam in one—I know but little of Little Ones, but love them very softly."

The years to come brought no disappointment in his high hopes and expectations. The love he had had in such abundance for every stranger's child, for roomfuls at once when he was a minister, for Margaret Fuller's niece and namesake, bubbled up from an inexhaustible spring. His second Mary, whom he called "Minnie," by a sort of tacit agreement so as to distinguish her from his first wife, was content to stay in the background. Her love was so suffused with admiration for Wentworth as a literary figure that she had written to her uncle, the poet, "Even if I should not in future do much literary work on my own account, I look forward with delight to helping him." It was with a similar submissive self-effacement that she allowed the child of his old age to make up for the many years he had missed.

During all of Margaret's childhood years she and Higginson would walk together, play together, or talk for hours on end. He never tired of her chatter, and she found him always acceptable as a playmate. She might interrupt his efforts to initiate her into the delights of literature by crying out while he was reading aloud, "Papa, play ball." When she did so, he was a good match. He remained fit and energetic enough to run up stairs two or three at a time until he was past seventy.

One of his private pleasures in his new household was to sing aloud while dressing or shaving, and he would often compose music of his own for ballads he remembered from his reading. He

Margaret Higginson and Papa, 1885.

COURTESY MRS. WILLIAM HALLOWELL AND MRS. W. J. WOODIN

had a fair musical sense, a good, if untrained, voice, and an appreciation of music that went back to his boyhood. Little Margaret often sang duets with him and did so with particular relish when he introduced her to the Sea Island spirituals he had written down and brought back years before.

In 1883, at the age of sixty he bought a new, and to modern eyes curious-looking, tricycle, built with a very high seat and center wheel and two much smaller balance wheels fore and aft. Behind the driver he had a seat constructed resting on a single long spring on which he perched his four-year-old daughter. The sight of the tall, distinguished man seated on this strange contraption with a tiny child behind caught the attention of an enterprising photographer. The picture was so successful he used it to advertise his establishment. It proved to be popular as a purely picturesque photo, and one day Colonel Thomas Wentworth Higginson wrote his daughter from New York:

This morning I went along a great big street called Broadway and what do you think I saw? Why, you and me riding on the tricycle; that is I saw the picture in a window, where the same photographers who took us have a store in New York! Some people stopped to look and one of them said, "I wonder who that man is with a little girl behind him." I could have told him, but I didn't. I might have said, "That's Margaret Higginson and I think the man must be her papa."

Good-bye, darling.
Your Own PAPA.

XXXVII

LITERATURE AND A BIT OF POLITICS

SIXTY YEARS OLD and back in Cambridge with a wife and baby daughter, Wentworth buckled down like any twenty-five-year-old husband to the problem of making a living. The Lyceum lecture circuit was drying up as a source of income for writers. The multiplication of newspapers and magazines, the gradual transformation of America from a rural to an urban nation, and the peopling of these cities with new Americans from abroad all contributed to the Lyceum's loss of popularity.

For Wentworth this was not a serious blow. It occurred at a time when he was so solidly established that there was demand enough for his writings to support the family. There was a fairly steady income from the *Young Folks' History*. Now that he was entranced with his daughter's companionship and the joy of bringing her up, the idea of the month's tour, sleeping in a different bed every night—often a primitive sleeping car—seemed much less attractive.

The return of a man of his age to dwell in a town where he had spent his boyhood and college years produced some troublesome sensations. After a decade and a half as resident of a resort town that was dominated by an older set, Wentworth was rather baffled by the flood tide of youth that dominated the streets of Cambridge. Gradually, however, he became fascinated by the young

Back in Cambridge to stay. Higginson's house on Buckingham Street.

COURTESY MRS. WILLIAM HALLOWELL AND MRS. W. J. WOODIN

people, without being resentful of his new position or concealing it from himself. He recognized that he was part of a generation that had been superseded. The students and the younger set of instructors and professors that made up the academic community sometimes seemed rather indifferent without being in the least disrespectful. They would no more be disrespectful to their great grandfather's portrait, he mused. The future was theirs and they knew it; for him it remained to be of such service as he could render, and he set about it.

He continued his writing on the rights of women to emancipation. He sought through regular articles in the *Woman's Journal* and many of his other essays to advance that cause by keeping the spotlight on the prejudices and fallacious habits of thought that preserved inequality. In his literary work he continued his efforts to serve the cause of a native literature. This was the freedom for which Emerson and the Transcendentalists had agitated, freedom from European domination and continental models, and especially freedom from British standards and habits of thought. Americanism in literature, he argued, must be based on a faith, above all, in national self-government. An American writer must have faith in this "as marrow in his bones and blood in his veins. He may still need culture but he has the basis of all culture."

The language we speak and write might seem superficially the same as that of the British, but even apart from Americanisms and slang expressions, there were five words that must be used as the touchstone of a distinctively American literature. Those five words were those in which "as Lincoln said, Jefferson embodied an eternal truth, 'All men are created equal'—that is," wrote Higginson, "equally men."

"From this simple assumption flowed all that is distinctive in American society. From it resulted, as a political inference, universal suffrage; that is a suffrage constantly tending to be universal, although it still leaves out one half the human race [the women]." American writers must boldly resist the attitude of British and continental who reject the common people as a subject of their art, he urged. "American literature must freely seek the common; its fiction must record not queens and Cleopatras alone, but the emotion in the heart of the schoolgirl and the sempstress; its history must record, not only great generals, but the nameless boys whose graves people with undying memories every soldiers' cemetery from Arlington to Chattanooga."

The urge to render public service remained with him. No longer did he have the thoroughgoing "attitude of revolution" that he had had before the war. He did not feel it necessary to place himself "outside of established institutions; to be obliged to lower one's voice and conceal one's purposes; to see law and order, police and military, on the wrong side, and find good citizenship a sin and bad citizenship a duty. . . ." as he described the period of

John Brown and the fugitive-slave cases. Quite the contrary. He was asked if he would accept nomination to serve in the Massachusetts State Legislature within two years after he returned to Cambridge, and he accepted and was elected. He served two one-year terms that were themselves an education.

He had some successes in his brief political career—abolition of the poll tax in Massachusetts and measures guaranteeing further religious freedom—and some failures, particularly in the area of women's suffrage. He was consoled to recall that four Irish American legislators respected him so for his work in behalf of religious freedom that they did not have the heart to vote against his woman's suffrage bill. Since it was counter to their convictions they merely went out to the lobby to abstain while it was being defeated.

On the whole the legislative and political process was disillusioning. He was repelled when he saw how political office came "to the man who works hardest for it, not to the man who is best fitted for it." The extent to which money and hypocrisy were involved in political advancement disturbed him:

> *The whole tendency of public life is undoubtedly to make a man an incipient boss, and to tempt him to scheme and bargain; and it is only the most favorable circumstances which can enable a man to succeed without this; it is mainly a question whether he shall do it in person, or through an agent or "wicked partner." The knowledge of this drives from public life some men well fitted to adorn it, and brings in many who are unfit.*

He returned to the full-time profession of writer with the reflection that a literary man lives in a world where these sordid devices are rarely required. He recalled that Goethe had said that the artist "is the only man who lives with unconcealed aims." For himself he observed that it is "very rarely intrigue or pushing which secures fame."

When he said this he was repeating in a different form what Emily Dickinson had written to him twenty years before, although he may not have been conscious of the fact, "If fame belonged to me, I could not escape her; if she did not, the longest day would pass me on the chase. . . ." In the history of the world's literature it may well be that the greatest Americans of the nineteenth century, or any century, will prove to have been Emily Dickinson and Henry David Thoreau. In each case fame arrived after the writer died; in each case Higginson was a rare and early enthusiast. Wentworth lived to record with satisfaction an encounter in his quest, while Thoreau, recently deceased, was still relatively unknown:

When I was endeavoring, about 1870, to persuade Thoreau's sister to let me edit his journals, I invoked the aid of Squire Hoar, the lord of the manor in Concord, who heard me patiently and then said:

"Whereunto? You have not established the preliminary point. Why should anyone want *to have Thoreau's journals published?"*

The time had arrived for fame to catch up with Emily Dickinson and Thomas Wentworth Higginson played an important part. Just as he had helped her to survive as a human being by the warm and intimate friendship he extended in his correspondence, he was now to be the key figure in the publication that was to enable her poetry to win recognition.

Emily Dickinson died in 1886. Though his friendship had been with the poet-recluse herself and not with her family, Wentworth was summoned to attend the funeral. He was asked to take part in the services as a friend and literary figure. He did so by making a few brief remarks and then reading a poem by Emily Brontë, which he knew to be, as he said, "a favorite with our friend who has now put on that Immortality which she seemed never to have laid off."

It was no secret to the family that Emily had been writing poetry for at least thirty years, but it was a very great puzzle as to what was to be done with it. They had, perhaps, insufficient critical judgment by which to estimate its value. The fact that so distinguished a writer as Higginson had kept in such intimate touch with her must have persuaded Emily's sister Lavinia and sister-in-law Sue that something must be done with the poems. However, in the state in which the manuscripts were found it was impossible to do anything at once. The poems she had been hoarding, save for the very few she had mailed to Wentworth and a sprinkling of other correspondents, were in a form that would not have been so much as looked at by any publisher. They were written in an almost illegible script on both sides of tiny sheets of paper fastened together by fine twine into little booklets. Much as he had admired her work and given of himself in the correspondence that marked a unique friendship, Higginson could do nothing now to help find a publisher. He insisted that the poems would have to be recopied.

An Amherst neighbor of the Dickinsons, wife of a faculty member, undertook the long, difficult task of transcription. She brought the completed product to Wentworth at Cambridge two years later. Seeing for the first time a large number of her poems at once he began to realize how really fine a genius she had been. He summed up his thoughts in an introduction he wrote for a proposed first volume of her verse:

> *In many cases these verses will seem to the reader like poetry torn up by the roots, with rain and dew and earth still clinging to them, giving a freshness and a fragrance not otherwise to be conveyed . . . we can only wonder at the gift of vivid imagination by which this recluse woman can delineate, by a few touches, the very crises of physical or mental struggle. . . . But the main quality of these poems is that of extraordinary grasp and insight, uttered with an uneven vigor sometimes exasperating, seemingly wayward,*

but really unsought and inevitable. After all, when a thought takes one's breath away, a lesson on grammar seems an impertinence.

It was not without difficulty that the poetry of Emily Dickinson found its way into print in book form. The distinguished position of her sponsor and his reputation as writer and critic, were not enough to overcome the initial opposition.

It was thirty years since his first trip to the post office, the walk that was marked by receipt of the questioning letter from the quiet poet. Her artistry remained in advance of her era: it was work, as he had invited in "Letter to a Young Contributor," of that rare quality that would make it necessary for it to create the taste by which it would be appreciated.

Wentworth confidently approached his own publisher, for whom he was also a reader of manuscripts. He was now a writer of forty years' standing and had come to be something of a revered figure in Cambridge as well as Boston, practically the last surviving link to the golden age of Emerson, Hawthorne, and Thoreau. After reading the Dickinson poems Higginson had selected for an initial volume, however, his publisher almost began to wonder whether the Colonel had begun to lose his mind, recommending such stuff.

"The poems, my dear Higginson, are much too queer. The rhymes are all wrong," they told him, pushing back the manuscript.

Fortunately there was an executive at another company, Roberts Brothers, a more broadminded gentleman, who remembered with affection Helen Hunt, whose *Ramona* he had successfully published. He had heard about Emily's poetry from this other protégé of Higginson's. The company submitted the manuscript to their own poetry reader and received a negative report. Despite this, as a courtesy to Higginson and in tribute to the memory of Helen Hunt, they reluctantly agreed to take the project on. There was one condition. To cut down their own expected loss, someone would have to pay in advance for the plates on which the poetry was to be set up in type. Emily's surviving sister agreed, and the project became a reality.

By the time the day of publication had arrived, Wentworth had put all reservations behind. "Books just arrived—bound. I am *astounded* in looking through. How could we ever have doubted about them?" he wrote. He recognized a duty to posterity, adding "I am distressed exceedingly to find that among E.D.'s countless letters there are poems as good as any we printed. . . . This shows we must have another volume, by and by." He rejoiced to learn that the foremost writer-editor of the era, William Dean Howells, had got wind of the forthcoming publication and was plugging it. Howells' daughter Mildred had been won by a reading of proof sheets of the verse and selected a favorite:

I died for beauty, but was scarce
Adjusted in the tomb,
When one who died for truth was lain
In an adjoining room.
He questioned softly why I failed?
"For Beauty," I replied.
"And I for truth,—the two are one;
We brethren are," he said.
And so, as kinsmen met a night,
We talked between the rooms,
Until the moss had reached our lips,
And covered up our names.

It was not very long after the publication of the first book that it became evident that the moss would never cover Emily Dickinson's name. Reviews appeared promptly, not all wholly favorable, but every one was struck by the work. One critic who had as advance reader disapproved the publication ate his words and said, "It is seldom that the reviewer is called upon to notice a book so remarkable as the 'Poems' of Miss Emily Dickinson."

The first edition was sold out within a month. While the second was being readied for shipment, the publisher planned a third. By the end of six months there had been half a dozen printings. The pleased publisher wrote to Wentworth's co-editor that he was quite willing to modify the original agreement by paying for the printers' plates plus a royalty of 10 per cent, just as if the work had been contracted for originally as the product of an established poet.

There was one special feature of the literary success that pleased Wentworth above all else, as he wrote exultantly to his co-editor:

> *I feel as if we had climbed to a cloud, pulled it away, and revealed a new star behind it. I have just been going over the reviews & noting in the book who quotes each poem. Have you observed how they are* distributed? *Sooner or later each poem, it would seem, must find its one admirer.*

In his advocacy of Americanism in literature, there was one theme that Higginson had stressed above all else. "Do not fear to excel in the particular, for only that can have universal appeal." He insisted that American writers should turn to the themes and subjects at home and in their region; there only, in dealing with the material they knew, could they win a wider fame. And so it proved with Emily Dickinson, who had barely ever left her tiny New England village except to roam through the universe of the soul. The visible setting of her poems was the New England countryside, a later critic and historian was to write;

> . . . *the village, the garden, the household that she knew so well, a scene, the only scene she knew, that she invested with magic, so that the familiar objects became portents and symbols. Here were the hills, the changing seasons, the winter light, the light of spring, the bee, the mouse, the humming bird, the cricket, the lonely houses off the road, the village inn. . . . She domesticated the universe and read her own experience into the motions of nature and the*

world she observed. . . . Her style, her stamp, her form were completely her own.

So wrote Van Wyck Brooks, in *New England: Indian Summer,* our foremost literary historian, reaffirming Wentworth Higginson's reflection, "The impression of a wholly new and original poetic genius was distinct on my mind."

Unfortunately he was unaware at the time of the initial publication of a developing three-way feud in Amherst. It was between his co-editor, Mabel Loomis Todd, Emily's surviving sister Lavinia, and her sister-in-law, Susan. As the smoldering bitterness of their quarrel flared up after his death, a quarrel taken up and made worse by their descendants, each of the feudists turned on him in reprisal, as it seemed, for his courtesies to or cooperation with the others. Scholars who have examined the documents of the day have refuted the charges made against him of careless or officious editing or lack of capacity to appreciate the genius that would never have been shared with the world without his intervention.

XXXVIII

A GLIMPSE OF UTOPIA

THE CITY OF BOSTON had lost a distinguished citizen. John Boyle O'Reilly, who died suddenly in 1890, was not at all what we would think of as a proper Bostonian. An immigrant who had landed after the Civil War, he had come as a fleeing criminal: an Irish revolutionary plucked from a British prison-in-exile by a Yankee whaler in the South Seas. Under the immigration laws in force when he died, twenty years later, O'Reilly would not have been admitted to the United States. Poet and community activist, O'Reilly had supported himself for two decades as writer and editor for the Boston *Pilot*. This newspaper served the Catholic community that Higginson had lived to see grow from a persecuted handful to a dominant group in the city.

In the poetry written during his lifetine, O'Reilly had more than once celebrated the memory of a fellow Bostonian. When a handsome civic monument went up to mark the Boston Massacre, O'Reilly wrote:

And honor to Crispus Attucks, who was leader and voice that day:
The first to defy, and first to die. . . .

When Higginson's abolitionist comrade Wendell Phillips died, O'Reilly, who had not arrived until most of Phillips' life work was done, paid him the outstanding poetic tribute.

Come workers; here was a teacher, and the lesson he taught was good;
There are no classes or races, but one human brotherhood. . . .

When O'Reilly died, the Mayor and the Common Council of Boston called an official memorial meeting. They sent across the river to Cambridge for the most distinguished speaker on the platform, Thomas Wentworth Higginson. An immense crowd was present, described in the city's official printed report of the proceedings as "the Irish-American and the Anglo-American and the Afro-American, in short, the people. . . ."

Higginson's tribute covered a number of O'Reilly's claims to recognition. Then, giving voice to a subject that had increasingly troubled him, he said:

And on the other questions that lie before us in the future—on the questions that are gathering behind all the present questions and that bid fair to give the next generation a harder problem, much harder to solve than the mere question of slavery, Boyle O'Reilly is lost at the beginning of a contest where his fire and his judgment will be greatly regretted.

It is not for nothing that, as the last generation grew up reading Harriet Beecher Stowe's "Uncle Tom's Cabin," so this generation grows up reading Edward Bellamy and listening to Henry George, and wondering where it is all to end. We none of us know where it is to end. We none of us know even how to state the new problems of the future.

During the first years after the Civil War, Higginson had been an interested spectator rather than a participant as the "new problems" were developing. His long isolation in Newport—from which he sallied forth occasionally to tackle the old problems of women's rights and Negro's wrongs—kept him from closer observation. The need to change his habits and begin a new life with a new family when he was almost sixty years old was a further deterring factor. He could see that there was a great change overwhelming the country he knew and had loved and had served. He recorded in his essays his concern and opposition to new aspects of American life that came with that great change. He knew that the clock could not be turned back, but he was never quite certain what side of what fight he should join.

He had seen the evils of an uncontrolled factory system in his early days in Newburyport. He saw how those who had invested their capital in buying or building the factories, the capitalists, resented and resisted his efforts to reduce the working day to ten hours. He had seen the growth in the size of the factories and the expansion of the railroads on the eve of the Civil War. The war and its needs unleashed an even more accelerated increase in the size and power of the aggregations of capital invested in factories, railroads, and mines. As he viewed from a distance the nature of the change, on his return to Newport to convalesce, he wrote a friend that he really wondered "whether the citizens of the United States would choose organized capitalism or organized government" to determine their fate and their future.

"Giant monopolies, colossal trusts," he said in another lecture in 1890, "begin to have power to control government, and to tax people indirectly without their consent. It must be admitted that the possible growth of trusts is a menace to republican institutions. . . . More than one great trust already has power to crack the domes of legislative halls like egg-shells."

In his essays during the years that saw this growth of economic power that seemed greater than the political power of the people, he would deplore the social effects. "It is almost as difficult to reconcile the principle of republican society with the existence of billionaires as of dukes," he said. He recalled sadly how in the colonial period, which he knew almost at firsthand, there was "nothing like the vast remoteness between poverty and wealth" that now afflicted the nation. He warned his fellow countrymen against the replacement of a hereditary nobility with a new "Aristocracy of the Dollar," quoting Emerson's observation that, "The whole interest of history lies in the fortunes of the poor."

Wentworth had an abiding faith in the common people, the "plain people," as he preferred to call them. "The republic rests upon its masses, upon those who not only do not appear in the society columns, but do not even see them." He disagreed violently with Charles Francis Adams who had grown wealthy in railroad operation and had suggested that Boston schools be run differently for children of day laborers and children of professors or the "better classes." He sharply reminded Adams that when he was school committeeman in Newport he never saw any difference in receptivity or intelligence to depend on the "ward" the children came from, as long as they were treated like human beings. He insisted that more of intellect dwells in workshops and factories "than in the majority, not merely of counting rooms, but even of court-rooms and pulpits."

Despite the virtues of the plain people, America had come to a state where, as he told one audience, "two thousand capitalists own more than all the rest of our 65,000,000 population." With this concentration of wealth had come the evils of corporate control, the power of the trusts, the insecurity of the poor. There was no easy answer. John Boyle O'Reilly had proposed socialism as a remedy and told him how impressed he had been with the writings of a German refugee, Karl Marx. In an obituary on Marx published in the *Pilot,* official newspaper of the diocese, O'Reilly had written that "no socialist reasoned closer" and agreed with Marx's theory that labor created value that was taken from the worker by the capitalist's control of the machinery.

Wentworth did not fear the idea of socialism or think it the least bit alien. He was old enough to remember Brook Farm and other cooperative colonies that had flourished in America before Karl Marx had written a word about socialism. His model, Theodore Parker, had defended the superiority of labor's claims to those of capital, and Parker's ideas, transmitted by Lincoln's law partner William Herndon (a lifelong admirer of the radical minister) had found their way into some of Lincoln's speeches. Although he did not fully accept the idea of socialism, Wentworth had nevertheless appeared before the Massachusetts legislature to urge that the state permit public ownership of electric and gas companies, then new on the scene, as well as street railways. All were monopolies that could oppress their workers and their customers as well, since there was no competition to deter them.

He had an ally in this, his friend Edward Everett Hale (only preacher to exchange pulpits with him back in Worcester). Hale, even older than Wentworth, stood up before the assembled legislators and ridiculed the opposition to government ownership; the very idea, he said, that government should stay *out* of business was un-American! "It was the most natural thing in the world, when I was a boy in New England, for the government to build and operate canals and roads, lighthouses and docks."

While Wentworth was on a speaking tour in the Midwest one day, in 1887, a friend pressed a book upon him. "The workingmen say I must read it," said he, "they affirm that it is what is coming." The book was called *Looking Backward: 2000-1887*, and it was written by Edward Bellamy. This was the book he was to compare with *Uncle Tom's Cabin* in his talk to the assembled citizens of Boston, to pay tribute in the name of the city to John Boyle O'Reilly.

Wentworth remembered Bellamy from letters they had exchanged. A younger man, born just too late to have fought in the Civil War, Bellamy knew Wentworth by reputation and correspondence with him, from time to time, from his own home in a western Massachusetts town. Bellamy had written for guidance and encouragement after he had chosen to become a journalist and writer upon graduation from law school. The more he learned about the ways of lawyers, the less he had wished to be one of them, and he abandoned the profession before entering it.

Wentworth had begun to read Bellamy's book with eager interest. He saw in it a restatement of the question that had been troubling him since the Civil War, "Shall industry be placed under public control for the public advantage, or under corporate control for corporate advantage?" He had seen, with Bellamy, the growing conflict between labor and capital, in which all the advantages seemed to lie with capital. He had sensed, as he told one audience, "If you dam up the stream of labor reform, you prepare an era when it will burst forth with havoc." Now he found, in *Looking Backward,* a possible answer to the questions that had given him such concern.

Bellamy used the form of a novel with a romantic plot to convey his message, just as Mrs. Stowe had in her story of Uncle Tom and Simon Legree, and Helen Hunt Jackson in the story of Ramona and the wrongs inflicted upon the Indians. This time the author did not emphasize and describe existing and past evils in an attempt to appeal to the conscience of the reader. Instead it was a novel of the type called Utopian, a depiction of how life could be beautiful in the cooperative society of the future.

Wentworth was fascinated as he read the story of Julian West, a young Bostonian who had been placed in a life-suspending trance in 1887. Forgotten by his contemporaries when his house burned down, while he slept underground in a sealed-off room, West was recalled to life when discovered by a doctor and his beautiful daughter in the year 2000. The society in which Julian awakens is one in which hunger, war, inequality, and injustice—all the problems that had plagued humanity in 1887—had been removed. Recollections of the beautiful dream of Brook Farm flooded his mind as Higginson read on.

In Bellamy's book Brook Farm was the whole nation and the world as well. All private enterprise was consolidated into one huge trust, operated by all the people in the interests of all the people. In the year 2000 money had been abolished. It was no longer permitted to serve as the key that opened all doors to the rich nor to be the club they held over the poor. Every able-bodied person worked; all received the same income; distribution of goods was organized to eliminate all waste; farms were operated on a collective basis with the aid of mechanization. Individual differences were encouraged and the aim of education was to develop the special talents of each child to the highest degree. The benefit of the industrial system was extended to all by permitting retirement at the age of forty-five.

In telling the story of the wonderful world of Julian West, Bellamy did not explain in detail how all this had come about. There were hints of a spontaneous movement called Nationalism (whose name meant simply public ownership by nationalization) that had led in taking the wealth of the nation and the instruments of production and distribution away from the few who controlled them. "At last, strangely late in the world's history," said one of the principal characters, "the obvious fact was perceived that no business is so essentially the people's business as the industry and commerce on which the people's livelihood depends, and that to entrust it to private persons to be managed for private profit is a folly similar in kind, though vastly greater in magnitude, to that of surrendering the functions of political government to kings and nobles to be conducted for their personal glorification."

Later on, when the book had become a definite success and a best-seller, Wentworth chuckled as he read Bellamy's answer to an interviewer who pressed him for details on how the new society was to be achieved. Would the government have to be overthrown, they wanted to know, or would it be changed by an election? How could you get round the fact that each of the two major parties supported private enterprise so loyally? "When you want to induce a bachelor to enter matrimony," answered Bellamy, "you don't go on with a lot of particulars about the marriage license and the gloves and the ceremony—you just show him the girl and let him fall in love with her and the rest takes care of itself."

It began to seem, soon after the publication of the book, that Bellamy was right. The American people found the attractions of a cooperatively run commonwealth irresistible in the pages of a book and almost so in real life. The seeming virtues of the socialism that the author called Nationalism were enhanced by the contrast with the seamy sides of poverty and exploitation under capitalism in the late 1880's. The book was an immense success and sold into the hundreds of thousands. Pleased, Bellamy modestly insisted that his book was successful only because it anticipated "what everyone was thinking and about to say."

Two of the book's admirers went beyond merely urging others to read it. Their admiration for the society imagined in the pages of *Looking Backward* impelled them to want to bring it into being. They proposed the formation of a Nationalist Club in Boston. Bellamy assented and the Boston Club became the first of more than one hundred and fifty that were spread out across the country. One observer wrote, "Copies of 'Looking Backward' are in every community. Probably every village has at least one man who is a thorough nationalist, while hundreds of his neighbors are in sympathy with its principles."

Reverend Hale and Colonel Higginson were intrigued by the movement. They debated with each other whether the complete collective ownership of factories and fields might impede the individual liberty that all Yankees cherished. Bellamy assured Higginson in a letter that Nationalism did not mean merely "economic reform, but its most important aspect is that of a moral movement for uplifting, enlarging, and ennobling the individual life." While remaining somewhat skeptical, Higginson persuaded Hale to come along with him and join. "The tendency of events is now toward Nationalism," he announced, "or State Socialism if you please."

After having supported the cause of Nationalism for a period of time, Wentworth began to have doubts again. Overwhelmed at the amount of political corruption he saw in Boston and Washington, he was not sure that such corruption was simply one of the evils of capitalism. "How far under national control of great industries can we keep the workshop out of politics?" he asked. "Shall we not open the way to prodigious political corruption if, besides political parties, we have political land, political coal, political cotton, political sugar, political oil?"

Disenchantment with the details of the Bellamy scheme did not lead him to denounce the dream of a cooperative society or to turn his back on Bellamy as a man. When he had first joined the Nationalist Club he had been asked to contribute an article to its newly founded magazine. Carried away by the spirit of the thing, he wrote a poem and inscribed it to Bellamy. To show that he remained loyal to the sentiments that made him join, he repeated the stanzas of the poem at the end of the public address in which he announced that he was no longer a member of the Nationalist Clubs:

From street and square, from hill and glen
Of this vast world beyond my door,
I hear the tread of marching men,
The patient armies of the poor.
Some day, by laws as fixed and fair
As guide the planets in their sweep,
The children of each outcast heir
The harvest-fruits of time shall reap.
Some day, without a trumpet's call,
The news will o'er the world be blown:
"The heritage comes back to all!
The myriad monarchs take their own!"

XXXIX

ANTI-IMPERIALIST

As THE YEARS PASSED BY, the old gentleman was less and less likely to run up the steps of his house or the Boston Library two or three at a time. His hair whitened, his skin began to tighten on his hands and face, and sometimes he'd stumble over a word or two when speaking. He carried himself always with a nobility and dignity that few failed to observe and admire. He was regarded in Boston as well as Cambridge as a "grand old man," a living monument to a radical past of which a conservative city was proud.

Around his seventieth birthday he began to count names in the *Harvard Graduate's Magazine* and was conscious of an ambition: to live to become the oldest surviving Harvard graduate. His birthdays began to be marked by the arrival of flowers, telegrams, and letters, and he appreciated the attention he received. Dozens of cousins made up for his having but a single child of his own; there was now always a nephew, grandnephew, or second cousin in attendance at Harvard in whom he would show interest. He would call on these and upon descendants of his friends and comrades of the antislavery fight at their rooms in the college. The visit would be followed by an invitation to tea at his Cambridge home, crowded with mementoes and souvenirs, where he spent his last thirty years.

In 1895, when he was seventy-two, he suffered a digestive attack that seemed to develop into a serious illness. One doctor warned him that he might not recover. Higginson refused to believe it, but he decided that he had better act as if the doctor knew what he was talking about. He was confined to bed for a year and sentenced to a milk diet. The years of incessant traveling and lecturing, the railway station meals, and the small town hotel dining rooms had taken their toll. The overwork of carrying a number of literary projects at once also had a price.

Temporary retirement, yes, but not surrender. He could not be content merely to lie in bed and read. He put the finishing touches on a military and naval history of Massachusetts in the Civil War, a task for which his state had drafted him five years before. He continued with occasional reviews and essays. Soon he undertook a major new assignment, most of which he did while he sat propped up on pillows. Four editors who had learned of his illness pressed him for a book about the person who had appeared in the background of his sketches and articles on others: Thomas Wentworth Higginson. He began to work on a series of autobiographical sketches after notifying the successful bidder of the competing offers, "with the courtesy," he added, "of an engaged maiden who wished her betrothed to know that he was not her only chance."

In keeping with his character, his lifelong outlook of sunny optimism, he titled his book of reminiscences *Cheerful Yesterdays.* He did not cover the entire story of his life; he concentrated more on the early years, especially the prewar period of "the newness," when the Transcendentalism and the socialism of Brook Farm were the glowing ideas that lit up the landscape for his generation. He added, in an epilogue to the book:

> *It must be borne in mind that one who has habitually occupied the attitude of a reformer must inevitably have some satisfactions, at the latter end of life, which those who are conservative by temperament can hardly share. To the latter, things commonly seem to be changing for the worse,*

At his summer home in New Hampshire.

COURTESY MRS. WILLIAM HALLOWELL AND MRS. W. J. WOODIN

and this habit of mind must be a dreary companion as the years advance. . . .

To those who were living when the American nation lifted and threw off from its shoulders the vast incubus of human slavery, what other task can seem too great to be accomplished? In the presence of such a step in human progress as this, how trivial and unimportant are all personal ambitions! The high-water mark of earthly endeavor is to be found in the sublime prayer of the French iconoclast, Proudhon, "Let my memory perish, if only humanity may be free."

Not very long after the publication of *Cheerful Yesterdays,* Wentworth's loyalty to the ideals of his youth was to be tested, and he responded to the call of freedom, as did practically every American writer and surviving abolitionist of the day. The challenge to freedom came from the McKinley administration's actions abroad. McKinley had been elected in 1896 on a pledge of peaceful foreign policy. "We want no wars of conquest; we must avoid the temptation of territorial aggression." Unfortunately, William McKinley was not the last American president to forget after election a platform pledge of peace.

After he had backed away from the initial enthusiasm with which he had welcomed the socialism of the Nationalist movement of Edward Bellamy's followers, Wentworth had not been actively engaged in politics. The Massachusetts military history, the Dickinson manuscripts, the regular flow of his literary work, followed by his breakdown and illness, detached him from the American political scene in the middle 1890's. Some of the members of the Nationalist Clubs formed by Bellamy enthusiasts had found their way into the then tiny American scientific Socialist movement. The Indiana-born Socialist leader of later years, Eugene V. Debs, called the writings of Higginson's friend "valuable and timely contributions to the literature of Socialism" that "started many on the road to the revolutionary movement."

These were only a minority. The great bulk of the believers in Bellamy's Nationalism, the enthusiastic readers of *Looking Backward* in villages and hamlets across the land, were persuaded that the promise of the future was in a new radical political movement. This was the People's Party, the result of a coming together of a chorus of rebel voices who were principally the spokesmen of discontented farmers of the South and West. They were putting into action the ideas that Wentworth had expressed years before, when it became increasingly evident that both major political parties were controlled by and acting for the benefit of the great money interests:

> *The young men read the proceedings of the two national conventions at Chicago, and they find no perceptible difference. I myself live at Cambridge, near the Botanical Gar-*

den and the Observatory; there are men there who spend their lives in using the most powerful lenses, and it may be that with the utmost power at their command some of them can discern faint differences between the Republican and Democratic Platforms; I confess that I cannot, nor can the young men who study them.

By the time these ideas of a decade before were put into effect by the Populists, as the followers of the People's Party were called, Wentworth's overwork and his illness kept him from active participation in this new movement to restore popular government to the plain people. As he was recovering from his illness the new movement had been submerged in a wider popular enthusiasm that took control of the Democratic Party for the time being. The Free Silver movement successfully appealed to an American instinct for slick or trick solutions to the problems of the poor and debtor classes. Bryan, the Populist and Free Silver candidate who had the Democratic nomination in 1896 was nevertheless defeated; his defeat was partly due to a belief that the incumbent Democratic administration had been on the road to war, and Higginson was among the many who believed the election of McKinley was the endorsement of a policy of peace.

The foreign policy issue was new to American presidential campaigns in 1896. Though subsidiary to the silver question, it had been injected as a result of the public reaction to a crisis over a Venezuelan border dispute of 1895, the closest the nation had come to a foreign war for half a century. On a literary pilgrimage to London in 1878, Wentworth had learned at firsthand of the addition of a new word to the English language during that very year. There had been a threat of war as a result of a clash between British and Russian empire-building activities in the Middle East, and a popular music hall comedian sang:

We don't want to fight
But by JINGO, if we do,

We've got the ships
We've got the men
We've got the money, too.

The word jingo had caught on and come to mean a superpatriot, one who loved war for his country more than peace for his people.

Higginson had quietly applauded from his sick bed when candidate McKinley had promised that there would be no "jingo nonsense" during his adminstration. "The so-called 'jingo' feeling," wrote Wentworth in an essay he dashed off, "is a peril and an anachronism." In a gentle warning to his countrymen he reminded them that nations "like individuals, reap what they have sown; if we do injustice, we may awake too late to the discovery that we must pay the price."

The nation nevertheless was to learn that the promise of a president to pursue a path of peace was not inviolable. There had developed during the latter part of the nineteenth century a movement within the industrialized nations to conquer or dominate other lands. The principal beneficiaries of Imperialism, as this movement was called, were the business interests of the conquering powers. It was, however, as Dr. Hannah Arendt has called it, "an alliance between mob and capital," meaning that the success of the policy depended not only on the push of the business interests and the use of troops and navies, but also on the civilian groups whose greed and lack of morality were played upon to back up territorial seizures.

America's revolutionary past and tradition of supporting freedom fighters abroad did not immunize it from the swing to Imperialism as a foreign policy. Once our native business interests, which had grown so strong and wealthy in the period after the Civil War, realized the need for markets and places to export capital, they began to look abroad. The drive to conquest or control that had sent European armies and navies to ravage Africa and Asia found its advocates here. Their first great success, the conflict that marked the beginning of the use of American arms to control other nations, was achieved behind the pretense of aiding small nations who sought freedom. The Spanish-American war was begun on the wave of great popular feeling of sympathy for Cubans fighting their Spanish oppressors. It ended on quite a different note, with American soldiers fighting to put down a patriotic effort by Philippine natives who had welcomed our fleet and troops in the belief that we were bringing them the freedom from Spain they had long sought.

Men of conscience in America did not hesitate, once they realized what had happened, to join in condemning their government for its policies and their president for his betrayal of his own campaign pledges of peace. A movement arose, the first of its kind in the history of the world, called the Anti-Imperialist League, and Thomas Wentworth Higginson was one of its first members.

What provoked the organization of the Anti-Imperialist League was a chain of events that occurred in quick succession in which efforts by the Spanish to seek peace were brushed aside, followed by a rapid series of American attacks on Spanish positions all over the world. The status and future of the Philippines had not been mentioned in the Congressional action—seemingly limited to freeing Cuba—under which the President had launched the war. Acquisition of a base in Southeast Asia was a concealed aim of the administration elected on a pledge of "no jingo nonsense."

This new war aim led to a bloody conflict never authorized by congress. There was a native independence movement in the Far East island group that was quite prepared to take over self-government after the United States destroyed Spanish rule, that had, in fact, aided us in destroying that rule. Once the Spanish were beaten, the administration turned about and sent out soldiers throughout the islands to destroy the native freedom movement.

There was a great national debate as the war of suppression continued, a war that was to cost more American lives than all the battles of the war with the Spanish. One side, the pro-Imperialist side, was summed up by Massachusetts Senator Henry Cabot

Lodge, whose grandson of the same name is well known in current public affairs:

> *To a naval and commercial power the coal mines of the Philippines will be a source of great strength and of equally great value. It is sufficient for me to indicate these few elements of natural wealth in the islands which only await development. A much more important point is to be found in the markets which they furnish. . . . Even as the islands are today there is opportunity for a large absorption of the products of the United States, but it must not be forgotten that the islands are entirely undeveloped.*
>
> *But the value of the Philippine Islands, both natural and acquired, and as a market for our products, great as it undoubtedly is, and greater as it undoubtedly will be, is trifling compared to the indirect results which will flow from our possession of them. From the time of the war between China and Japan it became apparent that great changes were impending in the East, changes which many economists and publicists believed would play the master part in the history of the next century. The struggle for the world's trade, which has for many years been shaping ever more strongly the politics and the history of mankind, has its richest prize set before it in the vast markets of China. . . . There is the greatest opportunity in China for trade expansion which exists anywhere in the world.*

So spoke Henry Cabot Lodge. Ranged against him and the President were many artists, writers, and intellectuals. Practically all the great American writers of the day, Mark Twain, William Dean Howells, William James, and many others spoke against the idea that aggression was to be justified for the sake of its material fruits. Their ideas were well expressed by Thomas Wentworth Higginson in an essay that was also a lecture in American history and that was reprinted as an Anti-Imperialist Pamphlet by a league formed to oppose the President's unjust war against farmers and native revolutionaries on the Philippine Islands.

To begin, he reintroduced his countrymen to Tom Paine, whose "book 'Common Sense' had probably done more than any other book to bring the American Revolution to a point, and his other publication, 'The Crisis,' to carry it safely through." Paine, he reminded his readers, had retired with honor, been pensioned by Congress, and was granted five hundred acres of land by the state of New York, "but he was not content to live on these comforts when he could help the cause of freedom elsewhere . . . and so he went to Paris and took a hand in the French Revolution."

For a century since the days of Tom Paine, "the American nation has habitually acted on his motto "and given its sympathy to the underside." Here was the essential point omitted by Henry Cabot Lodge in his concern with raw materials, exports, markets, and strategic bases for controlling China.

"Greece, Poland, Hungary, Italy, Ireland, Mexico, Cuba, the South American republics, have all called forth the national sympathy, because they were or seemed to be oppressed. No one has asked whether their heroes were all Washingtons and their generals all Grants. Probably they were not." In this, Higginson was alluding to the storm of propaganda directed against the Philippine freedom movement; the newspapers had repeatedly called their leaders outlaws and traitors and terrorists:

> *No doubt the prominent insurgent leaders, Bozzaris, Kossuth, Garibaldi, called forth plenty of criticism. Bolivar was called more than once a braggart and traitor, yet it was practically due to him that South America is now republican and not monarchical, and it is for this that his statue adorns American parks. So much for the leaders; and as for the people, there were always plenty who doubted, while the struggle lasted, whether the insurgents were worthy of freedom or could ever sustain a government of their own. . . . Probably there never yet was an insurrec-*

tion, large or small, in which the party apparently stronger did not honestly believe the weaker party to be utterly incapable of self-government.

The flaw in the whole reasoning in such cases is in leaving out the principle of liberty. When a nation, or even a family, once enters on the project of managing the affairs of its neighbors, it is on the wrong track.

In response to those who condemned the Anti-Imperialists for opposing their own government's policy, Higginson summed up their case:

The whole early history of free states usually consists in rebellion against the interference of other states which think themselves wiser and stronger. But the men who are remembered in history the longest are sometimes those who raise their voices against such aggressions, even when their own country commits them. Probably the thing by which the great Lord Chatham will be longest remembered will be his exclamation in Parliament, on November 18, 1777, "If I were an American, as I am an Englishman, while a foreign troop was landed in my country I would never lay down my arms—never, never, never!"

In saying this, Higginson was very pointedly suggesting that one could be a good American and still understand and sympathize with the Philippine rebels. A few months later an assembly of the Anti-Imperialist League at Chicago adopted a statement of principles that expressed the same thought:

We earnestly condemn the policy of the present National Administration in the Philippines. It seeks to extinguish the spirit of 1776 in those islands. We deplore the sacrifice of our soldiers and sailors, whose bravery deserves admiration even in an unjust war.

It was all in vain. After a long and costly struggle the rebels were overcome and American rule established on the islands, where it was to remain for half a century. Higginson could not forgive President McKinley for betraying the platform and principles on which he had been elected, for becoming the instrument and the advocate of the "jingo nonsense" that he had pledged himself to oppose. He reversed himself when Bryan ran against McKinley again in 1900, saying to one Boston audience that if Bryan, the man he opposed in 1896, were elected, "from imperialism back to civilization will be the result."

XL

HARDER TO SOLVE THAN SLAVERY

When it became evident that the efforts of the Anti-Imperialists were doomed to fail, a bitter note of triumph was sounded by one white southern senator. He taunted his opponents with being unable to "dare to wave the bloody shirt and preach a crusade against the South's treatment of the Negro." This was all over and done with, "The North has a bloody shirt of its own. Many thousands of them have been made into shrouds for murdered Filipinos, done to death because they were fighting for liberty."

The phrase "bloody shirt" was one that had long been familiar to Wentworth Higginson. It was a tragic reminder of the recent decades during which the achievements gained at the time of The Negro's Hour were nullified, seemingly for an indefinite time to come. The culminating achievement of that hour had been the event that his friend Wendell Phillips had called the victory that "washed color out of the Constitution," the ratification of the Fifteenth Amendment to the basic document of our government. This Amendment forbade the denial of the vote to American citizens by any state on grounds of race and pledged the national honor to back up the guarantee.

Soon afterwards another Massachusetts man, the former General Butler, now a congressman, held up the bloodstained sleeping garment of an American who had migrated to the South and there been the victim of an underground terror band. This display on the floor of Congress was for the purpose of arousing the conscience of legislators who could not realize how serious the situation in the South had become. It contributed to the passage of laws, some still on the books, to make it a national crime to use violence or intimidation to undermine civil rights.

In the years that followed, a remarkable transformation took place. The phrase "wave the bloody shirt" came to be used as a derogatory criticism of election oratory. It was considered a sign of cynical and insincere tactics to stress the crimes against the freedmen of the South, especially the violations of their Constitutional and human rights by those intent on repressing their instincts for freedom and self-respect.

Many of the orators who waved the bloody shirt when it suited their purpose were insincere, but the crimes against the freedmen and the Constitution were very real and very frequent. Some of those who committed these crimes or newspapers that mentioned their occurrence would seek to justify them on various pretexts. The freedmen did not want the vote; they were ignorant, animal-like, misled by so-called carpetbaggers; the South had to be saved from corruption by eliminating the Negro vote. Higginson knew how false these arguments and explanations were and often wrote to rebut them.

Higginson was there at the beginning with the knowledge and experience to answer allegations that increasingly were used to justify subversion of the United States Constitution in the South and the growing indifference to such subversion in the North. Not interested in freedom? He compared the newly recruited slaves who had served in his regiment with the northern women who were so often dull and apathetic when it came to fighting for their own rights:

> *I am bemused with the wonder why the instinct of freedom seems to be so nearly eradicated among women, when*

I found at the South that no oppression could blunt it among the Negroes.

He spoke up when an issue was presented on which he could bear personal testimony. One of the junior officers of his former regiment, a white Massachusetts man, Niles Parker, had chosen to stay on in the South, make his career there, and enter local politics. There was nothing new or unusual about this in American history. Wentworth could still remember how as a boy he had seen the Conestoga wagons headed on the pike to Concord, the first leg of the long and weary road to Ohio and beyond, and that was how the nation had grown and flourished. White southerners who stubbornly resisted the new constitutional requirements for biracial justice began to attack this old American tradition by condemning as carpetbaggers the migrants to their region, if the migrants practiced the preachings of the Bible and the Constitution.

His former Lieutentant N.G. Parker came under scathing criticism. It was said that he had been inefficient and worse in his handling of accounts as state treasurer of South Carolina. One writer who had rushed to condemn Parker without a trial went so far as to ask with sneering overtones, "What kind of an officer had Colonel Higginson found him?"

Wentworth answered very promptly that Parker had "proved himself a very efficient and valuable officer whom I should have been very sorry to lose." Moreover, he added, showing that in his seclusion in Newport with his invalid wife in 1870 he had kept close touch with affairs in the state where his regiment had fought for freedom:

After the war he settled in Charleston. He was appointed by the military authorities as an alderman. He was then elected a member of the Constitutional Convention where he was Chairman of the Finance Committee. The printed record of that convention shows how laboriously and faith-

fully he discharged his duties. As Treasurer of the State, he brought order out of chaos and made South Carolina the first seceded State to pay interest on its debt.

Even worse than the readiness of northern whites to accept the attacks made on men like Parker was a willingness to forget the services rendered the nation by the southern Negro during the war. The very proof the ex-slaves had given of their manhood was forgotten. Persons of liberal pretensions began to throw up their hands in despair at the seeming hopelessness of the national effort to oppose a subversive southern white movement to restore domination of one race by the other. In state after state the use of violence and fraud and threat of violence brought about the overthrow of the biracial governments.

Since the states had been readmitted to the Union, there seemed no way for the national government to interfere, and there was deep division in the North as to whether it should. Faced with this, most northern white liberals, persuaded themselves that there were good excuses for the violations of the express command of the United States Constitution. Many were anxious for a restoration of business as usual in a reunited country. Since enforcement of justice seemed to bring only turmoil, it became a trend to turn one's back on injustice. It was not enough to accept the often false attacks on northern migrants as crooked carpetbaggers. It was also considered necessary to accept the argument of white southerners that Negroes were not fit to vote.

Typical of the kind of comment that began to appear widely in the North was an item Higginson read with anger in the weekly white liberal magazine, *The Nation*. It said that all except a small number of South Carolina Negroes were "so low that they are but slightly above the level of animals."

Higginson immediately took pen in hand and wrote the editor of *The Nation* that he was appalled to find "such a slur in a journal claiming some deliberation and something of a judicial character." Slightly above the level of animals? "When I remember," he wrote sadly, "that the class here mentioned is one which I have known very intimately, and have reason to remember all my life with love and gratitude, I certainly ought not to withhold my frank dissent." He reviewed his military experiences with men who had been slaves in isolated island plantations until but a few months before they came under his command. "I saw the colored race under the conditions of solitude and society, and saw them tried by one of the severest of all tests—that of military discipline. I also knew a great deal about the family affairs and social relations of my men, and of the life on the plantations, where the slaves were just freed. And so unlike was my whole experience to the verdict of the *Nation,* as above quoted, that I should almost suppose that we were speaking of different races of men."

Higginson was blunt and frank about his knowledge of the comparative performance of white and Negro, for he had seen both at firsthand:

> *There was no more of lying, stealing, or unchastity in the regiment of which I speak than in the average of white regiments. There was decidedly less of drunkenness; and the absence of profanity was remarked by all visitors. I did not create this state of things; I found it on arriving. Nor did I find it in consequence of expecting it, for it was quite unexpected. I was prepared to see much more degradation than ever showed itself, and to use much severer discipline than was ultimately needful. And if this was the condition of the people after years of slavery, it is impossible for me to believe that the few years since the war have deprived them of human attributes, and even of intelligible speech.*

This last was a response to an added insult by *The Nation* writer, declaring the South Carolina Negro's speech was incomprehensible. The Massachusetts man added pointedly, "I often see Irish men and women who are far more obtuse, and who use a far more perplexing dialect than I ever encountered on the Sea Islands."

This was in 1874. Congressman Thaddeus Stevens and Senator Charles Sumner, who had led Congress in passing the civil rights amendments to the Constitution, had died without leaving political heirs having their courage or vision. President Grant faced a hostile Congress that would no longer support a policy of enforcement of national protection of national rights. The federal presence in the South had been reduced to token forces that were no more capable of protecting the great mass of freedmen than a troop of boy scouts. A rising chorus of northern voices, many Massachusetts men among them, began to murmur that the Negro problem had best be left to the South to solve, that it had been a great mistake to force Negro suffrage on the white South.

To these men Higginson retorted sharply that "the enfranchisement of the colored race was wise statesmanship, and indeed the only wisdom under the circumstances." He quoted in one of the regular articles he wrote for the *Woman's Journal,* the concession of a noted antiradical journalist, Charles Nordhoff, who had said "Negro suffrage was not a mistake," and that it was "absolutely necessary to the security of the blacks and the permanent peace of the Southern communities."

These voices were rare in the moral jungle that the United States had become by 1876. There seemed to be no hope of rallying a new host of abolitionist-minded men of conscience to inform and rally the rest of the nation. It seemed clear that no matter who won the 1876 presidential election, the Negro and the Constitution would be the losers. Higginson heard liberals talk of the tranquility and lack of turmoil in the southern states where the biracial governments had been ousted and wrote sadly, in December 1876:

> *This assertion of peace and order in Southern States controlled by the whites is precisely like the old assertions of Northern travelers that the slaves were happy and well off in slavery. "Who knows? Who has heard the slave's side?" said the abolitionists. Horace Mann said that a single slave, on a Georgia plantation, had about as much chance of mak-*

ing his wrongs known as has a man falling overboard in the middle of the Atlantic of swimming to the shore. The chance is not much greater now.

The apathy of the great majority of northerners and his own experience with an innate sense of decency shown by some white southerners led Higginson to take a new approach to the problem of securing interracial justice. Genuine and wholehearted national action for civil rights had become an unattainable ideal. The very laws that Congress had passed to uphold the new provisions of the Constitution were being rendered ineffective by the Supreme Court. Court and Executive seemed intent on restoring to the states the power to discriminate among their citizens that the War Amendments to the Constitution had been designed to remove.

In the face of this seemingly hopeless situation, Higginson thought he saw an answer in the words of a Confederate general who, in campaigning for the governorship of South Carolina had pledged, "Not one single right enjoyed by the colored people today shall be taken from them," and had run on a platform stating, "We declare our acceptance, in perfect good faith, of the thirteenth, fourteenth, and fifteenth amendments to the Federal Constitution." Perhaps, Higginson thought, there was more hope for justice in reposing trust in men like Wade Hampton, than in the northern politicians who waved the bloody shirt when it suited them, but were as prejudiced as the most benighted southerners.

After Mary's death in 1877 he had gone to South Carolina to revisit the scenes of his army experience. A lifelong tendency to be an optimist and to repose faith in the word of men who seemed to be gentlemen, plus favorable reports from those of his old soldiers whom he met, combined to give him a good impression of what he saw. Feeling that the only chance for a measure of justice was to look to the "better class" of southern whites, he wanted to encourage them in carrying out pleges like those made by Hampton. There were, in fact, Negro policemen and militia still, something that New England lacked, and "no conspicuous outrages." For the moment, at least, Governor Hampton had kept his pledges. The heart of the problem of restoring a two party system, Higginson was told, was not so much in the South as in the North. "The colored voters need to know that the party at the North has not deserted them," said one.

Three years later Higginson was sent by Massachusetts to represent his state at the centennial of a decisive battle of the revolutionary war. There in the presence of an integrated audience, and without interference or reproach from his hosts, he said, after dealing in the main body of his address with the event being commemorated:

> *No State can dare to be permanently clouded by the ignorance of any class of its people, or to allow any class to oppress any other. The bad effect of a single act of injustice may be felt among children's children.*

In keeping with the spirit of his optimistic southern report of 1878 was his major 1884 policy paper, "The Young Man's Party." This was a leading statement on behalf of the group that became known as the Mugwumps (an Indian name for Chief), so called because as independent voters who put the character of a candidate above party loyalty they were derided as self-appointed chiefs. In cartoons they were depicted as sitting on a fence "with their mug on one side and their wump on the other." While the candidates are making "appeals to the people to stand by the party of their youth, they behold their sons and nephews hard at work organizing bolters and distributing documents in behalf of revolution, which is, in turn, the party of their youth." On race relations, Higginson continued the policy to which he had turned in 1877 of encouraging and hoping for the best from the so-called better classes of southern whites. "I know of nothing more manly in this generation," he said, "than the manner in which the Southern whites, since the war, have addressed themselves to the problem of educating the blacks." Anticipating the criticism of those Republican "stalwarts" he said, "It is no doubt desirable that there should be a larger colored representation in Congress for the Southern states—but how large is the colored representation from the Northern states?"

By the time the century drew to a close he reluctantly realized that he had been too optimistic about the southern white political leaders who had pledged obedience to the Constitution. Many went back on their word and those who remained faithful to their pledge were unable to survive the rise of racist politicians who vied with each other in their appeals to the prejudices of white voters. He wrote, in a symposium on "The Colored Vote in the South" (referring to a black corporal who had said, thirty years before, "dese yere Secesh neber gwine be cibilized in my time"), "It is not being civilized, for the rich and powerful leaders of society to announce their purpose of taking from their humbler fellow citizens the one point they hold in common, the vote." Of recent outrages in the Carolinas, whereby riot and plunder was employed by the whites to insure the legal steps to outlaw the last vestiges of color-blind suffrage, he said "those who were thanked by southern statesmen for being willing 'to trust the new south' now feel most deeply the new outrages, both as a wrong and as a terrible political blunder. Of these persons, the writer is one."

With this bitter observation, he launched on a new round of activities in support of the cause of justice. He chaired a protest meeting called to condemn "Southern Barbarity," at which the recent upsurge of lynching was vigorously denounced. He rebuked the editor of *The Nation* for an attack on carpetbaggers and declared that "Negro suffrage was absolutely the only method by which the Negroes, who had proved almost the sole southern friends of the Union, could be protected in their most ordinary rights from those who had tried to destroy it. Anything less would have been an act of desertion on the part of the nation which would have disgraced it for ever." Rebutting the principal argument that had been used to excuse the decades of desertion he added "the persons mainly responsible for the misdeeds of the so-called 'carpet-baggers' were the people of the South themselves.

There never was a Western state which received into itself a better class of immigrants than those who entered the South after the Civil War." In introducing with a short preface a new book by a Negro historian he lashed out at the novel from which the film *The Birth of a Nation* was later made, decrying its "demagogic glorification of the Ku Klux Klan." With a prevision of the turn of the tide that he knew just *had* to come, he said at a Boston meeting called to celebrate the centennial of his old comrade, John Brown:

> *I wish I had the voice to take part in the new abolition crusade that is coming.*

He had thought he was doing so when he began to support the work of Booker T. Washington, the only Negro leader of national stature at the turn of the century. Washington had emerged to fill the void left after the death of Frederick Douglass, but with a new and different philosophy. He believed that southern whites had to be persuaded gently, not compelled, to accept the idea that education of the Negro was in the best interests of the South. He felt that the businessmen of the North should be cajoled and begged into giving the financial support the schools needed to make up for the neglect by southern lawmakers. The price he paid was a policy of accommodation: to accept, at least for the time being, the barbarism of segregation and the nullification of the United States Constitution. In deferring demands for equality, his purpose was to wait until a base for Negro power could be created by self-help.

Washington was so successful in his efforts that he became for a time a one man repository of such black power as there was in the nation. Philanthropists backed him, and national politicians looked to him for guidance in policies and appointments. Seeing no other sign of hope or help on the horizon, Higginson supported his efforts. The Colonel acted as trustee for one of the schools that Washington had developed and expanded in the South. He was confident that the policy of accommodation was but a phase, a mere temporary tactic, when he read Washington's tribute to the black regiments of the Civil War—a tribute that implied that abandonment of constitutional rights should not be thought permanent:

The services which the Negro troops performed in the Civil War in fighting for the freedom of their race not only convinced the officers who commanded them and the white soldiers who fought by their side that the Negro race deserved to be free, but it served to convince the great mass of people in the North that the Negroes were fit for freedom. It did, perhaps, more than any other one thing to gain for them, as a result of the war, the passage of those amendments to the Constitution which secured to the Negro race the same rights in the United States that are granted to white men.

After some years of Washington's ascendancy, Negro voices of protest that had never been stilled grew louder. A group of Negro intellectuals took exception to his philosophy and his style. The foremost among them was a Massachusetts man, holder of a Harvard doctorate, W. E. B. DuBois. He opposed the limitations of the Washington program to industrial and vocational education. He saw in the breadth of his own learning the proof of the inherent injustice of stifling the varied talents of his people. He felt that acceptance of temporary inferior status and stilling of protest would combine to make second-class citizenship permanent. He believed with Frederick Douglass, as the latter had written:

If there is no struggle there is no progress. Those who profess to favor freedom, and yet deprecate agitation, are men who want crops without plowing up the ground.

Wentworth saw with sorrow the development of the split between Washington and the DuBois group. It reminded him of the divisions among abolitionists and feminists, just as it may suggest to us a parallel with the diversity of voices of the present. He ruefully observed:

> *Internal feuds among philanthropists* [in his day the word still kept its literal meaning, "lovers of mankind," rather than the present, narrower, donors of charity] *are, alas, no new story, and few bodies of reformers have escaped this peril. . . . we must not censure the warring Negro reformer too severely. Nay, consider the subdivisions of the Garrison Abolitionists themselves, after slavery was abolished, at a period when I remember to have seen Edmund Quincy walk halfway up a stairway, and turn suddenly round to descend, merely to avoid Wendell Phillips, who was coming downstairs! . . . In the present case, as in most cases, the trouble seems chiefly due to the difficulty found by every energetic and enthusiastic person, absorbed in his own pursuits, in fully appreciating the equally important pursuits of others. Booker T. Washington, in urging the development of the industrial pursuits he represents, has surely gone no farther than Frederick Douglass, the acknowledged leader of his people, who said, "Every colored mechanic is by virtue of circumstances an elevator of his race." On the other hand, the critics of Mr. Washington are wholly right in holding that it is as important for this race to produce its own physicians, lawyers, preachers, and above all, teachers, as to rear mechanics. . . . It is infinitely to be regretted that everybody cannot look at every matter all round, but this, unhappily, is a form of human weakness in which there is no distinction of color.*

Less than two years before Wentworth's death, there came to his desk an invitation to a conference on the status of the American Negro. The conference was a preliminary step in the organization of the National Association for the Advancement of Colored People, which was to arise from a fusion of the efforts of white radicals, shocked by the worsening of the conditions of the Negro, and Negro intellectuals and militants led by Dr. DuBois. Influenced, in all probability, by Washington's opposition, his memory and his judgment impaired at the age of eighty-five, Higginson declined to attend the conference. He declared, contrary to the facts, that "In 1868 and ever since" he had opposed the indiscriminate extension of the suffrage; he added, in words that contradicted what he had written in a magnificent essay of 1904, called "Intensely Human," that the Negro "would better turn himself to his industrial and educational development than to strive for the establishment of a civil and political status which . . . can never be attained."

What has remained true is that the problem of prejudice, discrimination, and deprivation has continued to be, as Wentworth had said of the labor problem, "much harder to solve than slavery," and that the complexity of the problem produces the diversity of voices offering solutions. It is to be regretted that Higginson in abstaining from the movement that became the N.A.A.C.P. did not follow the lead of his fellow Bostonian of abolitionist background and fellow Anti-Imperialist, Moorfield Storey, who saw no incompatibility in supporting both leaders. Storey went on to become president of the N.A.A.C.P., and one cannot help thinking that Thomas Wentworth Higginson would have approved.

EPILOGUE

END OF A LONG JOURNEY

HE HAD WON MANY HONORS and received recognition for his achievements as writer, critic, historian, and reformer. He had been president—to mention only a few—of the Association of American Authors, Phi Beta Kappa, and the Board of the Boston Home for Aged Colored Women. Until he reached seventy-five, he had not received an honorary degree from the college whose child he was and whose town he graced for the last three decades of his life.

Finally notice came that the honor, so long overdue, was to be granted. The degree was to be conferred at commencement exercises the day after the graduation of a young Negro protégé from Radcliffe. When he saw her receive more applause than any other member of her class he said, "I felt that I would rather give up my degree for tomorrow than that all her efforts and mine should fail." Still, there was pleasure and gratitude when he was called on to step forward for his own Doctor of Letters, to be greeted with a tremendous roar of applause by the audience. "It was wholly a surprise to me," he jotted down in his dairy, "and it was something to have lived for."

The following year he had the pleasure of presiding at a coming-out party for his daughter, attended by six hundred guests. He continued to be one of her favorite escorts until a few years later, when he gave her hand in marriage to a young Boston doctor at a

His first two grandchildren.

COURTESY MRS. WILLIAM HALLOWELL AND MRS. W. J. WOODIN

little New Hampshire church near his summer home in Dublin. He had been old enough to be a grandfather when he had married Minnie and he was to have the joy of becoming a real grandfather at eighty-two. When his second grandchild was born he inscribed in the diary, "One of the happiest days of my life. . . ."

He was never content to rest on his laurels as a grand old man. He would often walk from his home to Harvard Square to board the trolley to the Boston Public Library, when it was necessary to put in a day's research there. On one occasion the old gentleman hastened to help an awkwardly plump lady up the high step of the car—and was to read of the incident in a poetic newspaper report by an anonymous observer that concluded:

The noble man by whom this deed was done
Was Colonel Thomas Wentworth Higginson.

The trolley car conductors enjoyed chatting with him. One gained immortality of a sort, in the Colonel's diary, when he told the old man that he had just taken *Cheerful Yesterdays* out of the library and that this would be the thirty-second volume by Higginson that he had read.

The Colonel did not shrink from automobile rides—still a risky enterprise, as he learned on one trip when his host had to abandon a car with the motor smoking—and just six decades ago the Colonel made a prophetic observation: the trouble with the new gadget was that it had "a general tendency to make all rural places suburban."

He never ceased to be interested in Cambridge and its undergraduates. He was glad to receive young men and women who called upon him for interviews. One of them, a young novelist named Upton Sinclair was gathering material for a novel based on the abolitionist period, and the old Colonel told him when they were through, "You must not leave Boston without meeting Mrs. Howe. Here is a note of introduction." Two years later, in 1906, Sinclair was interested in getting a list of sponsors for a new radical organization he was forming, to be called the Intercollegiate Socialist Society. Higginson agreed readily to be a sponsor. He explained:

I have for many years had some leaning toward Socialism, I suppose, but the thing for which I joined the College Association was because I thought it very undesirable

Grand old man, 1903.

COURTESY MRS. WILLIAM HALLOWELL AND MRS. W. J. WOODIN

> *that colleges should ignore the very* word *as they almost uniformly did then. . . . As for the name "Socialist," I never either claimed or disclaimed it, regarding it merely as a feeler in the right direction.*

He had enlisted in a new cause the year before his confession of partial socialism, that of simplified spelling. In this matter he was too set in his ways, at eighty-four, to practice what he encouraged the new movement to preach. His biographical sketches and essays continued to be turned out in the old style. In 1908 he was encouraged by a then new and very young publisher, B.W. Huebsch, to put together some reflections at sunset of a man's life, *Things Worth While*. Huebsch, as publisher for the next five decades, was to honor the traditions of dissent and defense of freedom that Wentworth had espoused all his life. One request for an advance on royalties that the young publisher received in October 1908 was a touching reminder of the precariousness of a writer's economic condition:

> *Pressed for the money by the necessity of keeping a double household at Ipswich (where my married daughter became the mother of a lovely little daughter) and my wife had to be with her and keep house. This was joined with the fact that our own summer residence at Dublin, N.H., failed of being let as we had expected on account of hard times. I have to draw about me every little sum. . . .*

During that winter his strength began to fail. Nevertheless he read a paper on Dickens before a round table in February and revised it for publication—which was to be posthumous. His last weeks were serene, and his death came naturally and without pain on May 9, 1911. He was buried in the Cambridge cemetery next to the tiny grave of his first child.

At his funeral an honor guard of Negro soldiers paid tribute to his unfailing loyalty to the cause of freedom by bearing his casket down the aisle of the Cambridge First Parish Church. When the pastor heard the bugle sounding "Taps" he thought, as he told Mary afterwards, "of the passing of Mr. Valiant-for-truth in 'Pilgrim's Progress.'" As John Bunyan had written, "he passed over, and all the trumpets sounded for him on the other side."

One of the verses that was read at the service was a poem written by Thomas Bailey Aldrich on the death of Wendell Phillips. The verse, alas, was prophetic in an unintended way:

One by one they go
Into the unknown dark,—

Thomas Wentworth Higginson was an uncommon American who deserved better of his countrymen than the oblivion that has closed around his name. He deserves to be remembered as a fighter for freedom—an all too rare breed.

READING AND REFERENCES

FOR THOSE WHO would like to see a full-scale bibliographical essay, I suggest the last thirty pages of Anna Mary Wells' recent *Dear Preceptor*, the only published biography of Colonel Higginson since his wife's of 1914. The unavailability in all but the largest reference libraries of the Colonel's own writings makes it desirable that E. L. McCormick's projected anthology be published. *Army Life in a Black Regiment* is in print in three different editions now, including my own, offering what Van Wyck Brooks has justly called "one of those rare books that recall a passage of history as the works of the formal historians cannot recall them."

Youth and Ministry: Transcendentalism

The best single historical work dealing with what Henry S. Commager has called in his own brief treatment *Era of Reform*, is Alice Felt Tyler's *Freedom's Ferment*. As a literary history, Van Wyck Brooks' *The Flowering of New England* covers the period and subject well. Lindsay Swift's *Brook Farm* is available in paperback, as is Hawthorne's *Blithedale Romance*, although the latter is a caricature rather than a picture. The late Perry Miller's anthology *The Transcendentalists* gives a range of firsthand material. Professor Commager's *Theodore Parker* helps fill out the picture, as does Mark Van Doren's *The Portable Emerson*. Thoreau has come a long way since Higginson was one of the few besides Emerson who appreciated him. W. W. Norton & Co. has in print his *Walden and Civil Disobedience, The Maine Woods,* and *Cape Cod.* The best available current biography is Walter Harding's *The Days of Henry Thoreau.*

Abolitionism.

One standard and still exciting general work is Henrietta Buckmaster's *Let My People Go.* Lawrence Lader covers the subject well in *The Bold Brahmins.* Louis Ruchames' *The Abolitionists: A Selection From their Writings,* Dwight Dumond's *Antislavery,* Herbert Aptheker's *To Be Free* and especially his *Documentary History of the Negro People* are useful. I was influenced by and read with enthusiasm John Jay Chapman's *William Lloyd Garrison,* as well as Irving Bartlett's *Wendell Phillips.*

Women's Rights

The current general works, like Eleanor Flexner's otherwise useful *A Century of Struggle,* tend to neglect Higginson's role in the first two thirds of that century. Yuri Suhl's *Ernestine Rose* and other biographies of the leading women of the nineteenth century, like Dorothy Sterling's *Lucretia Mott,* Katherine Anthony's *Susan B. Anthony,* Alice Stone Blackwell's *Lucy Stone* and Alma Lutz' *Created Equal* (Stanton) , piece out the history.

Kansas and John Brown

Louis Ruchames' *A John Brown Reader* was most useful to me, next to the Colonel's own recollections. Biographies of Brown by Oswald G. Villard and W.E.B. Dubois and such works as Barrie Stavis' play, *Harpers Ferry* round out the picture.

The War and the Sea Islands

The best single work from the point of view here involved is Dudley T. Cornish's *The Sable Arm.* James McPherson's *The*

Negro's Civil War has many contemporary documents. Wille Lee Rose's *Rehearsal for Reconstruction* gives the picture of civilian life in the territory of the Black Regiment; Katherine M. Jones *Port Royal Under Six Flags* has many pertinent portions. Ray Billington's editing of the Charlotte Forten papers, in print under the title *A Free Negro in the Slave Era,* also presents history as the works of formal historians do not. Mark Miles Fisher's *Negro Slave Songs* gives credit to the Colonel's contribution to the literature of Negro Spirituals and belies Kenneth Lynn's observations in his *Christian Science Monitor* review of *Dear Preceptor.*

Three Women

Three Saints and a Sinner by Louise Hall Tharp is the biography of Julia Ward Howe now in print. More material on the Higginson relationship is in the out-of-print biography by Mrs. Howe's daughters. Helen Hunt Jackson's *A Century of Dishonor* is in paperback, but Ruth Odell's adequate biography of its author who is remembered less than she deserves, is out of print. Emily Dickinson is the subject of a mass of literature. Her own letters and poetry are the best introduction to her life and work. They have been published complete by the Harvard University Press. The best single biography is George F. Whicher's *This Was a Poet.* There are many paperback editions of Miss Dickinson's poetry, and the Anchor edition is prefaced by Higginson's own essay on their friendship. "Letter to a Young Contributor" was reprinted in the Spring-Summer issue of *The Massachusetts Review,* Vol. VI, No. 3.

Reconstruction and Post-Reconstruction Race Relations

For a lengthy treatment of the first four decades of betrayal of the black regiments there is nothing to equal the combination of W.E.B. DuBois' *Black Reconstruction* and Rayford W. Logan's *The Negro in American Life and Thought,* both in paperback, the latter reissued as *The Betrayal of the Negro.* DuBois' *The*

Souls of Black Folk completes the picture as it appeared in the Colonel's last decade. General books of Negro History, such as Lerone Bennett's *Before the Mayflower,* and *Confrontation: Black and White,* John Hope Franklin's *From Slavery to Freedom,* furnish summaries of value for this and the abolitionist period and enable the reader to follow the path from past to present. My own Grant biography, *Let Us Have Peace,* gives a compressed summary of the Reconstruction. I should not overlook Henrietta Buckmaster's *Freedom Bound.* A swift and exciting journey through highlights of what is called "Negro History," but is really the missing keystone of the story of how America came to be what it is, will be found in Martin B. Duberman's play *In White America.*

A Glimpse of Utopia

A fine summary of the period of ferment, especially the latter part, is contained in Arthur Mann's *Yankee Reformers in the Urban Age.* Edward Bellamy's *Looking Backward* is durable enough to keep reappearing in paperback. The early years of the modern American socialist movement are covered well in Howard H. Quint's *The Forging of American Socialism.* I cannot mention in the space allotted the many out-of-print books that were useful in this and other sections.

Anti-Imperialist

Leon Wolff's *Little Brown Brother* tells much of the story of the dishonorable role of our Army in slaughtering Philippine guerrillas. *American Imperialism in 1898* (D.C. Heath, pub.) has valuable texts, as does Snyder's *The Imperialism Reader.*

INDEX